# EKKLESIA

# RISING

The Authority of Christ

in Communities

of Contending Prayer

# DEAN BRIGGS

Foreword by Lou Engle

CHAMPION PRESS
*Fuel for the journey*

*Ekklesia Rising*
The Authority of Christ in Communities of Contending Prayer

Copyright © 2014 by Dean Briggs
Published by Champion Press
Kansas City, MO

Cover images courtesy of Unsplash.com.
Cover design by DBB.
Book design by Eugenia Brock.

ISBN-13: 978-0692339381
ISBN-10: 0692339388

First Printing—December 2014
Second Printing — March 2016
Printed in the United States of America

# PRAISE FOR EKKLESIA RISING

"Dean Briggs has given the 2.0 upgrade in the study of the ekklesia and its relevancy to the true meaning, mission, and methodology of the church. This carefully researched book offers vital observations and principles designed to alter and align the church with Christ's true purposes for it. I not only strongly recommend *Ekklesia Rising*, I am grateful for the additions it makes to see the church change the world."

— **Dennis Peacock, President and Founder, GoStrategic and The Statesman Project**

"*Ekklesia Rising* is replete with truth born of genuine revelation. Its pages contain biblical truth that may extend beyond the reach of the casual reader but will surely ignite a fire in the heart of anyone searching for a deeper understanding of God's design and purpose for His saints on earth today. I highly recommend *Ekklesia Rising*."

— **Richard C. Durfield, PhD., M.Div., M.A.T., B.A.**

"*Ekklesia Rising* is not just revelatory, it is revolutionary. For far too long, we have been held captive by a church structure that paralyzes groundbreakers and transforms warriors into victims. It's time for change. With great clarity, Dean shines a biblical spotlight on what Jesus really meant when He declared the gates of hell shall not prevail. With passion and depth, he then illuminates the way forward. Warning! The anointing on this book is destined to unleash seismic shifts, even in your own life. But you will become strong, victorious, and free."

— **Jon and Jolene Hamill, Lamplighter Ministries**

"*Ekklesia Rising* is a paradigm-shifting book! A must read for all Houses of Prayer, Pastors and Church Leaders who want a greater revelation of the nature and authority of Christ in transforming culture and cities."

— **Greg Simas, Senior Pastor, Convergence House of Prayer**

"Once you understand what the ekklesia actually is, from its original state to what it has sadly become, you can't help but seek to inform, transform and reform our current 'church culture.' Honestly, I believe this book is a watershed that will mark you for life. *Ekklesia Rising* is one of the best books on this subject I've ever read. Biblically sound, with great historic references, this is a must read that scholars and laymen alike will heartily sink their teeth into. *Ekklesia Rising* will transform your purpose from merely attending your local congregation to realizing we gather together as members of the 'Divine Senate.'"

— **William Ford III, author of *Created For Influence*, Director of Marketplace Leadership at CFNI**

"*Ekklesia Rising* is seriously revolutionary and I don't say that lightly. I have never heard this subject treated with such depth, skill and inspiration. As director of a prayer and missions ministry, this book has become mandatory reading for my whole team. Something like scales fell from my eyes after reading *Ekklesia Rising*. After I closed the last page, I had a sense that the 'church' will never be the same."

— **Andrew Whalen, Director, Prayer & Justice Center**

"*Ekklesia Rising* lands like a timely, prophetic truth hammer on the heart, shattering religious paradigms that keep the church in a culture of resigned unbelief, comfortable indifference and safe prayer meetings. As you read this book, an intercessory groan emerges in the deepest recesses of the soul that culminates in a prophetic roar: 'We were made for so much more!' May the Lord establish His House of Prayer in the earth and may this be the hour that His ekklesia arises and lives up to our true name."

— **Tammy Riddering, Co-Director, Gateway House of Prayer**

# CONTENTS

Dedicated to all the small, faithful clusters
of three or four or five who gather and pray
in the simple belief that Jesus said exactly
what He meant to say.

# FOREWORD

I t was said that Winston Churchill "mobilized the English language and sent it into war." So, too, did Jesus marshal the language of Matthew 16 for the purpose of war on hell. *"Upon this rock I will build my church, and the gates of hell shall not prevail against it..."*

You know the story. After Peter understands that Jesus is the Christ, Jesus responds with mind-bending language that shatters our small thinking. He tells His followers that the measure of authority He will supply to praying disciples is sufficient to prevail against the gates of Hades, the very powers of death. If ever we truly laid hold of this declaration, we would fearlessly transform every place where Satan's shadow falls. With "red letter" certainty, we would know that every gate of hell, every spiritual power, is but a prayer target awaiting enforceable submission to the name of Christ. For some, this poses troubling questions, because if true it necessitates a realignment between popular church culture and what Jesus pledged Himself to build. For me it poses both answers and hope.

Let me illustrate my point. The story is told of the great conqueror Napoleon who, while inspecting his troops prior to battle, came upon a young man who trembled and shook with fear. When Napoleon asked the young man's name, the soldier responded, "My name is also Napoleon, sir." To which the general replied, "Young man, live up to your name or change it."

In *Ekklesia Rising,* my friend Dean Briggs offers hard-hitting, brilliant exposition to uncover the true meaning of what Jesus said He would build, along with challenging questions as to whether we have veered off course. Is our current church mindset sufficient for the binding, loosing and war which Jesus unleashed that fateful day? More to the point, since Jesus did not actually name His people the "church," but rather declared them to be His *ekklesia,* what is the difference at the root of our identity? As you will soon discover, the difference is significant. Clarification is long overdue. Dean unflinchingly commits himself to that task.

Furthermore, I know for a fact that Dean deeply loves the church as the people of God. He has been a church pastor, and is now a teacher among God's people. While some of his thoughts may seem aggressive in these overly sensitive times, this book is actually a solid call for maturity and balance. As a dynamic culture of prayer sweeps the planet, what should it look like? Again, *what* is Jesus building? While I fully rejoice in the tender revelation of Bridal love (among other important insights), Matthew 16 endorses a masculine spirit committed to war. Surely, what Jesus builds *will prevail* against the gates of hell. But are we prevailing? Have we become the church, or have we become the ekklesia? These are hard questions.

I recently watched a rather intense war movie with four of my praying friends, the kind not recommended for the weak of heart. The conclusion witnessed a lone, vastly outnumbered armored tank crew defending a critical supply route against hundreds of approaching Nazis. Facing certain death in the belly of the tank, the men steeled their courage for the final fight by reciting the prophet Isaiah's confession after he had glimpsed God on His throne: "Here am I, send me!" For me, the scene was almost mystical. Something in my spirit roared, "Yes, here am I! Send me! Deploy me in prayer against every principality and power, every high thing which exalts itself against the knowledge of God!" I want my life to be marked by that sort of fearless, holy aggression.

*Ekklesia Rising* will fuel such a flame of intercessory dominion in your soul. The revelation contained in these pages has launched me into a whole new paradigm of prayer, one I believe will fuel a reformation of missions and bring back the King. If we have captured the mind of Christ rightly, I believe an ekklesial paradigm can produce a movement of men and women who specialize in fasting and prayer for the sake of "air supremacy" over dark powers. This book is theological, foundational DNA for that movement. I want it in all my internships.

Thus, as Churchill marshaled language for the purpose of war, I believe the Biblical concepts Dean explains are more than recoveries of truth, they are catalysts to mobilize the body of Christ in a new way. We can't completely fulfill God's purpose unless we truly become the ekklesia and begin to produce bold, imperialistic praying. Let the ekklesia arise!

— **Lou Engle, co-founder**
  **TheCall**

"There is not a square inch in the whole domain of our human existence over which Christ, who is Sovereign over all, does not cry, Mine!"

– **Abraham Kuyper (1837-1920)**

# INTRODUCTION

One of the major obstacles the Allies faced during World War II was the superior industrial capacities of the Third Reich. The British Air Ministry had already identified Germany's heavily industrialized Ruhr Valley as a critical strategic target. This network of dams provided hydro-electric power, drinking water and an important canal transport system. These assets made the German war machine a model of efficient mass production. It didn't matter how successful an Allied counter-strike might be; the war machine could grind out more weapons.

Thus, one of the British Bomber Command's clearest objectives was to destroy as much of Germany's industry as possible. In-depth studies of previous attempts revealed a glaring problem: after each attack, the factories were not only rebuilt, but were spread over a wider geographical area. This made them more difficult to attack again. However, since industry requires power and must therefore be located within reasonable distance from a power source, they could only spread so far. Instead of simply attacking factories, Bomber Command realized that *attacking the power sources was a much better strategy.* Destroying one shared power source would have a trickle-down effect, disrupting numerous factories and industries.

Operation "Chastise" was developed to interrupt these supply lines by breaching the Möhne, Eder, Sorpe, Lister and Ennepe dams. An unconventional weapon was employed that, if success-ful, would direct 330 million tons of flood damage into the Ruhr Valley. The technology was a bomb named "Upkeep," an ingenious

bomb-in-a-barrel that skipped on water. No one thought it could
work, but since conventional aerial attacks were being thwarted,
they didn't have much choice. Upkeep was designed to breach various defensive measures by ignoring them altogether, using the
waterways themselves to reach the dams. Lancaster planes would
approach their target at 230 mph, descend to an altitude of only 60
feet above the lake's surface, then release their payload precisely 120
feet from the dam wall. When the bomb struck the water, the initial
impact would be cushioned by the mahogany case that enabled it to
skip like a rock across the lake surface before submerging near the
lakeside base of the dam and exploding. Tricky, at best.

Twenty-five year old Wing Commander Guy Gibson formed
a squadron of the finest pilots and crews the RAF could assemble for
the task. Two hundred elite, international volunteers from Australia,
Canada, Great Britain, New Zealand and the United States signed
up. The men knew up front that casualties would be high. They also
understood that failure was not an option. Gibson had two months
to get his squadron ready and train them to mark targets...while
flying at a dangerously low altitude...in the dark.

Worst of all, Upkeep wasn't even ready to test. By the time
the mission date was finally established, crews had only three weeks
to master the technology and approach. In addition, if lake waters
swelled from rain, mission specs tightened. But on May 16, 1943,
under a full moon, nineteen Lancasters scrambled out of Lincoln-
shire, setting a course over the Channel toward the Netherlands,
headed deep into the heart of Germany. The first and largest target,
the 30 year-old Möhne dam, 25 miles east of Dortmund, required
five tries before it was completely breached. The last of three bombs
destroyed the Eder dam. Flood damage inflicted a heavy toll all along
the Ruhr Valley, including the destruction of 11 factories and 25
bridges, plus damage to 114 hydraulic power plants and munitions.

But it was not without cost. Eleven of the 19 planes were lost, and 53 of 133 men did not return, a 40 percent casualty rate.

Yet the Dam Busters helped turn the tide of the war. Sir Winston Churchill was given a standing ovation when he visited the U.S. Congress, largely due to the success of Operation Chastise. The mission earned the Dam Busters a place in aviation history and the right to bear the motto, *"Aprés moi, le delúge,"* which means, "After me, the flood."

It is time for God's people to get a vision of the cost and glory of becoming Hell's Gates busters. Air superiority in prayer is a mission for heroes. We must identify clear targets: those supply lines and factories belching immorality, perversion and demonization into our culture. Gates of death must be brought down. Frankly, there is no other way to win. This book is about winning, which I define as loving Christ enough to govern the Earth in the manner intended when He commissioned His disciples in Matthew 16:18-19.

# REVELATION

---

*"Flesh and blood did not reveal this to you,*
*but My Father who is in heaven."*

---

"A mighty fortress is our God,
a bulwark never failing;
our helper He amid the flood
of mortal ills prevailing.
For still our ancient foe
doth seek to work us woe;
his craft and power are great,
and armed with cruel hate,
on earth is not his equal."

Verse 1: *A Mighty Fortress is Our God*
**– Martin Luther**

# 1

## CAESAREA PHILIPPI

Imagine for a moment that you've just stepped inside a time machine, closed the door and set the dial for 29 A.D. Now close your eyes as you travel back 2,000 years. When you finally open them again, you are standing at the base of the tallest mountain in northern Palestine, gazing upward. A brilliant sun rises in the east, capping the snows of Mount Hermon with a glowing, phosphorus white. Along the southern foot of this mountain, atop a terrace 1,150 feet high, lies a small city overlooking a fertile valley. This lush region is one of the greenest in the area, thanks to its abundant water supply.

But it has a dark side, too. In fact, the darkness is so strong, so entrenched in the history and geography, you cannot help but feel it. You've studied this region. Now it has come to life.

Watching impassively from a distance, you notice merchants, peasants, soldiers and robed magistrates all mingling together. You look closer, tracing the darkness. Yes, there it is. Clusters of people are thronging to the temple—travelers and pilgrims—to offer sacrifice and pray to their gods. Nearby, at the bottom of a massive cliff ledge, countless votive shrines are etched into the stone face. You understand anew why the locals call this imposing wall 'The Rock of the Gods,' for butted against the sheer bluff is a temple dedicated to the Greek god Pan. Pan is nothing but the latest incarnation of

Baal, the Canaanite deity who has been worshipped in this region for thousands of years, but with the influx of Greek culture, he has been given a facelift.

You've heard enough stories about the dark world of Pan's temple to know about the deep pool in the inner recesses of the cave. Though this is the headwaters of the Jordan River, faithful Jews never visit here. The city's hellenized pagans[1] believe this to be the great abyss, which makes the entire cave a frightful doorway to the underworld, one of only a handful of portals in the known empire. They call it the "Gate to Hades." If a pilgrim were to linger long enough, he would witness perverse rituals involving sexual acts with goats and temple prostitutes, in honor of the goat-god Pan, lord of shepherds and music, god of pleasure and fear. On the outer wall, carved recesses in the cliff celebrate other deities, too, such as Echo and Galerius, possibly also the fertility goddess Nemesis. It is believed that both Baal and the spirits of the dead enter the underworld through these gates into Hades, because the cave entrance looks like a yawning mouth on the naked stone.

Yes, you definitely feel it, the foul traffic of demons. Shuddering, you set your dial back to the present day. But even after you comfortably emerge from your time travel machine, you know that important secrets remain back there in Caesarea Philippi. Not only secrets of darkness, but more importantly, a brilliant, invading light. You know, because one of the most important events in the entire Bible took place there, directly orchestrated by Jesus Himself.

• • •

Seven short verses. Matthew 16:13-19. You've probably read this passage at least a hundred times. Countless sermons have been preached on it, yet something has always been missing. Though the passage feels like a full meal, we rarely come away from it satisfied.

Here, in Caesarea Philippi, the Bible tells us that Peter made a profound declaration regarding Jesus. In turn, the Lord replied with a profound declaration regarding His disciples. This book contends that this brief exchange is crucial—like eleven on a scale of one to ten—for effecting true reformation and preparing the people of God for the last days of history. Furthermore, the location is not accidental, it's instructive. In fact, the precise language of their conversation becomes far more potent when we understand the local context, setting the stage for a bomb of revelation. But you'll miss it if you don't know the backstory[2].

So let's look closer and set the scene again. First, you need to know that Caesarea Philippi was reviled by devout rabbis, so *why* would Jesus go there? The city's reputation was on par (or perhaps worse) than that of the wretched region of Samaria. In fact, if you understand the offense Jesus triggered when He spoke to the Phoenician woman, or dared tell a story about a *good* Samaritan, it will help you understand the repugnancy of Caesarea Philippi. With shrines to Caesar and other false gods, including a large statue of the goat god Pan in a state of exaggerated sexual arousal, surrounded by attending nymphs, Caesarea Philippi was the opposite of holy Jerusalem. It was a place of darkness, debauchery and occultism—the modern equivalent of Las Vegas, San Francisco and New Orleans rolled into one. No good Jew would defile himself by traveling to such an accursed place.

Until one day, inexplicably, Jesus comes to visit. He makes sure to take His group of twelve eager, young, impressionable men with Him. These are blue-collar working guys, not well-educated elites, nor respectable, well-heeled leaders. Fishermen, tax collectors, Zealots. Immature men who blunder and boast and make huge mistakes on a regular basis. For some reason, Jesus decides to take them, metaphorically, to the gates of Hades.

If you wish to fully comprehend the staggering scope of what follows, you must keep these images firmly in mind. Otherwise you'll be at a cultural and historical deficit, unable to read between the lines. We need to be attuned to our surroundings. Something critical is about to happen.

Let's also notice that this is not just one more, random leg of the journey for Jesus. When the Bible tells us, "Jesus came into the district of Caesarea Philippi" (Mat. 16:13), it leaves a nugget of revelation in what is *not* said: that Jesus went out of his way to go there.

---

**Light bulb: something *deliberate* is afoot. The rabbi, Jesus, is carefully staging His next lesson.**

---

Many times during the travels of Jesus, we don't know exactly where He was. But here, speaking to a primarily Jewish audience, Matthew notes the locale. If you compare the parallel passage in Mark 8:22 and 27, and correlate this information with one of the maps in the back of your Bible, you will notice that, having journeyed from Tyre and Sidon to Bethsaida,[3] Jesus must now go way out of His way 30+ miles (round trip on foot) to visit this perverse locale. This is a little confusing. In Tyre, it appears He wanted to lay low, maybe for privacy, maybe for some much needed R&R.[4] Also, in this same time frame, Jesus clearly states that His mission is limited to the Jews: "I was sent only to the lost sheep of the house of Israel" (Mat. 15:24). So why is He now heading north to a pagan, Roman stronghold? The route south from Sidon to Judea via Galilee is clearly the way back home. Vacation is over. Time to get back to work. A sharp turn north to Caesarea Philippi doesn't make sense. Plus, He's contradicting His own territorial boundaries, and furthermore, backtracking to do it!

Light bulb: something *deliberate* is afoot. The rabbi, Jesus, is carefully staging His next lesson. Much like the director of a play, He's framing the scene for maximum impact. As readers, we have the assurance of knowing the end of the story, but Jesus, in this moment, has a real and vulnerable question in mind. A fulcrum point in His ministry has arrived. Have these twelve young men been with Him long enough to know the truth? If so, *if* His disciples truly get it, then everything shifts from here on. But there's only one way to find out. So, "when Jesus came into the district of Caesarea Philippi, He began asking His disciples, saying, 'Who do people say that the Son of Man is?'" (Mat. 16:13).

This is hardly idle conversation. Starting at the perimeter with other people's opinions, Jesus invites the disciples to contemplate Him. Up until now, public speculation has been all over the map. Essentially, Jesus was asking, "What's the buzz about Me?"

> "And they said, 'Some say John the Baptist; and others, Elijah; but still others, Jeremiah, or one of the prophets'" (v. 14).

These are reasonable guesses as far as rumors go, but they're also way too small, too third-hand—"a friend of a friend told me" kind of deal. Jesus can go no further with followers operating at this level of revelation. Loyalty and courage will not be enough in the days ahead. To initiate the deep desires of His heart, His friends must really know who He is.

Did you get that? They must *know* it. It won't work if He has to tell them. It's personal.

> "He said to them, 'But who do *you* say that I am?'" (v. 15).

On the one hand, we can easily hear a confident Master leading His students. Jesus knows who He is. He doesn't need human affirmation, nor is He fishing for compliments. As the God-man, He lives in the constant pleasure of His Father. Yet there is another side. Listen also to the heart of one who "existed in the form of God...(yet) emptied Himself" (Phil. 2:6-7). Humans have questions. Humans want answers. In His own humanity, *Jesus wants to know if He is known.* Has His mission achieved its intended impact to date? He is the long-awaited Messiah with a clear destination in mind, but are the disciples ready to follow Him *there?* So with hope and longing, He personalizes the equation. "Okay, the poll numbers are in. Some say I'm John or Elijah or some other prophet. But what do *you* believe?"

> "Simon Peter answered and said, '**You are the Christ,** the Son of the living God.'"

Ahh! Though Scripture is full of transcendent moments, a few, truly special ones seem to leap from the pages and pivot history:

- Abraham on Mt. Moriah, knife drawn, ready to sacrifice his promised, beloved son.
- Moses at the burning bush, receiving his commission to deliver a nation of slaves.
- David, facing a giant with nothing but his sling and a burning heart for God.
- Simon Peter, in a burst of spiritual clarity, recognizing the one who stands before him. Was this man, Yeshua, just a wise rabbi? A prophet? No.

"You are *the Christ!*" Peter realized. He got it. He knew and believed. It wasn't full understanding, as later verses will soon prove. But for the moment, it was enough. Jesus was and is the Promised One. The mission could now proceed. In my mind, I see Jesus smiling. While He is proud of Simon, He is also grateful to His Father. No more delay is needed. Phase Two is ready to launch.

> "And Jesus answered and said to him, 'Blessed are you, Simon Barjona, because flesh and blood did not reveal this to you, but My Father who is in heaven.

'And I also say to you that you are Peter, **and upon this rock I will build My church;** and the **gates of Hades** shall not over-power it.

'I will give you the **keys of the kingdom** of heaven; and what-ever you shall **bind** on earth shall be bound in heaven, and whatever you shall **loose** on earth shall be loosed in heaven.'" (Mat. 16:16-19, NASB).

Now you see why the cultural subtext of Caesarea Philippi is critical. With all these kingdom-displacing references to rocks, might they be standing in sight of the Rock of the Gods when Jesus prompts this conversation? Is it an accident that He speaks of assail-ing the gates of Hades at an earthly locale that fits the bill, a place of legend that claimed men's souls, fed their fears, inspired their wor-ship? Did He travel 30 miles out of His way for nothing?

No, clearly Jesus is making an object lesson. The Lord of Heaven and Earth stands before twelve mortal disciples, and in a burst of insight more brilliant than the snow-capped glow of Mount Hermon, Peter becomes the first human to recognize Christ for who He really is.

The Ancient of Days has come. Lord of hosts. Captain of the armies of God.

The promised Messiah. *The Christ!*

When a man gets even a small glimpse into the total rulership of Christ, he stands at a new threshold for understanding his own purpose on earth, for Christ not only possesses all authority, He also bestows it. Understanding this far better than His disciples, Jesus seizes the moment to declare nothing less than war on hell.

With just twelve guys.

As we'll later discover, it's not the size of the group that mat-ters, but:

1.   The unity of their constitution

2. The clarity of their voice, and
3. Above all, their revelation of the One who directs them.

Jesus answers Peter's revelation with, of all things, a building plan. In the Greek, He said, "I will build my **ekklesia**." Now you probably thought He pledged to build His *church*, right? That's what we've all been taught because that's how nearly every Bible version renders it. But church is the wrong concept because *it's literally the wrong word*. It's not a poor translation, but a *mis*translation of the original language. While such a suggestion is no doubt controversial, please bear with me and I'll prove it in time. Furthermore, *if true, it is critical that we admit our error*. Why? Because we want to discern *Jesus's* actual mission, not some historically entrenched mistranslation, however dear it has become to our hearts. What if the church can't actually do what Jesus said we were supposed to do? What if it takes an ekklesia?

"But they're the same!" you say. "My pastor said so."

What if they aren't the same? Are you willing to discover the difference?

The central premise of this book will be first to prove, then correct this error. The very idea challenges our propriety, as new believers are typically trained to love and revere the church, largely because we have understood Christ to also love and adore the church. Actually, He cherishes his *Bride*[5] and identifies with his *brothers*[6], but what He convened in Matthew 16 and promised to build was an *ekklesia*, not a church. Please hear me. Over the centuries, church as an institution has no doubt offered many good and worthy spiritual and emotional harbors: pastoral care; a warm, social environment for godly friendships to flourish; a hub for teaching and edification. We cherish the institution, because by it, a corrupt world has gained a measure of salt and light. This is no small thing! I was raised to love the church. I planted and pastored a local church for many years. But there is no way around it: the Greek word *ekklesia* means something more and different than the English word *church*, and let me tell you, the gap is meaningful and real. Since language produces culture, we will always exist at a deficit in our mission until we confront the chasm between these two words. Church produces one thing. Ekklesia produces another. Which did Jesus intend? You know by the word He used, and also the word He did not.

---

**There is no way around it: the Greek word *ekklesia* means something more and different than the English word *church*. The gap is meaningful and real.**

---

Let me illustrate. Hendrik Kraemer, a bishop in Denmark during World War II, described the panic that overtook the clergy of his diocese as the Nazis marched in to take possession of their country. As priests and pastors gathered to his home, they asked, "What should we do?" He answered, "First, we must ask who we are! If we know who we are, then we will know what to do." [7]

How can we know what to do if we don't know who we are? Volumes have been written about our individual identity in Christ and many excellent books have also been written about our communal identity as "the church." But this begs the question: if Jesus didn't say we're His church—and He didn't—then what does it matter how well we answer the wrong question?

I must admit, the contents of this book might make you mad. While that's not my goal, it's not entirely the wrong reaction, either. To a certain degree, we've built our spiritual house on shifting sand, rather than the eternal Word, and that is a most grievous thought. By the last page, however, I believe you will have glimpsed the person and mission of Christ in a bold, new light, which also means—taking your stand in Caesarea Philippi with the first twelve apostles and comprehending Matthew 16 in its original intent—you will see yourself in a new light. Together, we'll gain a new and powerful identity as the ekklesia of Christ.

Please be patient and let me unpack this. We're laboring against at least four centuries of wrong thinking based on a mistranslation which nearly all scholars readily acknowledge, yet strangely few contest. Instead, everyone does gymnastics to make the wrong word fit. This dishonors the Word. If we are to reclaim the heights to which we have been called, we must first recognize the depths to which we've fallen. If we do not, the consequences will continue to play out in our homes, communities and nation every day. The good news? It can be fixed.

But first, like Peter, we need to get our own revelation of who Jesus really is.

# 2

## THE CRITICAL NEED
## FOR REVELATION

**T**his is less a book about spiritual warfare, and more a book about divine government. It is less a book about prayer, and more a book about paradigm. However, since a primary role of any nation's government is to declare war should that nation be threatened or attacked, and since prayer is central to any human/divine transaction, especially in the conflict between good and evil, this is also a book about prayer and spiritual warfare.

Why does government exist, if not to ensure a nation's well-being? The basic charter of any government is to protect land and people, root out enemies, and thereby secure a stable and lasting peace. War is part of this book because war is part of life. To contemplate or pray "Thy Kingdom come...on earth" must necessarily conjure images of D-Day and the beaches of Normandy or it is a pacifist delusion.[8] While the grace of Heaven may be embraced by humans, demonic ideologies are like terrorists. You don't negotiate with them, you must bring superior power and authority to bear. Paul could not have been more clear. Every day, we contend with principalities and powers in heavenly places. Robert Arthur Mathews was part of Britain's Force 136, a special force operating out of India into Burma and Malaya (modern Myanmar and Malaysia) during World War II.

He also served for many years as a missionary with the China Inland Mission. In his book *Born for Battle,* Mathews writes,

> "What all this is saying is that the 'principalities and powers in heavenly places' have mustered their unseen array, rigged their Trojan horse, infiltrated society, and opened the gates for a flood of evil to take over.

> "The Bible has alerted us to the possibility of supernatural evil powers establishing themselves in local cultures and then controlling life and custom. The messenger of the church at Pergamos is reminded of the grim fact that he dwells 'where Satan's seat is.' The obvious implication of this is that Satan's infiltration had reached its intended climax in the establishment of a control center on earth from which to direct the powers of darkness in their opposition to God's purposes of grace."[9]

War is not pleasant, but it can be just. To qualify, war must serve the *cause* of justice by *just means*, such as liberating the oppressed and halting the spread of evil, as in World War II. Unfortunately, the history of war has all too often involved aggressor nations wickedly attacking others motivated by things like racism, despotic ambition, rigid national self-interests, and plain old greed. Yet whether just or unjust, wars involve power, guns and bombs, i.e. weapons. Also: people, strategy, tactics, training, resources and diplomacy. Many factors.

As such, the dynamics of natural war form a template for insight into spiritual matters. In mission and method, right down to the great risks of hubris, natural warfare can help us better understand spiritual warfare. Obviously we must apply the comparison with care and great wisdom. For Christians, "war" is a spiritual enterprise. It is about defending the poor, honoring the Genesis template of Creation, exposing corruption and idolatry, creating equitable scales, expanding the culture of life, and protecting the weak and the widow. We do not take life, or battle people, we nurture life and care for souls. We do not war by amassing political power or forcing others to think and act like us. We war with prayer, mercy, truth and servanthood. These are our weapons. They are spiritual. But to diligently guard against carnal motivations, we must continually return to square one: Jesus. Over and over, we put our eyes on Him.

**The Cornerstone of Christ**

In the last 2,000 years, the slow, creeping influence of carnal thinking has led the institution of Christianity to build much that has little to do with Jesus. He must be the cornerstone, or the building will be unlevel, out of plumb, and out of square. This is always true, but especially when the subject is spiritual warfare! So if Martin Luther's great hymn were the template, some books about spiritual warfare might begin their battle treatise with the part about the ancient foe whose "craft and power are great." In this book, we choose to begin with the mighty fortress of God, who prevails over the mortal ills of sin and demonic rage. Luther rightly saw God as a "helper...amid the flood."

King David was even more clear: "The Lord sat as King at the flood; yes, the Lord sits as King forever. The Lord will give strength to His people" (Psa. 29:10, 11). In only 23 words, God is described as Lord three times, and King twice. David's revelation of the Kingship and Lordship of God translated immediately to "strength (for) the people." This is what a king does. He establishes government to help his subjects and expand his rule. Human kings do this imperfectly. A perfect King does it flawlessly.

We desperately need fresh revelation of this *perfect King* who is utterly committed to expanding His rule. The question tackled in this book is: *how* does He plan to expand it?

It is interesting that the cherubim and seraphim in Isaiah, Ezekiel and Revelation are described as being full of eyes. These creatures operate at the highest levels of divine interaction in the universe, yet it seems as if they can't get enough. Two eyes are simply insufficient, they are *full* of eyes.[10] The imagery of constantly beholding God is striking.

Our vantage is considerably more limited. We live in a fallen world and see in a mirror dimly.[11] This diminished capacity brings our need for revelation into sharper contrast. If winged creatures of heavenly radiance never stop gazing upon Him, how much more do we need our own eyes opened? Alignment of our vision with Heaven's reality is critical. Redemption is a process which God has already initiated and completed in eternity, but which you and I are called to implement in time and space. How can we expect the world to change when God's own people are not entirely committed to His purpose? The Kingdom is near, Jesus said, but if it is to come fully, it must first come *inside* us—you and me. For this, we need many eyes, i.e. many encounters with Christ, many downloads from Heaven.

Is it any wonder that the great, apostolic prayer of Paul is related to vision and revelation? "I pray that the eyes of your heart may be enlightened, so that you may know what is the hope of His calling" (Eph. 1:18).

So that *you* may *know.*

*The Message* says, "to make you intelligent and discerning in knowing him personally."

In *Shaping History Through Prayer and Fasting*, Derek Prince says,

> "This revelation cannot come by natural reasoning or by sense knowledge. It comes only by the Holy Spirit. He is the One who enlightens the eyes of our hearts and shows us two interwoven truths: first, that Christ's authority is now supreme over the universe; second, that the same power that raised Christ to that position of authority now works also *'in us who believe.'*"[12]

Other than Jesus, has anyone ever lived with more focus than the Apostle Paul? He described himself as being apprehended by something. Gripped. Yet what gripped him wasn't some random idea or strong, inward conviction. It was Christ! Paul said, "I count all things to be loss in view of the surpassing value of *knowing Christ Jesus*," and again, "I press on in order that I may lay hold of that for which also I was laid hold of *by Christ* Jesus" (Phil. 3:8,12). In the Greek, Paul says "that I may *katalambano*," a word which means to "seize or take possession of." Paul had been *katalambanoed* by Christ, therefore his life's obsession was to *katalambano* Christ even more. Every day was spent unto more of Christ. Unceasingly, with every breath...more! Notice also, it is no small thing that Paul attaches Christ as the title of Jesus in both passages. He does not say more of Jesus, he says more of *Christ* Jesus. Some may quibble with this, but the point of this book is to bring to light the vast implications of Peter's confession of *Christ* in Matthew 16.

The revelation of Christ is the sun around which the solar system of the kingdom orbits. It is therefore the means by which God assembles His people, and the cause to which He commissions them.

Not only does Paul describe revelation as the key to a focused life, but verse 12 also begs the question: *when* was Paul first seized? The answer is almost certainly *in previous moments of revelation,* from his first encounter on the Damascus road, to the time when he speaks of a man (almost certainly himself) who was "caught up to the third heaven...and heard inexpressible words, which a man is not permitted to speak," because of "the surpassing greatness of the revelations" given as part of the "proof of the Christ who speaks in me."[13] On the strength and authenticity of these revelations, Paul defended his apostolic ministry to the Corinthians.

In short, Paul was seized by revelation of Christ in such a way that he forever desired to seize more. Using the motif of cherubim and seraphim, we could paraphrase Paul thus, "In certain encounters, I was given eyes to see. Now all I want is *more* eyes." Herein lies the vitality and utter necessity of personal, present-tense, divine revelation. Individually or corporately, we will never become what Jesus promised to build without it. This is why Paul was such a wise master builder. For him, "Christ Jesus himself (was) the chief cornerstone" (Eph. 2:20) of all that he preached, wrote and labored for.

Yet Paul wasn't actually first with this revelation, Peter was; and Jesus praised the insight of this rough, uneducated fisherman as central to His plans. In fact, he pointedly contrasted the common process of sense knowledge with divine revelation. "Flesh and blood did not reveal this to you, but My Father who is in heaven."[14] Peter didn't consult focus groups to solve the question of Jesus's identity. This wasn't a Gallup poll, nor was it the result of brilliant human deduction. The word translated "reveal" (Gr: *apokalupto*) is a frequent New Testament term for the supernatural and often mysterious disclosure of truth. Simon's confession was divinely inspired.

In other words, while Peter's brain comprehended, and Peter's mouth spoke, the source of Peter's confession was in fact God Himself. The divine origin of true revelation imparts knowledge, wisdom and understanding which transcend human knowledge by infinite orders of magnitude, both in quantity and quality.[15] Yet, though they are inscrutable to human faculty, the Holy Spirit graciously draws forth the depths of God and permits us to drink. Deep, divine counsels are available to us. My friend, you are a revelation receptacle![16]

Mahesh Chavda says, "When God speaks, His revelation is true *at every level*. It will be true in the natural, it will be true in the spiritual, it will be true in the realm of the soul, and it will be true historically...because the Lord's Word is *truth*. On every level in which you encounter His Word, the truth will be there."[17]

If unveiling our eyes to Jesus as the Christ of God is so important—and clearly, it is—then how does the human heart *katalambano* (lay hold of) Christ? Let's examine five components of revelation.

### 1. Revelation comes from God

In Paul's prayer, "I pray that the eyes of your heart may be enlightened," the Greek word rendered 'enlightened' is *photizo*, from which we can easily recognize our own English word, photo. It conveys the idea of a shining light—the process of illumination. Really, this is the need of our heart, to be enlightened. This is the Hubble Telescope of our mind and spirit peering into the vast, deep heart of God, returning images of wondrous and infinite mystery. This is Ansel Adams at the Grand Canyon, capturing beautiful forms of light and shadow in a way that distills the natural wonder of stone and sky down to an intoxicating, fine wine. In similar fashion, as the human spirit focuses upon God in prayer, meditation, and contemplation, we hear the whisper of Jesus asking, "Who do you say I am?"

Really, there is no other question. But you can't arrive at the answer on your own. You can't swim around in your own thoughts and figure this one out.

When I Am asks, "Who am I?", it is only because He is prepared to tell you. Turn your camera on. Turn the gaze of your spirit, your affections and your thoughts toward Him. Ask for revelation. As you do this consistently, every now and then, by grace, a flash bulb pops. *Photizo.* Light explodes. In those moments, you capture Him within, so that your inner man becomes a photo image of some facet of His will and personality. Though mysterious, this process is hardly abstract, because the results are so real and powerful. Something more than head knowledge transfers to our inner life, our understanding of God, ourselves, the world.

Some part of His identity becomes ours.

Some part of His mission becomes ours, too.

In those moments, you cannot help but wish you had more eyes. Everything seems so clear, so enriched with the purity of *that* moment's truth. On a soulish level, epiphanies bring your feeler and knower into total unison right down to your bones so that nothing else matters but the *aha!* Extending this, revelation is the process of spiritual epiphany. Revelation begins with God and ending with God. It distills one thing from many, penetrating the fog and clutter of life like a single ray of light, flooding the dark uncertainty of our mind and spirit with Christ. In revelatory moments, you are elevated above the fray. The magnet of Heaven attracts you upward, giving you vision you could not otherwise achieve from below. It is transformative.

I call this type of personal, divinely-inspired epiphany the "FedEx Effect." You may or may not have noticed the simple, compositional brilliance of the FedEx logo. I hadn't either until my son, Evan, pointed it out. He said, "Dad, isn't it cool how their logo forms an arrow?" I had never seen it, but he was right. Next time one of their trucks drives by, study it more closely. Look at the way the negative space between the 'Ex' letters forms a perfect, right-facing arrow. "When it absolutely, positively has to be there overnight," the FedEx promise is clear as an arrow, moving you forward. It's simple and brilliant, but if you've never seen it, you probably don't even realize it's there. On the other hand, once your eyes are opened—"Aha, I see!"—then you can't *not* see it.

Certain themes and promises of Scripture are like that. You can be blind to them for years, then revelation comes, and then every verse you read says nothing else. You can't imagine why you didn't see it there all along. Same verses, different understanding. What changed?

The FedEx Effect.

I just gave you the clue, but you have to get the revelation for yourself by looking at the logo. This is how it is with God and us. He gives so that we can receive, but we still have to "get it" in a personal, experiential way.

## 2. Revelation is about Jesus

Revelation always centers around the person of Christ.[18] As discussed above, Paul knew the seizing force of personal revelation. Saul the Jesus-hater became Paul the bond-slave, all because he *saw* the risen Christ and heard His voice. Later, he told the Galatians that the gospel he preached did not come from man, but from a revelation of Jesus Christ.[19] In Ephesians 3, we read that, "by revelation there was made known (to Paul)...the mystery of Christ." Jesus was and is the central message. "We preach Christ crucified...for I determined to know nothing among you except Jesus Christ...for we do not preach ourselves, but Christ Jesus as Lord" (1 Cor. 1:23, 2:2; 2 Cor. 4:5).

---

**The final, total, visible rulership of Jesus over planet Earth means there is a "a long-range plan in which everything would be brought together and summed up in Him" (Eph. 1:10, MSG).**

---

The final, total, visible rulership of Jesus over planet Earth means there is a "a long-range plan in which everything would be brought together and summed up in Him" (Eph. 1:10, MSG). When Scripture culminates with John's mind-bending "Revelation of Jesus Christ," it is not merely some bizarre map of past and future events, but rather it is entirely about the rule and reign of Jesus!

Are we consumed with this? If not, why not? Do we wrongly assume that the rule of Christ is predestined with no involvement from us? If so, this book will change your mind.

### 3. Revelation requires faith

Because the realm of "head knowledge" generally follows clear rules of logic, it typically operates by mental assent. In other words, I gain value by acknowledging or agreeing with the facts, then committing to a course of action based on those facts. Human knowledge is achievable on human terms. Meanwhile, God-ideas are only achievable by God, and by those willing to believe them—often in open defiance of the facts. This is why God *loves* faith, because it puts us in His dimension, His playing field. He operates almost exclusively through people willing to walk by faith, not by sight.[20] In fact, we are told that without faith it is impossible to please Him.[21] That's huge!

How much of church activity is dependent on faith? How much of your energy, money and time is spent in activities that *please God* based on the constraints of that verse in Hebrews 11:6? Be honest. I look at my own life and fall woefully short. Most of my life is spent nurturing my own sense of comfort and security. Faith is a word reserved for salvation, not daily life. Faith jeopardizes my control. Faith destabilizes my routine. But if I trace this problem to its roots, I'm simply confessing that I operate at a deficit of revelation. I'm walking by sight.

Revelation-energizing faith is a central premise of this book, since it will take both faith and revelation to prevail against the many, fearful gates of Hades in our generation. Early on, let me clearly state: our normal, modern Christian worldview has deviated *significantly* from that of first-century believers. Did we mean to do this? Likely not. Our slow drift is the direct result of an intentional mistranslation of our job description in Matthew 16:13-19. There, Jesus set a clear course for all who seek to be His disciples. When our forefathers substituted the wrong word, the result was a wrong mindset, wrong focus, and wrong actions. The consequences have been predictably tragic. Our boredom, our lack of faith, our dullness of heart, the grinding, religious ruts of "normal church life," along with our impotence in the world at large, all stem from watering down what Jesus said He would build.

Absence of revelation will produce absence of faith. On the other hand, if we will hunger for it, since revelation comes *by* faith, it will also *produce* faith. A number of immediate, practical reasons come to mind. First, it takes faith to gaze upon God in the first place, as the natural mind is scandalized by the folly of God. Second, to believe there is an answer in Heaven for the problems of Earth is a daring leap that challenges our humanistic assumptions and egotistic orientation. Third, and perhaps the most stretching implication, is that to truly qualify as revelation, *we must receive the answer as coming from God.* Implicitly, this requires faith.

The challenges are evident, in that the rules and mechanisms of revelation are intentionally fuzzy. That our spirit and soul could receive communication from God in the form of dreams, visions, circumstantial "coincidence," inner promptings, and the conviction of the Word, is to propose a human/divine interface subject to unbelief and ridicule at every turn. The very nature of revelation demands that we rely on some source of knowledge outside of our own to bring to light what was formerly darkness. Because of this, divine communication is designed to both *produce* and *release* faith into the earth. A mystery is not a mystery if it is easily deduced. Spiritual revelation requires a "breakthrough" of insight that cannot be obtained while working within the limitations of our own ability.

Ultimately, if our insights do not originate with God, they cannot produce God. (This should greatly sober our heavily rationalistic Western theology.) To be willing to believe that God actually speaks to us and entrusts us with His plans and authority is, in itself, an act of faith.

The difficult construction of the process is its own fail-safe. Evolutionists talk about the process of natural selection. Revelation is a process of supernatural selection. Only those willing to believe and receive, will. For example, if someone reads about the FedEx Effect, but refuses to ever gaze at the FedEx logo until they finally see it, then this is not my failure to invite, nor the failure of the logo to reveal. It is a failure of submission and faith. Though the offer to be a recipient of God's voice and conduit of His will is available to all, not everyone accepts.

### 4. Revelation is relational

"Who do you say that I am?" Jesus asked His disciples.

"Why are you persecuting me?" Jesus asked Saul.

The process of revelation can be thunderous and intimidating (as with the Apostle John, who trembled and fell down as a dead man in Revelation), or it may come softly as a whisper, as when "Your ears will hear a word behind you, 'This is the way, walk in it'" (Isa. 30:21). In either case, while revelation can often feel like a download, it is not just a download of information, but a divine, relational moment. Jesus is not an idea, therefore the unveiling of Him is not merely the transference of information. He is a person, and He reveals Himself in personal ways. In John 15, He told His friends, "All things that I have heard from My Father I have made known to you." Later, John clarified the nature of this interaction. Revelation of the God-man was a thoroughly hands-on experience. "What we have *heard,* what we have *seen with our eyes,* what we *beheld* and our *hands handled...*"(1 John 1:1, ASV). Jesus was not an abstract voice floating down from Heaven. Master, Savior, and Lord, yes, but also teacher and friend, with skin, eyes, fingers and a scruffy beard.

Amazingly, human. Yet somehow, also, God. How can this be?

Such apparent contradictions reflect the systemic limitations of finite beings attempting to interface with the infinite. (Thus, again, the need for faith.) Revelation challenges our comprehension today no less than it did for the disciples. How is it that the uncreated Logos of Creation deigns to speak to us via our own thoughts, with intimate knowledge of our lives? Yet He does, sometimes with comfort, other times with correction, always with love. As stated above, this is part of the value of revelation, in that we are forced to comprehend God on His terms, as He reveals Himself, rather than by our laughable attempts to intellectually unravel mysteries too deep to fathom. Left to our own devices, we will think God is one more puzzle to solve. He is not. He is beyond the scope of our faculties to such degrees of impossibility that unless He makes Himself known, we would never know Him. And so, in love, He *self-discloses*.

Relationship.

In different ways, the relational dimension of revelation is often overlooked by both Evangelicals and Pentecostals. Evangelicals may subconsciously defer too much to *Sola Scriptura,* and end up forming a deeper relationship with their Bible than with the Incarnate, Living Word. Charismatics err on the other side, forming more of a relationship with their experience than with the Man. In both cases, though facts about God are realized, revelation actually diminishes. If we wish to become a true ekklesia, we must always hold to Christ above all.

**5. Revelation must be nurtured**

Though epiphanies feel sudden in the moment, revelation is rarely instant. Typically, we must learn to persevere.

In 1996, thirteen years before my father died, I was given revelation in a dream, the details of which are not important here. Suffice it to say, I didn't understand the dream at all, I just knew it was from God. So I carried it in my heart. I struggled with it, and with God, over the vague, foreboding implications of this dream. The imagery seemed to represent a very difficult time, and who wants that? But I kept it close to my heart, I didn't dismiss it. Eight years later

I entered the darkest period of my life. During this period, I lost my wife to cancer. I lost my church and my friends due to my own failure. I was disgraced. My identity and purpose in ministry was cut off. A couple of years after that, my father-in-law died, a man I loved and respected greatly. Then, finally, my most formative spiritual influence, my father and friend, passed away in 2009. It was a brutal season of loss, disorientation and pain.

Shortly after all this, suddenly, and with great precision, I understood the dream. Though I had carried it for years without understanding, my flashbulb, FedEx moment eventually came. Though the "instant" revelation of the dream had come in 1996, I received the gift of understanding much later, when I needed it most. God had spoken to me in striking detail, well in advance, but in ways I could not possibly understand or appreciate at the time. In reality, if He had been more explicit, I almost surely wouldn't have been able to handle the weight of that season's grief prior to its unfolding. Afterward, however, I was given a window into the mind and kindness of God. I understood more of His sovereignty and lordship over my life. The dream reassured me: Though I felt alone at the time, I was not. I was known, I *am* known, and the book of my life is written in the ink of His grace. By showing me that via a mysterious process of revelation—spanning more than a decade, using the symbolic language of dreams—I also came to know Him more. In this way, ultimately, *He* became my revelation.

Bingo. That's the point.

In reflecting upon both the dream and my "Aha!" moment, I could honestly say to myself, "Flesh and blood has not revealed this to me."

Revelation was in the Garden of Eden, when God spoke intimately to Adam and Eve. It was by revelation that Noah built a boat, and Abram left Ur. It was a revelation that drew the father of our faith to Mount Moriah. From his agonized offering of Isaac, we all gain revelation into the Lamb of God. By revelation, Joseph was promoted to Pharaoh's right hand; Moses received the Law, drafted the tabernacle and built the Ark of the Covenant; Joshua conquered Jericho; Gideon defeated the Amalekites; Samuel anointed the king; Elijah challenged the prophets of Baal; and Daniel ruled in Babylon. By revelation, wise men from Persia, along with Anna, Simeon, and John, all recognized Jesus when no one else did. By divine revelation, Paul turned his missionary focus from Asia to Macedonia. Over and over again, the epochal moments of Scripture were the direct result of divine revelation.

Yes, the canon of Scripture is closed, but revelation continues. A famous story about St. Thomas Aquinas in the 13th century puts this into perspective. Aquinas had a brilliant mind and was a major architect of Christian doctrine. His *Summa Theologiae* is one of the most influential books ever written. Yet shortly before his death, Aquinas had some sort of mystical experience which ruined him forever. In 1273, Thomas was celebrating Mass when, according to some, he heard Christ speak to him. The Lord asked Thomas what he desired, to which Thomas replied "Only you Lord. Only you." After this exchange something happened, though Thomas never spoke of it directly, nor wrote it down. Even so, he abandoned every pursuit, refusing to dictate any further works. When pressed, his explanation was simple: "After what I have seen, and Whom, all I have written seems but straw."

For Peter, the episode at Caesarea Philippi was such a moment. Perhaps this book will be one of yours. Do you have faith for that? Can you, like the Seraphim, have *many* eyes? Jesus, the Christ, is ready to be known. He's the author. He's got the script. My words and your words are shifting sand, but His words are solid rock.

# 3

## SMALL ROCK, BIG ROCK

Jesus said, "Upon *this* rock I will build my ekklesia."

Which rock? *This* rock. That's a key word, isn't it? It's very important we know what rock He's talking about. You can't grasp the ekklesia that Jesus promised to build unless you grasp the rock upon which it stands. Matthew 16 is a watershed experience in the history of divine revelation. Prior to the Cross, it may be God's pinnacle self-disclosure. From Adam forward, all of history, all of prophecy, have been pointing to this moment. It also represents a turning point in Jesus's message. The trip to Caesarea Philippi takes place about six months before Golgotha's bloody tree. Up until now, He has mainly preached the kingdom. After this, the focus shifts to declaring His coming death and resurrection.

To begin, we must realize who He's talking to. Peter's old name, used as a point of contrast, is given as Simon Barjona. In Hebrew, this would have been *Shimon bar Jonah,* meaning Simeon, son of Jonah.[22]

As you may suspect, much of the rich wordplay of this passage is completely lost on us modern readers, being translated first from Aramaic to Greek, finally to English. To begin with, take the name, Simon. One spurious but popular rendering is that Simon means "wavering reed." Supposedly we are to see in this the foreshadowed transformation of a man named Simon from a fearful, wavering soul

*39*

who denied Christ under pressure, to the bold apostle who preached at Pentecost and never denied the Lord again. While interesting, this is an inaccurate claim. Simon is the Greek form of Simeon, which means, "Hearer." This is the name Leah gave her second son in Gen. 29:33, when she felt heard by God. The root of the word, 'shama,' means "to hear, listen and obey." Simon Barjona suggests a revelatory, listening ear when posed with the question: "Who do you say that I am?"

Of note, Peter is the only named person to receive a direct blessing from Jesus. "Blessed are *you*" is a phrase applied by Jesus to no other individual in Scripture. By this we are encouraged to be disciples who *hear* the voice of the Holy Spirit when He whispers commands and mysteries from God. Once more, we are also reminded of the urgency of revelation. Twelve disciples gathered, representing twenty-four ears, but only one heard God's answer to God's question.

Yet Simon's name is only the beginning. Simon is an old name. Jesus has given this disciple a new name. Even more clever is the comparison of his new name, Peter (Gr: *'petros'*), to the foundation rock (Gr: *'petra'*) upon which Jesus will build His government. Such wordplay was intentional. Jesus shrewdly employed a pun to add layers of meaning that would fascinate us for generations to come. Each layer is like a shaft boring through differing geological strata, first striking water, then oil, then gold, permitting additional riches to surface.

*Petros* means a small, detached stone, anything from a pebble to a boulder, while *petra* refers to a great, unyielding bedrock. A *petros* is moveable, a *petra* is not. Peter, the small stone, is contrasted with a great rock. Through the centuries, this has been a highly controversial passage. Millions of people base their denominational allegiances on this passage. Countless commentaries and volumes have addressed this topic, and much scholarship has been given to the Greek. For our purposes, I will simply summarize the four major interpretations of Jesus's words, "Upon this rock (*'petra'*) I will build..."

## 1. Peter is the rock

Our Catholic brothers would like us to believe that Jesus was basically installing Peter as the first Pope.[23] In this view, the Lord's reply to Peter's confession is meant to establish Peter's primacy not only in launching the church, but also governing the church. In other words, the Catholic position has Jesus saying, "Upon you, Peter, I will build..." This view may be strengthened when it is understood that if Jesus actually spoke the phrase in Aramaic (as He well might have), the word used for both 'Peter' and 'rock' would be identical—*'kepha'*—lacking the nuances of the written Greek.

"I also say to you that you are *kepha,* and upon this *kepha* I will build..."

Peter's leadership in responding to the Jews after Pentecost, and converting 5,000 souls with his first sermon, is obvious and beyond dispute. Clearly, he was the key figure among the twelve in founding the New Covenant faith.

But is he *the* Rock?

The Roman Catholic Church stakes their institutional soul on this claim, deriving authority from the notion that apostolic succession historically began in Matthew 16. Protestants agree that Peter launched the movement, but disagree that the movement is built on him. Also, it is worth noting that Peter's name had already changed prior to this confession.[24] Per the example of Abram, Sarai and Jacob, Jesus was grafting Peter into a larger prophetic tradition, but the use and repetition of his name in this story seems instructive more than institutional.

If we do not see this, we run the risk of making Peter the revelation of this passage. He is, and shall be (as prophetically revealed in the cleverness of Jesus's wordplay), a key figure. In a clever way, Jesus may even be describing Peter as a sort of chip off the old block—"Peter, I look at you and see a part of Me!"—rough stone being shaped into a glorious masterpiece. A follower of Christ being conformed to Christ. Even so, he is clearly peripheral to the central figure, Jesus.

### 2. Jesus, the Rock

The Bible repeatedly describes God as a rock. The imagery is meant to help readers understand the safety and protection He gives. God is solid, unchanging, faithful, strong. He is the foundation of all existence, the fountainhead of salvation. Comparing many passages, the rock motif is synonymous with God as fortress, strong tower, and refuge: "Who is a *rock,* besides our God?"[25]

The rock becomes salvific in the atoning work of Christ. Jesus describes obedience to His Word (and therefore, Himself), as being an unshakable foundation to build upon[26], while Peter and Paul make it clear that the Messiah is the rock of offense spoken of by the prophet Isaiah.[27] Likewise, Christ was the sustaining rock from which the Israelites drank in the wilderness.[28]

In Matthew 16, it requires no great leap to understand that Jesus is drawing a direct connection from the type of God as an immovable rock to Himself. Though the Bible is famously sparse in physical details, I like to imagine that Jesus might have used hand gestures to clarify His intent. As He answered Peter, might He have pointed to Himself?

"Upon *this* rock," He says, emphatically patting His chest. "Upon My own life, death and resurrection, My mission and mercy, My sacrifice and love—upon Myself, for there is none other more sure and true—I will build. I am the epicenter of Creation, the Alpha and Omega, the Ancient of Days. By Me all things were created, both in the heavens and on earth, visible and invisible, whether thrones or dominions or rulers or authorities. All things were created by Me and for Me. No man can lay a foundation other than that which has been laid. Who is the rock? I Am."

As Leonard Sweet and Frank Viola succinctly state in *The Jesus Manifesto,* "The Christian life properly conceived and experienced is simply a reproduction and a reliving of the life of Jesus. Your Christian life begins with Christ, continues with Christ, and ends with Christ. Simply put, the history of Jesus is both the experience and the destiny of every believer."[29]

Sweet and Viola further expound upon the all-sufficiency of Christ, properly framing this penniless preacher from Nazareth as the entire occupation of the heavens, the Old Testament, the New Testament, the apostles and history itself. "Christ isn't just found in the center. He's also found in the corners and on the edges, just as the light of the sun hits all of planet Earth. He's the God of the whole show. The Bright and Morning Star gives light to all that exists... Christ is the only *thing* that the Spirit reveals. He has no other revelation."[30]

Eternal life (for each individual) and eternal purpose (for the corporate body) necessarily must be built upon an eternal foundation. There is only one: the rock of Jesus Christ.

### 3. The ongoing revelation of Christ is the Rock

Layers upon layers of meaning.

The brilliant construction of Jesus's language in this passage allows multiple claims to be true at once, each with its own scale of priority and importance. Peter *was* a small part of that rock. Jesus *is* the ultimate realization of that rock. Yet we are not finished extracting all possible meanings. As the frame around this stunning masterpiece expands, we stagger back just enough to realize that it is actually the *ongoing process of revelation* that forms the foundation of God's work in the earth. Do you see?

---

**Christ *is ever being* revealed. What matters most is that each generation—man, woman and child—gains a fresh download of His glory into their own lives.**

---

In this scenario, Jesus is still clearly the rock, but a qualifier is attached. A subjective element threatens the primacy of His revelation, which is this: does anybody see or care or know? This is the reception issue I spoke of in the last chapter. Just as the disciples were continually stumped, so are we. We often live in a spiritual fog, clueless, distracted, tone-deaf, busy, bored and unfocused, yet God is talking all the time. His signal is strong and His broadcast is perpetual. Christ *is ever being* revealed. What matters most is that each generation—man, woman and child—gains a fresh download of His glory into their own lives. Otherwise, the heart of the gospel will grow stale, and the kingdom of God will not advance. If we are not continually enlarged in our understanding of His glory and kingship over the earth, we will hesitate in our purpose, becoming stunted, lethargic, and spiritually narcissistic. Life will be redefined as ours, not His. *Jesus must ever and freshly be seen.* The steady disciplines of worship, Word and prayer are meant to produce fresh seasons of renewal, where our spirit sees and says, all over again, "Aha! You are the Christ!"

Viewed from this angle, Jesus is saying, "Simon (the Hearer!), you have heard and seen me as I really am, and rightly so. Everything revolves around seeing *Me,* because I perfectly reveal the Father! Keep your eyes on Me. I am limitless, which means you can always see more. I am always speaking, which means you always need to hear Me. This interaction and the revelation which comes from it—*this* is what I will build upon!"[31]

## 4. The Rock of the Gods is the rock

Finally, the historic backdrop of Caesarea Philippi adds another possible interpretation. The reason for this will be explained in detail in the next section titled "Rulership," but suffice it for now to remember that Jesus has staged this scene very carefully. He likely stands within view of a well-known, demonic stronghold called The Rock of the Gods. Is it merely coincidence that the Son of God arrives and starts talking about building His kingdom on a rock? Not at all. It is a showdown, with one Rock challenging the claims of another rock. Who will win? Daniel 2:31-35 comes to mind, when a small rock cut out of a mountain smashes into another mountain and destroys it. God's kingdom against demonized, earthly pretenders. Caesarea Philippi is an early prototype of this conflict.

In essence, Jesus might well have been saying, "Look guys, look over there. Do you see that demonic fortress, with all those people trapped in idolatry? You know what that monstrosity is called. It's a big rock (petra). But as Peter has realized, I'm the Christ, which means the earth is mine and all the fullness thereof. Soon, I will take My rightful place at the right hand of My Father's throne. He will establish Me in Heaven. But one day, He will also establish me in total supremacy on Earth. When the seventh angel sounds the final note of history, all the kingdoms of the world will become Mine, and I will reign forever and ever in perfect justice, truth and love. But please get this: *I'm not waiting until then!* I'm starting now. I'm going to build My kingdom atop every outpost of darkness. Men call that thing over there 'god's rock.' It's a lie. I'm the One, true Rock. And I want My kingdom everywhere—not just in nice, beautiful places, but also in the hard, dark, evil places. *Especially* in those places. I want to capture back every square inch of the planet, until all is subsumed in My glory. So on *this* rock, I will build..."

**In summary**

Perhaps we can imagine the Lord pointing first to Himself ("upon this rock"), but then maybe also gesturing to The Rock of the Gods ("I will build") to firmly establish in the minds of His apostles that nothing was exempt from His rulership. Clearly, He wanted to link the two. Why? Because total dominion means that *every gate of Hades must be challenged.* Jesus went 30 miles out of His way to make sure His disciples got the point. The Acts of the Apostles clearly demonstrates the early believers got it. The question is, do we?

If you answer in the affirmative, what exactly would you point to, to prove your point?

The contemporary church has a revelation of many things. We have a revelation of church government (presbyterian, congregational, episcopal). We have a revelation of denominations or non-denominations. We have a revelation of successful marketing and organizational strategies, along with the usefulness of Sunday School and the value of tithing. We understand the enormous potential of technology to communicate our message. We understand building campaigns. Impressed yet?

The resounding question of this book: Do we have a revelation of Christ?

Is our message Jesus's message? Do we understand what Christ wants established on the earth? Read the Old Testament prophecies and one thing becomes abundantly clear: Christ has not only come to save, but to triumph over Satan. In other words, He has come to rule.

## MY NOTES

Every gate of Hades must
be challenged
Q. Do we understand what Christ ☆
☆ wants established on this earth?
A. Christ has come to save but also
to triumph over satan!

In other words, He has come to Rule!

# RULERSHIP

---

*"You are the Christ!"*

*"On this rock I will build my ekklesia!"*

---

"Did we in our own strength confide,
our striving would be losing,
were not the right man on our side,
the man of God's own choosing.
Dost ask who that may be?
Christ Jesus, it is He;
Lord Sabaoth, His name,
from age to age the same,
and He must win the battle."

Verse 2: *A Mighty Fortress is Our God*
**– Martin Luther**

# 4

## CHRIST THE LORD

**J**ust as Caesarea Philippi provided a microcosm to enrich the drama by which Jesus was revealed as Messiah, so too the broader Near East culture—already several millennia old at that point—provided a specific macrocosm into which the story of Christ was written. We must understand that Jesus was not arbitrarily proclaimed Lord of Lords and King of Kings. These lofty titles did not emerge in a vacuum. Rather, the terms meant something definite to the people that heard them. Intricate layers of cultural, historical and scriptural connections, like synapses in the brain, formed powerful, magnetic reference points by which the disciples and the broader community could recognize what was really going on. Twenty-first century readers live highly detached from this communal memory. We live in a constitutional democracy. We know about iPhones, cars, football and presidents, not Christs and kingdoms.

So before we can gain the full benefit of Peter's confession, "You are the Christ," as well as Jesus's reply, "Upon this rock I will build my ekklesia," we must quickly immerse ourselves in that world. I will utilize four arenas of thought to expand our understanding. I will summarize the first three in this chapter, but the fourth requires a chapter unto itself. We must understand Christ according to:

## 1. The Culture of Caesar

Ancient Near East rulers were regarded as gods. This was typical of both the region and the times.[32] Acts of fealty included bowing, along with vows of loyalty. No one was permitted to defy Caesar, who, along with his son, was regarded as divine. Emperor deification followed a clearly prescribed pattern, with fifty-five Caesars being deified after their death.

Pastor Ray Vander Laan has written a fascinating online essay on the roots of Roman Emperor deification. The writer describes how the people of Asia Minor viewed Croesus, king of Sardis, as partially divine, as early as in 550 BC, predating Rome. Sacred enclosures and temples sprang up, such as the acropolis of Pergamum, where "the rulers of the city were honored as gods, a practice which legitimized the absolute power of the king and his dynasty. They bore titles such as *Soter* (Savior) or *Epiphanes* (God Manifested), and were worshipped regularly, including a festival on their birthday... After (Alexander the Great) died his empire was divided among his commanders, each of whom continued the practice of declaring themselves divine. This added legitimacy to their rule." With the advent of the Caesars, more and more cities built similar temples, including Ephesus, Nicaea, Nicomedia and Caesarea Philippi, just to name a few.

The writer continues:

"When Julius Caesar became emperor the enthusiasm for his official deification grew in the East even though in Rome the rulers were not considered divine. When Julius Caesar was murdered in 44 BC; a spectacular comet passed by, so bright it

could be seen in broad daylight for eight days. This was interpreted as the divine authentication of Caesar's deity. His adopted son Octavian proclaimed his father 'divine' and himself
'Son of God' when he became emperor in 27 BC. He changed
his name to *Augustus,* a title of supreme majesty and divinity...

"(As a result of Caesar worship) the world of Asia was suddenly a very dangerous place for the rapidly growing Christian communities. The believers must be willing to call Caesar
'Lord and God' or risk death...(but) it is important to understand that the basic reason the believers were persecuted was
not the worship of Jesus...It was not one's allegiance to Jesus
that was considered dangerous, but the insistence that he
must be the only Lord. All other gods are not gods at all (Acts
19:23-26)."

The writer goes on to describe the importance of festival holy
days in which the emperor was worshipped throughout the imperial
cities. Statues of the emperors and other gods were given crowns
and paraded through the streets. Citizens were expected to offer sacrifices and eat the meat in honor of the gods, as recognition of the
emperor's divinity.

"(Since) Jesus, the Son of God, is 'Lord of Lords and King of
Kings' (Rev. 17:14; 19:16)...the witness of the disciples and the
believers was a declaration of war on the Roman state and its
Satanic foundation. What seemed religious to the Christians
was political to the Romans. There was no middle ground. Either Caesar was Lord or Jesus was. To his followers the basis
of life and faith was a total commitment to God who was 'the
blessed and *only ruler,* the *King of kings* and *Lord of lords,* who
*alone is immortal*'" (1 Tim. 6:15-16)."[33]

What is interesting in all these stories is the mythic yearning
for a human ruler who is also God. Did you notice? Pagan prac-
tices and thought systems simultaneously reveal and corrupt the
legitimate spark of God in the heart of man since Creation. If this

is true, we should view these errors not as less than erroneous, yet revealing an outline of truth much as the shadow of an object is shaped by the light. Being formed in God's image, it is inevitable that human history shares certain expectations, albeit tainted with sin. These repetitive themes are not pagan so much as human, and could be compared to the chipset of a computer. In a sense, we're all programmed by divine prerogative to anticipate certain realities. While the process of deifying mortal kings is a gross act of idolatry, it also represents a persistent tribal anticipation of the true Messiah. In every culture, something latent cries out for Christ to be revealed.

---

**In every culture, something latent cries out for Christ to be revealed.**

---

Emperor deification required material witnesses to vouch for having personally observed the newly deceased ruler rising into heaven.[34] Sound familiar? So when an unspecified number of ordinary Jews (as many as 500 according to 1 Cor. 15:6) bore witness to the improbable sight of a resurrected dead man rising into the clouds, they had no idea the enormous repercussions their claims would later bring.

Meanwhile, John 18:37 and 19:12-16 clearly show us that Jesus was not crucified because He preached a different religion but because He was proclaimed the only true Caesar[35] by His followers. Thus, the permanence of every earthly Caesar's crown was called into question. "The divine Lord of the world is not Caesar, bestride his brutal empire. It is Jesus, the Jewish Messiah, whom the Roman Empire crucified but whom Israel's God has now vindicated."[36]

The similarity in the political language used by both Jesus and His followers to proclaim the coming Kingdom of God and that of the secular kings of His time was intentional. When Paul and Silas arrived in Thessalonica, Paul followed his custom of proclaiming in the synagogue that "This Jesus whom I am proclaiming to you *is the Christ*" (Acts 17:3). The multitude got the message—they knew what Christ meant—and were greatly offended. A mob formed. How do we know they got it? Because when the mob complained to the city authorities, they said: "These men who have upset the world have come here also...and they all act contrary to the decrees of Caesar, *saying that there is another king, Jesus*" (Acts 17:6-7).

Revelation 1:5 tells us that Jesus is the ruler over all presidents, prime ministers, dictators and parliaments. When the Lord stood before Pilate, bound and bleeding, He calmly informed Caesar's tetrarch, "You would have *no* authority over Me, unless it had been *given you* from above" (John 19:11).[37]

### 2. The Messianic Psalms

While a first century worldview is helpful, ultimately, we understand the truth of Christ through the lens of Scripture, not culture. "Christ" is a title, not a last name; the simplest and most profound understanding of Christ is "The Anointed One." Likewise, to comprehend the magnitude of this title as the disciples would have understood it, the Jewish frame of reference rooted in Psalm 2 and Psalm 110 is most helpful. While many other passages are also messianic,[38] these two psalms penned by King David express the heart and soul of Jewish messianic expectation:

### PSALM 2

**1: Why are the nations in an uproar, and the peoples devising a vain thing? The kings of the earth take their stand, and the rulers take counsel together against <u>the Lord</u> and against <u>His Anointed</u>:**

> *The word 'Anointed' in Hebrew is 'Mashiyach,' rendered in English, 'Messiah.' In the Greek Septuagint, this is 'Khristos,'*

> *rendered 'Christ.' Earth's kings (and by them, prefigured, are all demonic powers) do not want to submit to the rightful rulership of God's chosen and anointed ruler. This is symbolic of every anti-Christ spirit, institution and ruler throughout history.*

**2: "Let us <u>tear their fetters apart</u>, and <u>cast away their cords</u> from us!"**

> *They are committed to removing all restraint. They will not submit. "Let's get free of God! Cast loose from Messiah!" (MSG)*

**3: He who sits in the heavens <u>laughs</u>, the Lord scoffs at them. Then <u>He will speak to them in His anger and terrify them in His fury</u>:**

> *God is entirely unfazed by this global rebellion. Divine laughter conveys total sovereignty through derision. Yet God's disdain is hardly laissez-faire. "At first he's amused at their presumption; then he gets good and angry. Furiously, he shuts them up" (MSG). God is not negligent or disconnected. He has a clear reply.*

**4: "But as for Me, <u>I have installed My King upon Zion</u>, My holy mountain."**

> *God's answer to the rebellion is not to personally overthrow the rebels, but to enthrone His own chosen King in Zion. This verse promises the future inauguration of a new regime. One day, the Christ will come!*

**5: I will surely tell of the decree of the Lord: He said to Me, "You are My <u>Son</u>, today I have begotten You. Ask of Me, and I will surely <u>give the nations as Your inheritance</u>, and the very ends of the earth as Your**

possession. You shalt <u>break them with a rod of iron</u>, You shall shatter them like earthenware."

> *The Messiah will be a son. He will also be given wide latitude, even to the point of asking for and receiving all the nations of the earth as His rightful inheritance. This Anointed One is under no obligation to be merciful. His actions of rulership are like a rod of iron shattering a clay pot. The rod of iron is actually a king's scepter in Psa. 110:2. The Messiah will demonstrate His total authority and power by shattering all resistance. "He will strike the earth with the rod of His mouth" (Isa. 11:4).*

6: Now therefore, <u>O kings, show discernment; Take warning, O judges of the earth.</u> Worship the Lord with reverence, and rejoice with trembling. <u>Do homage to the Son</u>, lest He become angry, and you perish in the way, for His wrath may soon be kindled. How blessed are all who take refuge in Him!

> *In light of this terrifying reality, all kings and kingdoms should take care to come into alignment with the will of God, expressed through the dominion of the Anointed One. Kings and judges should understand that the strength of their government derives from the justice of God, not any self-derived greatness or might. Participate with Messiah, in His values and truth—give Him homage—or face the consequences.*

## PSALM 110

1: The Lord says to my Lord: "Sit at My right hand, <u>until I make Your enemies a footstool</u> for Thy feet."

> *The Messiah rules at the right hand of God, and shall, until His enemies are completely subdued on earth. In 1 Corinthians 15, quoting Psa. 110, Paul says, "The last enemy that will be abolished is death."*

**2: The Lord will stretch forth Your <u>strong scepter from Zion</u>, saying, "<u>Rule in the midst of Your enemies.</u>"**

> *Here, the rod of Psalm 2 is revealed as a scepter stretched forth from Zion. Zion refers to the throne of Messiah, the seat from which He rules. Crucial to understanding ekklesia, Zion also refers to the mount of assembly. The rod extends from Zion. This enthroned ruler has dominion or "rule," though surrounded by enemies. Still, His victory is assured because all His enemies shall be subdued. Thus, though not yet fully realized in human terms, the Messiah's rulership remains constant and unchallenged. The marshaling of significant threatening resources against Him is of no consequence. It is actually a messianic priority to manifest His authority in the midst of the strongest, deepest outposts of darkness. The later section of the Psalm teaches this "Lord" is more than a king; He is also a priest (110:4).*

**3: <u>Your people will volunteer freely in the day of Your power</u>; in holy array, from the womb of the dawn, Your youth are to You as the dew. The Lord has sworn and will not change His mind, "You are a priest forever according to the order of Melchizedek."**

> *When God's Anointed One is revealed in full strength—i.e. the revelation of Christ—the natural heart response of those who follow Him is to yield even more completely to His will and plan. They "volunteer freely," meaning they commit to full*

> *participation on God's terms, with God's favor, acting in His name, for His glory. As we shall see, this is the ekklesia, ruling out of Zion, the ones who assemble around the revelation of Christ. For this reason, Psalm 110 is a precursor passage, mirroring Jesus revealed as the Christ in Mat. 16, and then immediately forming His ekklesia.*

**4: The Lord is at Your right hand; He will <u>shatter kings</u> in the day of His wrath. He will <u>judge among the nations,</u> He will fill them with corpses, He will <u>shatter the chief men over a broad country</u>. He will drink from the brook by the wayside; therefore He will lift up His head.**

> *This portion repeats the themes of the closing verses of Psalm 2. The Messiah will shatter the governmental authority of rebellious kings—both spiritual and earthly. He will "shatter the chief men over a broad country," meaning influential men, but also "rulers, against the powers, against the world forces of this darkness, against the spiritual forces of wickedness in the heavenly places" (Eph. 6:12).*

The Latin Vulgate gives us the traditional title of Psalm 110, *Dixit Dominus,* referring to the announcement of a ruler. The first verse of Psalm 110 is directly quoted or referred to in the New Testament more than any other Hebrew Scripture (21 times). Seven additional references to later verses (all in the book of Hebrews),[39] brings the total number of New Testament quotations to 28. Obviously, this passage is highly significant for an adequate theology of the Messiah.

Notice also that the rebellion of Psalm 2 is specifically against the rule of Christ. Buddha, Allah, Shiva and Baal are of no account. It is the rulership of Christ which the kings of the earth despise, and to Jesus alone that they refuse submission. Even so, the Son of God is installed in Zion. With a rod of iron, He will crush the rebellion and exercise dominion in the midst of His enemies.

> "For a child will be born to us, a son will be given to us; *and the government will rest on His shoulders;* and His name will be called Wonderful Counselor, Mighty God, Eternal Father, Prince of Peace. There will be *no end to the increase of His government* or of peace...The zeal of the Lord of hosts will accomplish this" (Isa. 9:6; cf. 2:1-4).

Hundreds of years after Isaiah, a child was born in a stable as the human son of God. This child was chosen to fulfill the work of salvation, walk in power, "anointed...with the oil of gladness above Your companions" (Heb. 1:9) as the "firstborn of many brethren" (Rom. 8:29), "the first-born of the dead, and *the ruler of the kings of the earth*" (Rev. 1:5).

---

**Get this: Jesus *the lamb* and *human Son of God*, brings *salvation* in mercy and grace.**

**But Jesus as *the Christ* brings the *government of God to the earth*.**

---

Get this: Jesus *the lamb* and *human Son of God,* brings *salvation* in mercy and grace. But Jesus as *the Christ* brings the *government of God to the earth.*

Read that again: Jesus's anointing brings the government of heaven to planet Earth. Daniel prophesied as much. "And in the days of those kings the God of heaven will set up a kingdom which will never be destroyed, and that kingdom will not be left for another people; it will crush and put an end to all these kingdoms, but it will itself endure forever" (Dan. 2:44).

In short, the full expectation of the Jewish people, and thus the disciples, was that the promised Messiah was a *ruler.*

"Let all kings bow down before him, all nations serve him" (Psa. 72:11).

Clearly, the Christ is a threat to every worldly king on earth and every demonic throne in the high places. Herod understood this threat. Later, as the gospel spread, Caesar would come to understand it. At first, per Psalm 2, the strategy of earth's rebellious kings was to stamp it out, quash it, kill it; Herod slaughtering male children under two years of age, Nero slaughtering Christians in the Coliseum. But under Constantine—a dubious convert at best and more probably an immoral, brutally shrewd politician—the stratagem changed: If you can't beat 'em, join 'em. Or, stated more directly, if you can't kill it, co-opt it. Thus began our descent into "church culture," as opposed to organic body life and praying ekklesia.[40]

### 3. The Christ of Philippians 2

One of the clearest explanations of the impact of Jesus the Christ is found in Philippians 2:6-11. Here, we read that "(Jesus) existed in the form of God" but did not regard "equality with God a thing to be grasped." Instead, God became a normal, working guy. A carpenter from Nazareth. He emptied Himself, took the form of a servant, humbled even to the point of crucifixion. In light of His severe humility and total fidelity to the mission of God, Paul declares that,

> "God highly exalted Him, and bestowed on Him the name which is above every name, that at the name of Jesus every knee will bow, of those who are in heaven, and on earth, and under the earth, and that every tongue will confess that Jesus Christ is Lord, to the glory of God the Father" (Phil. 2:9-11).

We must not miss this astonishing statement, that "at the name of Jesus *every knee shall bow*...and *every tongue shall confess* that Jesus Christ *is Lord*" (Phil. 2:10-11). This is not poetry, it's both prophecy and actuality. The reference point for this claim is Isaiah chapter 45.

> *"I am the Lord, and there is no other;* besides Me there is no God...A righteous God and a Savior...Turn to Me, and be saved, all the ends of the earth; for I am God, and there is no other...*to Me every knee will bow, every tongue will swear allegiance"* (vs. 5, 21-23).

For simplicity, I'll condense God's claims to four key points:

1. There is only one Lord
2. God the Lord is also our Savior
3. Every knee will bow to this Lord
4. Every tongue will confess (swear allegiance)

God's definition of His own personhood is forceful, decisive and exclusive. It expresses supreme authority, confidence, and ultimately, dominion, though this dominion is clearly unrealized at present, at least in human terms. Even so,

"To me every knee *will* bow."

Bowing and confessing God's right to rule is at the heart of the human story. At present we are free to choose. You either bow or you don't. Relative to the size of the population and the length of history, God rarely wins this freewill test. Since Adam, people have stubbornly refused to recognize His rulership. However, while the trend is growing worse,[41] it is a temporary state. One day, they *will*.

By contrast, those loyal to God will *never bow to anyone but God.* Numerous biblical passages warn against bowing to idols. While Moses "made haste to bow low toward the earth and worship" Yahweh (Exo. 34:8), and the psalmists declare, "Because He is your Lord, bow down to him" (Psa. 45:11) and also "Come, let us worship and bow down. Let us kneel before the Lord our maker" (Psa. 95:6), yet the people were continually warned against giving the same reverence to images of wood and stone:

> "You shall not make for yourselves idols, nor shall you set up for yourselves an image or a sacred pillar, nor shall you place a figured stone in your land **to bow down to it;** for I am the Lord your God" (Lev. 26:1).

> "(Do) not associate with these nations...or mention the name of their gods, **or make anyone swear by them,** or serve them, **or bow down to them**" (Josh. 23:7).[42]

While the claims of Isaiah 45 are clear, their application remains somewhat abstract. After all, how shall the true God to Whom all must bow be recognized? How will He be made manifest in such a way as to receive complete allegiance? In response to this lingering question, Jesus strides onto the stage of human history, and Peter, drawing upon the collective messianic memory of the entire Jewish race, proclaims, "You're the One!" Paul was more explicit. Jesus was not only the Messiah of God, he *was* God. Thus, God's oath in Isaiah 45:23 is unequivocally and uniquely fulfilled in the person of Jesus. This is the backdrop of Philippians 2.

> "The central feature of (Paul's) reworking of Isaiah 45 [in Philippians 2]...indicate(s) the transferral of Old Testament language from God to Jesus Christ...Christ's lordship may well be an expression of Jewish monotheism, but it comes about precisely because he (Christ) is the human *embodiment* of that monotheistic God."[43]

To this day, Isaiah 45 is still read by rabbis around the world, eagerly awaiting their Messiah. Yet Paul audaciously claims that this passage belongs *exclusively* to Jesus and no one else. The implications are vast. "The name above every name" can be none other than the holy name of God first revealed to Moses, *Yahweh.* Thus, Jesus the

Christ ('*Yeshua Hamashia*') is now given this name, and by rights, the very authority of *Yahweh* himself.[44]

N.T. Wright says, "If you read *Christos* here as merely a proper name, or as simply a divine title, it won't make nearly as much overall sense as if you read it as 'Messiah.'" If Jesus Christ is Messiah and Lord as the Jews would have understood the totality and severity of those terms, then nothing is exempt from His Lordship or Anointing. By extension, Caesar is *not* Lord, he merely pretends at the title.[45] Both Paul's Christology and the kingdom of God are clearly presented as a counterpoint to Caesar, Empire and every God-opposed governmental structure they represent. Before the throne of Christ, every worldly ruler is not merely demoted, but dethroned. When Paul tells the Colossians, "In Christ, all the fullness of the Deity lives in bodily form" (Col 2:9), the profundity of the statement is so complete that we are meant to understand, quite literally, *everything* by it. All world systems are re-prioritized in response to the revelation of Jesus as Lord.

In *With the Grain of the Universe,* Stanley Hauerwas, professor of Theological Ethics at Duke, says Christ is not only a Christian truth for everyone, but He is also the *absolute truth* about "the way things are...the way the world is."[46] In other words, the prevailing reality of Christ is so woven into existence that submission to Him is the only way to live with the grain of the universe. Do you see?

If this is real, then there is nothing more real, and if it is true, there is nothing more true.

Before all is finished, good angels and redeemed people will worship Him, but no less, rebellious angels and rebellious people will also worship. He has power "even to subject all things to Himself" (Phil. 3:21). *Everyone* will worship the Christ of God.[47] All people, principalities and powers will one day bow.[48]

Paul was unabashed about this reality, instructing Timothy to shepherd his flock with the understanding that right in the midst of imperial Rome, Jesus was the "*only* Sovereign, the King of kings and Lord of lords" (1 Tim. 6:15). John also understood what this meant. In his letter to the churches, he called the resurrected Christ "the ruler of the kings of the earth" (Rev. 1:5-6).

If Jesus is Lord, King and ruler over all, then Caesar is not. This is not a small matter, for it bears directly on any group formed or authorized by Him to act on His behalf, *vis-a-vis* the ekklesia. It means any authority the ekklesia is given, if it comes from Him, is the highest, most potent form of authority possible. It means the tools He gives are real tools to effect real change.

It also means in Christ, Lord Sabaoth has come.

# 5

## LORD SABAOTH

God's name is sacred in the extreme among orthodox Jews. It is so holy that certain traditions closely guard its use. For example, before writing the divine name, a scribe must carefully prepare his heart and mind. Once he begins writing, he does not stop until it is finished. According to tradition, no interruptions are permitted, even to greet a king.

The most transcendent of all of God's names is YHWH (Yahweh). It was called "the ineffable name." To protect it, it was read aloud as Adonai, *"the Lord."* This name, along with the title Elohim, is frequently combined with other words. In this manner we obtain the familiar compound names, such as: "Yahweh-Jireh" (the Lord my Provider), "Yahweh-Shalom" (the Lord our Peace), "Yahweh-Rapha" (the Lord my Healer), and others. These names are meant to help us understand key components of God's nature, the sum total of which is God Himself. Compound names are used about 30 times in Scripture, with each uniquely fusing some aspect of human need to a corresponding attribute of divine supply (peace, healing, provision, etc.).

Yet there is one formulation of the compound name that is far more prevalent than all others, occurring approximately *290* times by itself—nearly ten times more than all the other compound names combined! This is Yahweh or Elohim paired with the Hebrew word *tzevaot,* translated "hosts" or "armies". In English this becomes Lord Sabaoth, the Lord of hosts.[49]

In *This Day We Fight,* Francis Frangipane says, "From the sheer number of references alone, we see that 'the Lord of Hosts' (or the God of Armies) is the revelation of the Most High most frequently demonstrated to mankind in the Bible."[50]

Lord Sabaoth paints God in the bold military colors of a divine warrior. Don't be fooled here. Angelic warriors are not cute, cuddly creatures, but fierce spirits of awesome power, so much so that when one appears in Scripture, he often has to tell the people around him not to be afraid.[51] Their number—"ten thousand times ten thousand" (Dan. 7:10, KJV)—is entirely at God's disposal, and cannot be defeated. The supernatural power of angels is evident in their capacity to:

- Strike men blind (Gen. 19:11, 2 Kings 6:18)
- Call down fire and brimstone from heaven (Gen. 19:13, 21-25)
- Move stones weighing many tons (Mat. 28:2, Mark 16:4)
- Unfasten iron manacles (Acts 12:7-11)
- Open locked prison cells (Acts 5:19)
- Kill rulers (Acts 12:23)
- Sweep through army encampments with plague and death (Sam. 24:15-16; 2 Chron. 32:21; Isa. 37:36)
- Release various calamities in the book of Revelation

In light of this, the New International Version's rather weak translation of "Lord of hosts" into "Lord Almighty" has been criticized for muddling the explicit military tone. Yet while the denotation of Sabaoth is "warriors," the connotation may be closer to "strength" or "power." In this view, the hosts of heaven are best understood archetypally as a real and present threat to evil, expressed in the ascendancy of justice, righteousness, truth and salvation, not guns, bombs and human striving. Justice is always at the heart of Lord Sabaoth's righteous warfare. The sum total of the observations below inform us of the Lord's priorities, methods and His purpose in man. I cannot be more emphatic on this point: the Lord of hosts is not drafting a camo-wearing militia in Montana, but a ruler-ship-minded people who are willing to contend in love, humility, prayer and fasting for the breaking of demonic strongholds.

---

**The Lord of hosts is not drafting a camo-wearing militia in Montana, but a rulership-minded people who are willing to contend in love, humility, prayer and fasting for the breaking of demonic strongholds.**

---

### The Divine Warrior and King

Elisha's apprentice was granted a literal sighting of God's heavenly army. As human armies with horses and chariots encircled the city of Dothan, Elisha calmly tells his servant,

> "Do not fear, for those who are with us are more than those who are with them. Then Elisha prayed and said, 'O Lord, I pray, open his eyes that he may see.' And the Lord opened the servant's eyes, and he saw; and behold, the mountain was full of *horses and chariots of fire* all around Elisha" (2 Kings 6:16-17).

While impressive, this is not the first revelation of God as warrior. The first came when Pharaoh's army was destroyed in the Red Sea. On the shores of victory, Moses and the sons of Israel sing a song:

"I will sing to the Lord, for He is highly exalted; the horse and its rider He has hurled into the sea...*The Lord is a warrior; the Lord is His name*... Your right hand, O Lord, is majestic in power, *Your right hand, O Lord, shatters the enemy*. And in the greatness of Your excellence You overthrow those who rise up against You; You send forth Your burning anger, and it consumes them as chaff...

*Who is like You among the gods, O Lord?* Who is like You, majestic in holiness, awesome in praises, working wonders? You stretched out Your right hand, the earth swallowed them... *The peoples have heard, they tremble;* anguish has gripped the inhabitants of Philistia. Then the chiefs of Edom were dismayed; The leaders of Moab, trembling grips them; *all the inhabitants of Canaan have melted away.*" (Exo. 15:1-18).

From this great hymn of praise, we realize:

1.  **God wants us to know Him as a warrior.** In light of His single-handed defeat of the most powerful nation (Egypt) and human ruler (Pharaoh), the people unequivocally acknowledge God as their dread champion, a warrior unparalleled.

2.  **The warrior was spoiling for a fight.** He had multiple objectives:
    *   To multiply signs and wonders throughout Egypt (Exo. 7:3).
    *   To humiliate the gods of Egypt (Exo. 12:2, cf. Num. 33:4).[52]
    *   To bear witness among the Egyptians that He was the true God (Exo. 14:4).
    *   To bring honor to Himself "through Pharaoh...his army...chariots...horsemen" (Exo. 14:17).

3. **God's triumph is on behalf of His people.** The direct recipients are oppressed and downtrodden humans. Slaves are liberated. The weak are made strong. As already stated, Lord Sabaoth fights to restore justice. (This will be explored more later.)

4. **God receives greater praise and recognition as a result of His victories in war.**

5. **Other nations and gods should fear Him.** The breaking of Egypt is a shot across the bow of other Canaanite tribes. Yahweh's clear intent is to continue His victorious march over other god-kings. Sensing this, the Canaanite rulers rightly fear Yahweh and His people.

For obvious reasons, Lord Sabaoth inspires terror in the heart of His enemies. Now pause and ask yourself, how much fear does the church inspire today? Do kings dread the prayers and service of the living army of God? Do principalities and powers tremble in their high councils in anticipation of our next frontal assault? If Lord Sabaoth is our leader, why not? I propose it is because we pose no real threat. We take no ground, we yield it. We exist in a static, perpetually defensive posture, surrendered to political correctness, feeling slightly embarrassed and at a loss to explain the ways of a Divine Warrior to our culture of "peace."

The Israelites had no such luxury. They understood themselves as a tribe of warriors. There are dozens of references to "men of war," "valiant men," "valiant warriors," and men "arrayed for battle" in the first fifteen books of Scripture. The Exodus was rightly understood as an act of war by God upon a corrupt human king and a depraved system of slavery. As such, the high drama of those events fundamentally shaped the new nation's identity, and later informed their conquest of Canaan. No less, Lord Sabaoth must inform our own tribal concept of God. If the Lord of hosts was so instrumental in founding the nation of faith, shouldn't He be allowed to define our identity, too?

The activity of Christ involves victory and dominion. Since the Messiah was regarded as a human king, and Jesus is King of kings, "God's warring activity is intimately connected with His kingship."[53]

> "Who is the King of glory? The Lord strong and mighty, *the Lord mighty in battle...* Who is this King of glory? *The Lord of hosts,* He is the King of glory" (Psa. 24:8, 10).

Moses knew this God intimately, but before Israel could take the land, Joshua needed his own introduction. So an early manifestation of the Lord of hosts appeared to him:

> "Now it came about when Joshua was by Jericho, that he lifted up his eyes and looked, and behold, a man was standing opposite him with his sword drawn in his hand, and Joshua went to him and said to him, 'Are you for us or for our adversaries?'

> And he said, 'No, rather I indeed come now as *captain of the host of the Lord.*' And Joshua fell on his face to the earth, and bowed down, and said to him, 'What has my lord to say to his servant?'" (Josh. 5:13-14).

### A Barren Woman's Prayer

Given the clear military themes surrounding the divine warrior, Scripture refuses to allow us to drift into carnal, selfish applications. Yes, the Divine Warrior is real. He is the Christ! But before you start to pound your war drums, pause and register with surprise that the first official use of the name, Lord of hosts, occurs in a passage not about war, but in the *prayers of a barren woman.* When Hannah desperately prays for a child, her petition is offered to the Lord of hosts. If God will grant her request, she will dedicate the child as a Nazirite.[54] Soon after, when Lord Sabaoth hears and answers, Hannah gives birth to the prophet Samuel. This is the first occurrence of *Yahweh Tzevaot* in the Bible.[55]

The second, being intimately connected to the first, is no less surprising. This time, a young shepherd faces a giant named Goliath and warns him that he is armed with "the name of the Lord of hosts" (1 Sam. 17:42-47). David had great confidence in Lord Sabaoth, to the point of declaring in advance that he would cut off Goliath's head and give his dead body to birds and beasts, "that all the earth may know there is a God in Israel" (v. 46).

Who anointed David? That's right, Samuel. Thus we see in the first two occurrences of Lord Sabaoth's name that 1) fervent intercession brings forth 2) Naziritic consecration which produces 3) a clear prophetic voice by which 4) anointed destinies are produced, 5) giants are challenged and overcome and 6) the king is made known.

Every single part of this equation contains DNA from the Lord of Armies. Do you see? Names are banners we come under. Specific DNA produces specific results in prayer. When we come into alignment with a focused aspect of God, as He has disclosed Himself, we stand in line to receive that part of God, because now we have faith for it. "Faith comes from hearing, and hearing by the Word of Christ" (Rom. 10:17).

Follow this: When God is revealed as provider, man receives provision. When God is revealed as savior, man receives salvation. When God is revealed as healer, man receives healing. *When God was finally revealed as the ruler and commander of armies, Israel received her king!* It is Samuel who anointed both Saul and David. As an intercessor, Hannah launched a process far greater than she could have possibly imagined. Each of the six steps listed above, from Hannah's prayer to David's crown, is meaningful in and of itself, but we must not fail to see the bigger picture. A specific revelation of God, released in prayer by a barren woman, became a seed that later bore fruit on the lips of a young warrior king, and this king was anointed by God to establish the throne upon which Messiah Himself would rule. Hannah likely had no idea the scale of events she set in motion. She just wanted a son. But in her passionate prayer (so fervent that Eli the priest finally accused her of being drunk), she appealed to the Lord of hosts for the first time in biblical history. And boy, did she get an answer! Samuel, the Nazirite prophet, was so dear to God that none of his words were allowed to fail.[56]

Do you see the ekklesia of Christ foreshadowed here? If not, don't fret. We have to unthink some wrong stuff before we can replace it with right stuff, so I want to make sure key themes in the Word are clarified to fully enable a revolutionary shift in the second half of this book. We're getting there! In Chapter 8 we'll begin a straight-forward discussion of how Jesus promised to build the ekklesia, not the church, but we have so much ground to cover first. For now, it is important to note that a barren woman's prayers (she who could bring forth no life) inaugurated God's name as Lord of hosts. Furthermore, the answer to her prayers was powerful not only in its time, but also timeless, leading straight from David to David's son, Jesus the Christ.

**War and Peace...and Justice**

Part of the reason Lord Sabaoth answered Hannah's prayers is because He is committed to restorative justice for all under the oppression of Satan, suffering in a fallen world. We must briefly examine this further. First, let's say what justice (and dominion, for that matter) is *not*. God's justice, along with His zeal to bring it to pass, is not about fists and a vengeful spirit, nor the demonization of those with whom we do not agree. In human terms, spiritual author-ity is the product of a humble heart, not "might makes right."[57] Dominion does not mean to behave domineeringly. We certainly need God's power—we're barren without it!—but He doesn't need ours at all. For this reason, David told Goliath, "(Lord Sabaoth) will *give you* into our hands...that all this assembly may know that the Lord does not deliver by sword or by spear" (1 Sam. 17:47). Though the fame of David's victory was rightly his, he deferred to the source, Lord Sabaoth. "God, not humans, is the one who wins victories... God's miraculous intervention provides the victory."[58]

So a loving God wages war. How can this be? It is crucial that we see God in His totality. He is not schizophrenic, one moment warring, the other loving. The virtues of love and mercy by which He extends salvation to sinners, tenderly cares for the weak and the broken, and also delivers the oppressed, are the same motivating passions which stir Him to wrath and war against His enemies, those who defile purity, obstruct justice, and oppress the weak. He is humanity's ultimate ally in that He is committed to destroy everything that is harmful to our lives. His warfare is an expression of covenantal love.

The wholeness and unity of God means every facet of His nature works in perfect harmony. So Lord Sabaoth is the divine manifestation by which Yahweh Shalom produces peace, Yahweh Jireh produces abundance, Yahweh Rapha produces healing, etc. God does not war because He enjoys violence, but because He delights in justice. He relishes the triumph of His own nature above every inferior substitute, including every demonic foe that seeks to oppose Him. As such, He is utterly committed to removing barriers to love, defilements of sin, and every last vestige of Satan's rule. Though we are continually beset by enemies, because of Lord Sabaoth, we emerge triumphant as recipients of grace.

So while military action seems the dominant motif, it is a mistake to get stuck there. Yahweh Sabaoth's zeal is most consistently demonstrated in His oversight of the downtrodden.[59]

> **"Thus says the Lord of hosts,** the God of Israel, 'Amend your ways and your deeds, and I will let you dwell in this place... For if you **truly amend your ways and your deeds,** if you **truly**

*practice justice* between a man and his neighbor, if you **do not oppress the alien, the orphan, or the widow,** and **do not shed innocent blood** in this place, **nor walk after other gods** to your own ruin, then I will let you dwell...in the land that I gave to your fathers forever and ever'" (Jer. 7:3-7).

Interestingly, Jesus quoted from this passage when cleansing the temple.[60] His indignation was that of Lord Sabaoth because Christ is the incarnation of the Lord of hosts.[61]

In Isaiah 3, it is the Lord of hosts who "enters into judgment with the elders and princes of His people (saying), 'It is you who have devoured the vineyard; the plunder of the poor is in your houses. What do you mean by crushing My people, and grinding the face of the poor?' declares the Lord God of hosts" (vs. 14-15). Lord Sabaoth also denounces the peoples' apostasies and wayward devotion to God's Word.[62]

Yet more surprises await. In the age of grace, Jesus deepened our understanding of the Divine Warrior. When the babe in the manger is first introduced to the world, the host He previously commanded in Heaven now bears witness in the skies over Bethlehem. Observing the scene, we become like Elisha's servant in Dothan; only this time, rather than sky squadrons striking us blind, we are granted sight. How will God's justice be revealed? With *mercy*. With *good news.* Instead of crying, "Death to the infidels!" the angel army sings, "Peace among men with whom He is pleased!" (Luke 2:14). Lord Sabaoth arrives to wage war on Satan, not man, securing peace for the human enemies of a holy God at the price of His own life. The increase of His government promises an unending increase of peace.[63] God, superior in strength in every way, conquers all demonic powers, why? For the sake of the *powerless.*

For this reason, we must take care how we treat the weak and underprivileged around us. Lord Sabaoth comes to defend those with no reputation, nor rights, and no recourse to achieve their own justice.

---

**Lord Sabaoth comes to defend those with no reputation, nor rights, and no recourse to achieve their own justice.**

---

"Behold, the pay of the laborers who mowed your fields, and which has been withheld by you, cries out against you; and the outcry of those who did the harvesting has reached the ears of *the Lord of Sabaoth*" (James 5:4).

In all of this, the principal revelation of Lord Sabaoth is not *that* He goes to war, but *why* and *for whom*. Triumph is a means to an end. His great arsenal contrasts with man's in that God is not motivated by the hopes of more war, but of paradise restored.

"The Lord of hosts is with us...He makes wars to cease to the end of the earth; He breaks the bow and cuts the spear in two; He burns the chariots with fire. Cease striving and know that I am God" (Psa. 46:7, 9-10).

Warren Wiersbe believes this entire psalm is a musical reflection on God's deliverance of Jerusalem from the Assyrians in the time of King Hezekiah.[64] It is also likely the inspiration for Martin Luther's famous hymn, "A Mighty Fortress is Our God," whose verses introduce each major section of this book. Read all of Psalm 46 and you will see several dynamics regarding the overshadowing protection and strength which the Lord of hosts gives His people:

1.  God is a refuge who is present to help us in our troubles.
2.  There is no need to fear, in spite of major upheavals and uncertainty

3.   Instead, joy and gladness flow to those who understand God's righteous strength

4.   He is not distant, but dwells in our midst. Since He helps us, we will not be moved

5.   As in Psalm 2, the nations rage against God's sovereign support of His people

6.   But ultimately, since *the Lord of hosts* is with us, we can be at peace.

---

**Lord Sabaoth does not emasculate His people to achieve peace. He empowers them. We must avoid human sentimentality in our conception of God's *shalom*. Peace is not some gauzy, idealized pacifist notion where everybody mutually agrees to lay down arms. Don't kid yourself. Satan will never behave with an ounce of restraint, kindness or due process. He must be forcibly restrained.**

---

Don't be fooled. The promise of peace will not occur by robbing God's victorious army of its weapons. Rather, as with the Assyrians, peace is secured when the righteous dismantle *the enemy's* war engines.[65] Lord Sabaoth does not emasculate His people to achieve peace. He empowers them.[66] We must avoid human sentimentality in our conception of God's *shalom*. Peace is not some gauzy, idealized pacifist notion where everybody mutually agrees to lay down arms. Don't kid yourself. Satan will never behave with an ounce of restraint, kindness or due process. He must be forcibly restrained. He must be disarmed. When Lord Sabaoth came in the flesh He "disarmed the rulers and authorities (and) made a public display of them, having triumphed over them" (Col. 2:15).

You may ask, if Christ has already triumphed, what is our role? Good question, since evil is still clearly at work in the world. In every generation, *Jesus gathers His ekklesia to enforce and expand the outworking of His victory in practical terms.* We are meant to achieve this with weapons of prayer, fasting, repentance, worship, confession, servanthood, sacrifice and truth. Before the Lord returns, war is the only path to peace. Otherwise, if we defer in our role, the enemy gains squatter's rights to the land, and the gates of Hades prevail.

"Possession is nine tenths of the law" is more than a proverb, it is a spiritual truism. We must not allow the enemy to possess our land by default. He must be challenged and cast down from every place and every person he seeks to control. The revelation of Lord Sabaoth authorizes us to displace every interloping spirit in this age. While this is true, our imperative to rule in Christ's stead must never be confused with attempts to personify power by fleshly means. We operate under constraints, in that His power is made perfect through our weakness.[67]

In the final apocalyptic closing of the age, when evil is entirely called to account and meted the justice it is due, God's retribution among the nations will be swift and shockingly complete. Yet both now and then, our weapons are the blood of the lamb (*not* the spilling of blood), combined with confession even to the point of martyrdom.[68] Once more, Lord Sabaoth will stride forth, no longer a babe, nor a crucified Messiah, but with armies from heaven and roaring lambs on earth, to rescue those this world had crushed. His eschatological ferocity will be justified in every sphere of human experience where our natural strength has failed: in the total elimination of tyranny, oppression, famine, war, usury, cruelty, trafficking and disease. He has a heavenly host, but as the contingent of His human host, we also have the full resources of Heaven at our disposal. Until He comes, we engage the enemy with an alert spirit, guided by clear objectives, refusing to negotiate with demonic principalities in their control of our world.

Our mandate of dominion yields no room for moral concessions, within or without. This is what it means to exert the escalating, total dominion of Christ until He returns.

# 6

## THE DOMINION THREAD

In Jericho, the harlot Rahab tied a "cord of scarlet thread" to her window, marking her home to be spared by Joshua's troops. Some see this as the origin of the "red light" tradition for houses of prostitution. This may be true. Yet for Rahab, that scarlet thread was the beginning of her redemption. Many years ago, W.A. Criswell preached a famous sermon that compared the Bible to a patchwork quilt sewn together with Rahab's "Scarlet Thread of Redemption," a long-noted symbolism dating all the way back to St. John Chrysostom. Along with redemption, Scripture's quilt is woven of other threads, too: rebellion threads, sovereignty threads, Messiah threads. In this chapter we will explore the dominion thread.

A story will help. Back when Shug Jordan was coach at Auburn University, he asked his former linebacker Mike Kollin if he would help him do some recruiting for Mike's old alma mater. At the time, Mike was with the Miami Dolphins and Shug wanted to skim the cream from the Miami area.

"Sure, coach. What kind of player are you looking for?"

The coach replied, "Well Mike, you know there's that fellow, you knock him down, he just stays down?"

"We don't want him, do we, coach?" Mike answered dutifully.

"No, that's right. Then there's that fellow, you knock him down and he gets up, you knock him down again and he stays down."

Mike said, "We don't want him either, do we coach?"

Shug shook his head, "No, but Mike, there's a fellow, you knock him down, he gets up. Knock him down, he gets up. Knock him down, he gets up. Knock him down, he gets up."

Mike smiled. He got it. "That's the guy we want, isn't it, coach?"

Shug Jordan shook his head, "Mike, we don't want him either. I want you to find the guy who's knocking everybody down. *That's* the guy we want."[69]

Perfect! That's the guy. Believe it or not, God is looking for guys like that, too. People with a dominion spirit. Precisely because Christ has come, Lord Sabaoth in the flesh, and because Lord Sabaoth is the manifest will of God for justice and redemption, God seeks men and women to join his Justice and Redemption Team with a contending spirit of dominion for the cause of Christ in the earth. Does the notion of rulership sound bold? It shouldn't.

Dominion was the original state of humanity.

**The Genesis Mandate**

Rulership has been the divine plan for man from the beginning.

> "Then God said, 'Let Us make man in Our image, according to Our likeness; and *let them rule*'...And God blessed them; and God said to them, 'Be *fruitful* and *multiply,* and *fill the earth,* and *subdue it;* and *rule over* the fish of the sea and over the birds of the sky, and over every living thing that moves on the earth'" (Gen. 1:26, 28).

God's first pronouncement was that Adam was meant to rule. While he was created in the context of divine fellowship—"let *Us* make man"—by which we understand that Adam's deepest source of life, joy and satisfaction was God Himself, Adam's *job description* was to rule! God was not apologetic about this plan. In fact, the proximity of the two phrases, "in Our image and likeness" to "let them rule," is meant to bring revelation: When we see God as He is, and by extension, man as he is, *an understanding of rulership is released.*

All of creation was to be subject to man. Why? This is a simple case of cause and effect. How can humanity bear God's image and *not* rule? It demeans the complete rulership of God to populate the earth with image bearers who have no capacity for dominion. Intimacy may be what moves God's heart, but dominion gives Him honor. This is part of the function of Christ, to restore the dignity and authority of man as God's co-regent over creation. To understand this, we must admit that the earlier-stated definition of Christ is incomplete. Christ literally means "The Anointed One," but implicit in this title is "The Anointing *of this One.*" You see, it is not only the person upon whom the Spirit rests, but the Spirit that rests upon Him. In a sense, the Anointed One merely implies selection. It is a designation. What does the Anointed One *do*? More importantly, how does He do it?

---

**It demeans the complete rulership of God to populate the earth with image bearers who have no capacity for dominion. Intimacy may be what moves God's heart, but dominion gives Him honor.**

---

Jesus answered this when He went about "for this purpose, that He might destroy the works of the devil" (1 John 3:8)—casting out demons, opening blind eyes, healing the lame, raising the dead, challenging corrupt rulers, preaching truth. It was the anointing *upon Him* by which the people understood that He was, in fact, the Anointed One. As the incarnate Lord Sabaoth, Jesus had an Isaiah 61 preaching-releasing-healing-liberating-comforting-devil destroying anointing upon Him *by the Holy Spirit.* Thus, an amplified rendering of Christ would be, "The Anointed One *and* His Anointing." This same Holy Spirit was then poured out at Pentecost, on Peter, on Philip, on Paul...on you! It is the Spirit of God which regenerates and recreates you.

Make this personal. Can you be filled with *Him* and not destroy the works of the devil?

## The Job Description

To exercise Christ's dominion over Satan is to rule on Earth.

Adam quickly failed his commission. He abdicated, and Satan began to reign on Earth with an iron fist. The world was so immediately plunged into darkness that just a few generations later, God had to wipe out the entire species and start over again with Noah. Yet God didn't alter His original intent for humanity. Thus, in every slice of redemptive history, we see God calling His people back to their rightful place of rulership.[69]

In the Garden, Eve was promised the seed of a ruler who would *"bruise (Satan) on the head, and you shall bruise him on the heel"* (Gen. 3:15). This prophesy is restated in Psalm 110, where the enemies of the Messiah are made His footstool. From the very beginning, God promises that the authority Adam forfeited will be restored.

Next, Abraham was granted an exalted, divine patronage. In modern terminology, we might call it "Favored Nation" status. God's language of covenant toward His friend is full of outrageous blessings, protection and rulership: "I will make you a *great* nation, and I will bless you, and *make your name great*; and so you shall be a *blessing*; and I will bless those who bless you, and the one who curses you I will curse...*and kings shall come forth from you*" (Gen. 12:2-3, 16:6).

In honor of His promise to Abraham, when Egypt oppressed God's favored nation, He rescued them from their powerful oppressor in the most sensational ways imaginable. The extraction plan was full of natural calamities that clearly expressed God's dominion over creation, false gods, injustice, and Pharaoh himself. But *divine* dominion was only a case in point. Later, in the promises of Deuteronomy 28:1-14, Yahweh makes it clear that the children of Israel are also meant to enjoy mastery over every sphere of life. If they would but follow God and obey Him, "all these blessings shall come upon you":

- Blessings wherever you live (v. 3)
- Blessings of increase: children, harvest, herd (v. 4)
- Blessings on provision and food (v. 5)
- Blessed at home and away from home (v. 6)
- Enemies will be defeated and forced to flee (v. 7)
- Future provisions will be safeguarded, labors will be favored (v. 8)
- They will be established in holiness before the Lord (v. 9)
- They will act as a faithful witness to others and earn their respect (v. 10)
- They will abound in prosperity: children, harvest, herd (v. 11)
- They will lack famine and drought, rain will be plentiful (v. 12)
- Resources will exceed need, so that they can lend and never need to borrow (v. 12)
- They will be made the head, not the tail; be above, not beneath (v. 13)

This is such a clear picture of productive, successful living that we are tempted to disbelieve. Yet God is committed to building a nation of kings and priests who understand and express His rule over the train wreck of sin's influence until the dominion of sin totally bows before the dominion of Christ. As others have said, we are being "trained to reign."

And so the history lesson continues with Joshua, who not only conquered Jericho, but displaced all other nations.[71] God promised him, "Every place on which the sole of your foot treads, I have given it to you...No man will be able to stand before you all the days of your life...that you may have success wherever you go" (Josh. 1:3-7). In one instance, God promised Joshua victory over the Amorites. When it looked like some of the enemy might escape, Joshua cried out to God for a miracle. He did not want victory, he wanted *total dominion!* In response, God moved miraculously to support Joshua's zeal for rulership to the point of raining large hailstones and stopping both sun and moon "until the nation avenged themselves of their enemies" (Josh. 10:13). The Bible says there was no day like it, when the Lord "listened to the voice of a man" (v. 14). This is the heart of God, that we partner with Him in prayer until the triumph of Lord Sabaoth is made manifest on earth. When we speak, He listens, unleashing the armies of heaven, dethroning rulers of iniquity,[72] bringing ruin to His enemies.

---

**This is the heart of God, that we partner with Him in prayer until the triumph of Lord Sabaoth is made manifest on earth.**

---

Later still in redemptive history, King David came to embody Messiah to such a degree that Christ was called the Son of David.[73] The fact that Messiah occupies a *human* throne (David's) means in part that His rulership is expressed in tangible, material, human terms. Jesus, the son of David, touched people. As a *man*, He touched lepers and the lame, He healed eyes and released demoniacs from their torment. As a man, He challenged oppressive rulers. He shifted regions and cities by demonstrating the dominion man had lost.

For this reason, the prophets of the Old Testament were fixated on the Messiah, because they fundamentally understood that His rule would also restore Israel to her glory, and dominion to the people. The lost blessings of Abraham—lost to Assyria, Babylon and Rome—would be restored. In true Davidic fashion, as when David's victory over Goliath became the people's victory, the natural consequence of Messiah's rule was understood to transfer to the entire nation. Daniel foresaw a time when "the *sovereignty*, the *dominion*, and *the greatness of all the kingdoms* under the whole heaven *will be given to the people* of *the saints* of the Highest One" (Dan. 7:27).

Finally, the book of Revelation confirms both the total victory of Christ and the fulfillment of man's role as overcomers. Reigning with Christ on Earth is the destiny of the redeemed.[74]

The role of king, priest and judge actually describes spheres of rulership. The priest was essentially ruler of covenantal *relationship*. He was given dominion in the form of rituals, wave offerings, an altar and a washing bowl, all for the purpose of achieving something: atonement. The priest was given authority to restore broken relationship. He was the channel of forgiveness for both national and individual guilt. Judges ruled the covenantal *society*. Using dominion tools such as a fair scale, the Law of Moses and an impartial heart, judges served to safeguard ethical business and family practice. They refused bribes, honored tribal and familial land boundaries, and also made sure orphans and widows had a voice. In criminal matters, they guaranteed that the accused were not unfairly conspired against, that witnesses were true. Finally, the king was ruler of the covenantal *nation*. Whereas priests and judges assured the rule of righteousness internally, the chief mandate of the king was to overcome foreign invaders, secure the peace, and enforce the values and priorities of the nation externally. Literally, the crown and the scepter were the king's dominion tools.

In other words, the notion of dominion must be holistic. We glimpse a fuller picture in the work of sacrifice and relational atonement governed by priests, the righteous judgment and social order established by judges, and the commitment to war led by kings. Yet war is only part of dominion, not the whole. Such types and shadows are meant to form a living picture by which we enter the more complete covenantal blessings of the New Covenant found in Christ alone. But make no mistake, if the people of the Old Covenant understood rulership, so must we, or the dominion of Christ will be found lacking in the earth.

# 7

## THE DIVINE COUNCIL

We have come to understand the critical need for revelation of Christ, and also God's original blueprint for
humans to possess authority over creation. In the process, we have
examined earthly things. Now we must consider heavenly things.
To do this, we must get comfortable with progressions of meaning,
such as moving from the literal meaning of a thing to its application
as an object lesson. Beyond both of these is the rich vein of symbols.

C.S. Lewis said, "Symbols are the natural speech of the soul,
a language older and more universal than words."[75] Given the con-
stancy and pervasiveness of symbolism in Scripture, it would seem
that God ordained a pattern wherein symbolic imagery serves as
a sort of visible theology. Obviously, there are limits to this claim,
and too many liberties will run us afoul of truth, but the principle is
sound. For the purpose of this book, two questions are necessary at
this point: 1) How does God structure the government of Heaven?
and 2) how might that govern the culture, constitution and mission
of the ekklesia? "Visible theology" is crucial to the deeper understanding that we seek. In the end, we'll better comprehend what
Jesus promised to build in Matthew 16.

While prophecy is full of symbolism, non-prophetic examples
of symbolism abound. The writers of the New Testament made ample

use of Old Testament imagery, utilizing former things to illuminate latter things. Examples include Adam (Rom. 5:14; 1 Cor. 15:45), Isaac (Heb. 11:19) and the Mosaic feasts, including the Sabbath, as types of Christ (Col. 2:16-17); the old covenant as a type and predecessor of the new (Heb. 8:6-12); and the Aaronic priesthood, surpassed only by the Melchizedek priesthood, as the symbol by which we understand the atoning priesthood of Jesus (Heb. 7-8). The Bible calls these types and shadows. What is a shadow? A shadow is an inferior representation of the real thing. If you study your shadow in late afternoon, the shape on the ground looks like you. It's recognizable, but it's only an outline, right? It is not, in fact, really you. You are much more than your shadow. So when the writer of Hebrews says the Mosaic law was "only a **shadow** of the good things to come and **not the very form** of things" (Heb. 10:1), he is making a bold, radical claim.

Jewish history was intentional. The Torah was comprised not only of teachings and wisdom, but a code. Paul cracked the code, then used it to transmit deep, spiritual ideas, as did the writer of Hebrews. Remember as a kid, those boxes of cereal with the hidden message and the decoder ring? The book of Hebrews is very much like a big decoder ring.

After listing numerous sacred items (real, physical objects with mass and form, and therefore hardly symbolic or abstract to their original users) such as a lampstand, a table with bread, a veil, an altar, incense, a box made of wood and gold, a golden jar holding something called manna, a wooden staff and stone tablets, the writer of Hebrews says that *by these things* (including an offering of blood), the Holy Spirit is "signifying" deeper realities. To signify is to *sign*-ify. The entire tabernacle system, we are told, is "a symbol for the present time...until a time of reformation."[76] Bear in mind, for Aaron, Moses and three million Israelites, these weren't signs, but objects of daily interaction. Imagine learning some day in the future that your computer and coffee cup were really mysterious symbols of a higher dimension of existence. You might be baffled. You drank coffee out of that cup! Certainly, the tabernacle paraphernalia were holy unto the Lord, but even those should not be considered mystical in the sense of possessing latent, intrinsic powers, like magic talismans. Instead, by virtue of their form and function, these "signs" are given to us so that we can comprehend profound mystical truths, and thereby recognize the outline of Christ. Afterward, because we have studied and understood His shadow, we are primed to recognize Him when He appears. Types and shadows are like clues sprinkled in a good mystery novel, so that the climax of the book makes sense. They are the footprints of Jesus in the Old Testament. This is not a game to God; it is quite necessary. Why? Because when dealing with the heavenly realm, language simply fails. And when language fails, we must turn to symbols to achieve depths of meaning unavailable to human speech.

---

**Types and shadows are like clues sprinkled in a good mystery novel, so that the climax of the book makes sense.**

---

Thus, when Hebrews 8:11 tells us that Christ "entered through the greater and more perfect tabernacle, not made with hands," we understand that the tabernacle and priestly symbols were not only for Israel. Their true purpose was to reveal to *us* important things about Christ.

In fact, we are meant to understand countless references in this light. Paul unabashedly broadened the scope of symbolism to include virtually every aspect of the Old Testament. These things, he says, "happened to them *as an example*, but they were *written down for our instruction*, on whom the end of the ages has come" (1 Cor. 10:11). Notice in this passage, he didn't limit the symbolism to a predetermined list of types and shadows. Biblical history is replete with object lessons: Noah's ark, Samson's hair, Gideon's trumpets and clay pots, the red heifer, the scapegoat, the brass serpent, Egypt, the gods of Canaan, Jerusalem, the fiery furnace and more. All these are ripe not only for illustrating basic moral truths, but also to capture and convey transcendent principles. The fact that we are given this latitude does not diminish their historicity or individual significance. When an object or event ends up demonstrating a larger principle, you know it is important. But when under the inspiration of the Holy Spirit it becomes a symbol, you can be assured that larger vistas of truth await.

### Wait, there's more!

This can get confusing because many scriptural symbols are not, in fact, merely symbols. Some represent a pattern of reality more concrete and "real" than the book you are holding in your hands right now. Heaven may be invisible to the naked eye, but it is not by its invisibility rendered immaterial or substanceless. Heaven is eternal, earth is temporal. The kingdom and throne of God has substance. It is not the popularly conceived softly ephemeral world of spectral mist and glowing wraiths.

Thus, certain biblical models surpass themselves as symbol to become a portal by which we perceive the literal order and structure of the kingdom of Heaven. The wilderness tabernacle is a marvelous case in point. The tabernacle, in plain reckoning, was not much more than a big tent. Yet Moses used very *precise* language to describe a *precise* process by which a very *precise* tent could become a tabernacle for God's presence in the wilderness.

Why the precision?

The writer of Hebrews says Moses was "warned by God...see that you make them after the pattern which was shown to you on the mountain." David stated almost exactly the same in his own construction of the tabernacle: "the Lord made me understand in writing by His hand upon me, all the details of this pattern."[77]

From Exodus 25-40, Moses gives 236 verses of detailed instruction regarding this pattern. If that's not enough, he gives 179 more regarding the tent's actual construction. The Bible doesn't waste space, ever. This was a precise blueprint. Every detail mattered.

Again, we must ask, why is this so important?

The book of Hebrews helps us interpret the significance. In commenting on the blood sacrifice which occurred in the tabernacle's inner court, we are told:

> "Therefore it was necessary *for the copies of the things in the heavens* to be cleansed with these, but the heavenly things themselves with better sacrifices than these. For Christ did not enter a holy place made with hands, *a mere copy of the true one,* but into heaven itself, now to appear in the presence of God for us" (Heb. 9:23-24).

Do you see what this is saying? It's saying this earthly construction of poles, sheets, rooms, tables and altars is "patterned" after something. The tabernacle isn't a prop, it's a copy of the real thing! Yes, it's a symbol by which we understand deep theological truths, but it's *not only a symbol.* It's also a specific recreation on Earth of something that actually exists in Heaven. This is confirmed in passages such as Isaiah 6, where the prophet sees God seated on His heavenly throne, while the "train of His robe fills the *temple*" and His "*temple* (filled) with smoke." This is profound! God has His own tabernacle/temple! This means the detailed instructions given to Moses and David were facsimiles of *the real thing.*

Consider: In the eternal dimension, while the throne is the ultimate Holy of Holies, there also exists an outer court and inner court. What are they? Where are they? Are they dimensional access points to His person? Or perhaps the outer court is Earth itself? Regardless, in each artifact of the tabernacle system (which later includes Solomon's Temple), we go beyond imagery as theology to a materialization of the divine.

Let me be more direct: in the tabernacle, a piece of Heaven literally touched Earth. God emailed the specs so that Moses, as general contractor, could build Heaven on Earth!

It is as if we are given an early snapshot of God's heart, as Jesus taught us to pray, that the kingdom of God would come "on earth as it is in heaven." This could be pictured as follows:

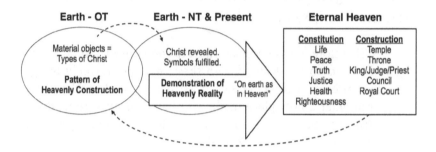

## Mirror vs. Symbol

Consider the difference between symbolizing beauty and mirroring it. The mirroring of Heaven opens gateways of power, beauty, grace and truth that words and symbols cannot attain, moving us from revelation to demonstration. Mirroring isn't imitation, but replication. It is molding the natural to the shape of the supernatural. In this manner, Moses's tabernacle and Solomon's temple are more than symbols, they are mirrors. They prefigure the heavenly temple, where God rules a court from a throne. The construction of that court bears directly upon our understanding of the ekklesia.

Thus we come, in Scripture, to the Divine Council.

## Throne Visions

Sumerian, Akkadian, Babylonian, Egyptian and Canaanite mythologies demonstrate an idea common to Mesopotamian religion, that the gods sit in council together, typically ruled by a supreme deity. We gain no truth from these facts, only context. Similar to our review of Caesarea Philippi and the culture of Caesar at the time of Christ, the prevailing worldview helps us understand how, and perhaps why, God chose to reveal Himself as He did. We also gain more evidence of the divine spark in man's imagination that shadows truth, though tainted by sin.

The Bible provides a handful of explicit "Throne Visions" which help us understand the construction of Heaven. I don't have time to examine each one, but I encourage you to take a moment and read each of the following passages before continuing.

- **Exodus 24:9-11**
- **1 Kings 22:19-23**
- **Isaiah 6:1-8**
- **Ezekiel 1, 10**
- **Zechariah 3**
- **Daniel 7**
- **Revelation 4-5**

Like curtains pulled open in a dark room so that morning's glory chases away the night, these powerful glimpses into divine reality greatly enhance our understanding of God's mind and plans. Perhaps for the first time, do you see that God assembles a heavenly council around Himself as King? For this reason, the court of human kings is no accident, because divine royal impulses manifest archetypally around human rulers. So a king sits at court. Now, the American form of government split the high powers of the king's court into three branches: Executive, Legislative and Judicial. This represents the king, his generals, advisors and judges. The court of Heaven consolidates them into a single, seamless government.

God is not a floating, detached spirit. He is seated. In heaven. On a throne. A host of spiritual beings form His court. Scholar Patrick Miller calls the imagery of the divine council "one of the central cosmological symbols of the Old Testament."[78] The divine council offers a model of how God operates the universe to achieve His aims for and through Israel and all humankind. In his essay entitled,

"Visions of the Divine Council in the Hebrew Bible," Paul B. Sumner says the divine council:

> "...is one of the Bible's ways of describing how God maintains order in the Creation. Working through innumerable hosts of angelic servants, God creates and rules the physical universe, as well as the world of men. In his position as head of the council, God holds three primary offices: King, Judge, and Warrior. He is absolute ruler over all. He makes judicial decisions about the activities of its occupants. And he initiates punitive actions against those forces (divine or human) which cause chaos and disorder (i.e. sin), in order to restore *tsedaqah* (righteousness) and *shalom* (wholeness, peace). His obedient angels serve him in each of his corresponding offices. In his royal throne-room, they praise their King and act as his official counselors, courtiers, and messengers. As members of the court, they act as witnesses, investigating detectives, bailiffs, and perhaps fellow judges. As members of the Warrior's vast army, they wage war on evil beings."[79]

---

**Certain prophets were allowed to audit the structure and proceedings of Heaven, then communicate to the people what they beheld.**

---

The possibility of a divine council might surprise many, because it smacks of Mesopotamian religion more than true revelation, but the reverse is more likely true. Scripture affirms that Yahweh's throne is comprised of a congregation of *bene elohim* ("sons of God" or "gods"). Obviously, such a notion threatens the clear monotheism to which Israel was called and committed in covenant relationship with the One, True God, yet the nation resolutely persisted in defending this council as integral to Yahweh's absolute control over the universe. This begs the question, how did they even know of its existence? The answer is because prophets were granted a "stage pass" behind the veil. Certain prophets were allowed to audit the structure and proceedings of Heaven, then communicate to the people what they beheld. The prophets ratified the divine council as a legitimate framework for understanding Yahweh. Sometimes the glimpse we are given is troubling. Consider the much-debated passage that initiates the trials of Job.

> "Now there was a day when the **sons of God** (Heb: *'bene elohim'*) came to present themselves before the Lord, and Satan also came among them" (Job 1:6, 2:1, also 38:7).

The Bible uses this phrase, *bene elohim,* only five times,[80] the first two being when "the sons of God" had relations with the daughters of men and produced *nephilim,* or giants (Genesis 6:2,4). The other two, in Job, reveal a meeting of spiritual entities around the throne of God, much as one might witness courtiers or ambassadors seeking audience with an earthly king. Though these are awesome beings, and in some sense regarded as gods, they are clearly not in charge. Though powerful, they must obtain permission to execute their plans. If the book of Job does anything, it affirms the absolute sovereignty of God—even in the most discomfiting of ways. As these lesser beings approach Him, they ask questions. They seek favors. They cannot act unilaterally. God alone is King of His court.

Interpretations of the *bene elohim* are as much debated today as they have been for millennia. While a full defense of my position falls beyond the scope of this book, the view of this author treats the *bene elohim* as an angelic company. In support of this, it is worth noting that the apocryphal *Book of Enoch,* a work that was favored by several early church fathers for canonicity, and quoted by both Peter and Jude (and possibly also referenced by John),[81] repeatedly utilizes the phrase *bene elohim* to refer to fallen angels, whom it calls Watchers. Jude 14-15 directly quotes Enoch 1:9:

> "And about these also Enoch, in the seventh generation from Adam, prophesied, saying, 'Behold, the Lord came **with many**

***thousands of His holy ones,*** to execute judgment upon all, and to convict all the ungodly of all their ungodly deeds...'"

Holy ones. Angels.[82] The *bene elohim*. It is also worth noting that the two archangels mentioned by name in Scripture, Gabriel and Michael, along with five other angels common to rabbinic literature (as well as the book of Enoch)—Uriel, Raguel, Saraquael, Ramiel, Raphael—all end with the syllable 'El,' which literally means "god" and is the root word in *El-ohim*.

So Job shows us a heavenly court, with powerful spiritual creatures assembled before Yahweh's throne. Other passages are even more explicit.

- "The heavens will praise Thy wonders, O Lord; Thy faithfulness also in the ***assembly of the holy ones.*** For who in the skies is comparable to the Lord? ***Who among the sons of the mighty*** is like the Lord, a God greatly feared in the ***council of the holy ones,*** and awesome ***above all those who are around Him?***" (Psa. 89:5-7).

- "God has taken his place ***in the divine council;*** in the ***midst of the gods*** ('elohim') he holds judgment" (Psa. 82:1, ESV).[83]

This divine council, while fundamental to the order of Heaven, also has direct impact upon the people of Earth. When Ahab, king of Israel, sought to go to war with Aram, he looked to form an alliance with King Jehoshaphat of Judah. Ahab sought and received approval from his hired prophets, but Jehoshaphat rightly perceived that they did not have the word of the Lord. They were just telling Ahab whatever he wanted. Jehoshaphat asked to hear from another prophet, Micaiah. Ahab complained that Micaiah, the true prophet of God, would not support him with a favorable prophecy. Micaiah responded by peeking behind the curtain to describe what was really happening in Heaven as it played out on Earth. He showed us the divine council at work.

> "Micaiah said, 'Therefore, hear the word of the Lord. I saw the Lord sitting on His throne, and all the host of heaven standing by Him on His right and on His left.
>
> And the Lord said, 'Who will entice Ahab to go up and fall at Ramoth-gilead?' And one said this while another said that.
>
> Then a spirit came forward and stood before the Lord and said, 'I will entice him.'
>
> And the Lord said to him, 'How?' And he said, 'I will go out and be a deceiving spirit in the mouth of all his prophets.' Then He said, 'You are to entice him and also prevail. Go and do so.'
>
> Now therefore, behold, the Lord has put a deceiving spirit in the mouth of all these your prophets; and the Lord has proclaimed disaster against you" (1 Kings 22:19-23).

In one sense, these are troubling images. We don't fully understand what is going on, and they do not fit with popular conceptions of God. It seems the heavenly host is involved in conversation and relationship as part of God's design, but what does that mean? Is God just one of many gods? Does He need advice? No, He rules in absolute power and wisdom, but the glory of His rulership is somehow enhanced when expressed through a council of servants who do His bidding, whose own glory might be perceived as godlike from a human perspective.

We see this practically applied on Earth, too. If a king sits alone in a small palace on a small throne, with no attendees or visiting diplomats crowding in to see him, how important is this king? Not very. By contrast, conjure images of the kings of England in their splendor, or the emperors of China, guarded by legions of trained soldiers, with rulers of other nations pressing for an audience, along with a council of very important men, generals, scholars, and judges, who advise the king, while singers and musicians fill the hall with song—now, how great is *that* king? You see, the council does not diminish His splendor, it *reveals* it.

More importantly, the council is fundamental to His government. As the prophet Micaiah shows us, it's how the business of Heaven gets done.

The compelling vision of Daniel 7 reveals God taking His seat amidst many "thrones."

> "I kept looking until **thrones were set up,** and the Ancient of Days took His seat; His vesture was like white snow, and the hair of His head like pure wool. His throne was ablaze with flames, its wheels were a burning fire. A river of fire was flowing and coming out from before Him; **thousands upon thousands were attending Him,** and myriads upon myriads were standing before Him; **the court sat, and the books were opened**" (Dan. 7:9-10).

As Daniel continues to look, he sees, "One like a Son of Man was coming, and He came up to the Ancient of Days and was presented before Him. And to Him was given dominion, glory and a kingdom" (vs. 13-14).

Clearly, this is governmental. The eschatological council scene is nothing less than the court of heaven, full of imposing thrones and books and judgment. If we overlay the content of other Throne Visions,[84] the council members are easily recognizable: Elders, Living Creatures, cherubim, seraphim, archangels, "myriads upon myriads" of angels, along with the assembled throng of humankind...and also false gods (demons) who seek audience with Yahweh. The court bears witness to the supremacy and rightness of Yahweh's selection of the Son of Man to receive all dominion and glory. This powerful scene is the same as Psalm 110: "The Lord said to my Lord, 'Sit at my right hand.'"

The vision of Psalm 110 and Daniel 7 is similar to Stephen's at his martyrdom, who "gazed intently into heaven and saw the glory of God, and Jesus standing at the right hand of God" (Acts 7:55). Likewise, John is taken to Heaven to witness "Him who sits on the throne, and...the Lamb" (Rev. 5:13). By these revelations, John and Stephen are verified as spokesmen[85] of the council, along with Ezekiel, Isaiah and Moses. This is a small, non-exclusive group of true prophetic voices. No wonder Paul chose to solemnly charge Timothy in his duties "in the presence of God and of Christ Jesus and of His chosen angels" (1 Tim. 5:21)—a sober reference to the heavenly council:

Christ is exalted to the right hand of His father amidst the council of Heaven. He is Lord Sabaoth, the commander of the armies of Heaven. "For You are the Lord Most High over all the earth; *You are exalted far above all gods*" (Psa. 97:9).

**From Yahweh to You**

This chapter develops both the significance of types and symbols, and also heavenly realities expressed literally, physically, on *terra firma*. When we realize that the tabernacle of Moses not only symbolizes the temple in Heaven, but actually *mimics* it, the only proper response is to be stunned. An entirely fresh view of our role on planet Earth opens to us, especially since each and every human is a divine image-bearer in our own right. *You* are a living revelation of God.

This means we've come to a turning point in this book. We've reached critical mass. Here's the teaser: If, under the inferior system of the Old Covenant, God allowed a tent to reveal a small piece of Heaven on Earth, how many other heavenly models might He desire to replicate, especially in the glory of the New Covenant?[86] The rest of the book ponders one central thought: If the heavenly temple is real and the tabernacle patterned it on Earth, what might the divine council look like, and what function might it serve—on Earth as it is in Heaven? Are you starting to glimpse where this is going? If not, Psalm 82 will be a huge help.

First, understand this: in the same way that numerous prophecies point to the coming Messiah, a handful of them also point to *us* as part of Messiah's mission. In Psalm 82, we see a direct connection from the divine council in Heaven to the ruling council Jesus formed on Earth.

> "God has taken his place *in the divine council;* in the *midst of the gods* ('elohim') he holds judgment" (Psa. 82:1, ESV).

After setting the scene in Heaven—lights, camera, action!—the camera suddenly jerks, shifting the frame toward the problem of injustice on Earth. In other words, verses 2-7 reveal God enthroned in the midst of the gods, passing judgment on them. But wait a minute, who is God talking to? Angels or men?

> "*How long will you judge unjustly*, and show partiality to the wicked? Selah. Vindicate the weak and fatherless; do justice to the afflicted and destitute. Rescue the weak and needy; deliver them out of the hand of the wicked. They do not know nor do they understand; they walk about in darkness; all the foundations of the earth are shaken. *I said, "You are gods, and all of you are sons of the Most High* ('bene elyon'). *Nevertheless you will die like men,* and fall like any one of the princes" (Psa. 82:2-7).

These "gods" will die like men? In John 10:33-36, Jesus quotes this psalm to defend Himself against charges of blasphemy. In what did He blaspheme? By calling Himself a son of God! In case we think the defense only applies to Jesus, the context of the Lord's rebuttal clearly refutes this, since "You are gods" (v. 6) was spoken *to men* "to whom the word of God came (and the Scripture cannot be broken)." The Scripture did not come to gods, but to weak and fallen men. How do we reconcile these things? Psalm 82 seems to have a dual meaning. It accurately portrays the heavenly council, but when it comes to matters of justice on the earth, God seems to use the council motif to summon mortals to His chambers, in the process disclosing that it is not really angels, but men who are (or will be) "sons of the Most High." As a promise of our future status, we know this was not true until the work of Christ was complete. But it was prophesied in Psalm 82!

---

**The idea of the divine council takes a radical turn when we realize that, in the New Testament, "sons of God" are the twice-born, new creations of the Holy Spirit—you and me!**

---

In the New Covenant, an interesting switch happens. The idea of the divine council takes a radical turn when we realize that, in the New Testament, "sons of God" are the twice-born, new creations of the Holy Spirit—you and me![87]

"For you are all sons of God through faith in Christ Jesus" (Gal. 3:26).

Scholar Lewis Sperry Chafer says, "In the Old Testament terminology angels are called sons of God while men are called servants of God. In the New Testament this is reversed. Angels are the servants and Christians are the sons of God."[88]

The gravity of our privileged position in Christ is made more weighty by the fact that, even under the Old Covenant, God allowed mortals to witness His council deliberations. In fact, not only were prophets given access to the court of Heaven, but on Earth, Abraham debated with God over the fate of *two entire cities* scheduled for judgment: Sodom and Gomorrah. In fact, God's reaction to the whole affair makes it seem as if this was the only natural course of events from His perspective.

"The Lord said, 'Shall I hide from Abraham what I am about to do?'" (Gen. 18:17).

Abraham was an amazing man, but was he exclusive in this regard? Could it be that humans are meant to operate at a far higher level of engagement in the divine process of governing the earth than we ever considered possible? Consider, if these privileges were true under the Old Covenant, how much more for those who are in Christ, as heirs to a "better covenant, which has been enacted on better promises" (Heb. 8:6)?

Could it be that *you* and *I* are meant to shape history? Save cities? Contend for nations?

In *Healing the Nations*, John Loren Sandford describes three aspects of cooperating with God in His work of redeeming and transforming nations. First, we must develop a deep relationship with the Father. Second, we "engage in burden-bearing intercession for the nations." Third, we "make ourselves available should we be summoned into heavenly councils, as nations hang in the balance."[89]

Not everyone will be summoned to councils in the heavens, where God is surrounded by twenty-four elders, cherubim, seraphim, and an angelic host beyond number. On the other hand, we know that God patterns on Earth what is constructed in Heaven.

If this is true, what is the court of God on Earth? What is His ruling council on Earth?

Sons of God, awake to your destiny. You are part of the ekklesia of Christ.

# 8

## EKKLESIA: THE RULING COUNCIL ON EARTH

We have come to the heart of the matter. Everything prior has been necessary, but preparatory, like beginning a puzzle with the outer edge pieces. Having suitably framed the conversation with understanding of the local culture, historical context, theological and prophetic implications, and also divine patterns at play, we are finally ready to directly explore the richness, nuance and revolution bottled up inside this single, mistranslated word: ekklesia. It is my aim to reclaim this word and uncork the uprising it contains. Ekklesia has to do with many things, but perhaps most of all, authority in prayer. The people of God *must* begin to pray. Not small, little polite prayers. Not ten minutes of prayer. Do you read the headlines? The earth is groaning, society is tottering, darkness is exalting itself like never before. Who among the people of God will rise in the Spirit to challenge the rising tide? Supplication, adoration, confession and thanksgiving are regular parts of a prayer diet, but contending prayer must dramatically increase! Day and night, prayer must shake the earth. When we realize we are the ekklesia, a "prayerdigm shift" is inevitable because the word itself properly aligns our identity with government and prayer as Jesus intended. There is power in this word to correct our function on Earth.

According to a Chinese proverb, the beginning of wisdom is to call things by their right names. This should be obvious enough. God was very specific with names all throughout Scripture, both for Himself and others. Names have meaning. Words have meaning. He even changed people's names to signify a change in their nature. Think of it this way: what if the Marines were called ballerinas, and vice-versa? Instead of *Semper Fidelis*—a motto reflecting the faithfulness, courage and sacrifice of men who are "first to fight"—what if their motto was *Motu Camena,* which is "poetry in motion"? Does it matter that a bear is a bear and a lamb is a lamb?

These are not cheeky, semantic questions. Massive consequences hinge on the meaning and intent of this word. Jesus promised to build something. What is it? Do we know? Is it okay if our replacement word is "close enough?" My friends, I appeal to you, do not stiffen your necks in pride or act like this doesn't matter. Tradition and inculcation have bred a deeply passive familiarity, yet *Jesus used a specific word with specific connotations,* and, as you will soon discover, our forefathers *willfully changed it!* Worse, every subsequent generation has defended the change. Can we afford to be casual about this? Do we value our cherished, traditional, *substitute* word above *His* word? For generations, the answer has been yes. Our negligence has created a false identity and misguided mission, and we don't even know it.

I am told that each September in northern Manitoba, the temperature drops and rain freezes. A sign by the road reads, "Choose your rut carefully. You'll be in it for the next 60 miles." Words create culture. By adopting the word *church* with its totally different etymology, instead of the more contextually accurate word of Christ, *ekklesia,* the movement of God has been in a rut for 2,000 years.

Don't believe me? Pick up any dictionary. Look up 'church.' See if it lists ekklesia as the Greek root. Hint: it won't. What it will tell you is that church derives from the Late Greek word *kyriakon,*[90] which eventually took an Anglo-Saxon twist to become "kirche" and the Scottish "kirk." Alternately, *Smith's Bible Dictionary* wonders if kyriakon isn't the root either, but rather, by virtue of the connection to kirk, church might be more related "to the Latin circus, circulus, the Greek kuklos, because the (early) congregations gathered in circles."[91]

---

**Don't believe me? Pick up any dictionary. Look up 'church.' See if it lists ekklesia as the Greek root. Hint: it won't.**

---

In either case, as even a nine-year-old can tell, our beloved word, church, doesn't even resemble the Greek ekklesia! A related form, *kyriakos,* appears only twice in the New Testament.[92] Since believers during the early centuries called the place in which they met, *Kuriake Oikia,* the Lord's House, this has become the common meaning.[93]

Obviously, translators broke the rules in a big way.[94] Virtually every major commentator over the last four centuries—Smith included—will readily admit that church actually comes from a different word, but then, in the same breath and with apparently no discomfort, defend the merits of this decision by appealing to the idea of "assembly," a meaning which both words share in a very general sense.[95] The unfortunate impression left upon both serious and casual Bible students is that the word church is an accurate translation of ekklesia in the Greek text, which is simply not the case. Once you see it, you will likely wonder how and why it has been allowed to continue. To validly interpret Jesus as telling Peter He would build His church would require Matthew 16:18 to read thus, "Upon this rock I will build my *kyriakon*," literally forcing a different word into the text! Simon Peter would have replied, "Huh? What's that?" because there is no New Testament Greek word to convey the equivalent of our modern English word.[96]

The irony is painful: What we claim Jesus to be building is founded on error and myth, not Christ. If we are building a church, we are building in vain.[97] Is it any wonder "church life" often feels like we're chasing our tail, traveling in circles, then cringing while our faith sometimes plays out like a circus on TV? It shouldn't. We chose *that* word to define us...not Jesus's word!

## Ekklesia means ekklesia!

An inevitable fact of travel is that orientation affects your destination. In Lewis Carroll's *Alice in Wonderland,* Alice asks the Cheshire Cat which way she should go.

"That depends on where you want to go," he replies.

Alice says, "I don't really care...as long as I get somewhere."

The Cheshire cat grinned. "Well it doesn't matter then, does it?"

In many respects, this has been our attitude, but is somewhere good enough? On the one hand, if all we want is church, we've got it. But if Jesus wants an ekklesia, we don't. Solomon offers a clear warning to those who would mismanage God's Word. "Every word of God is tested; He is a shield to those who take refuge in Him. ***Do not add to His words*** lest He reprove you, and you be proved a liar." David said God was "***justified in Your words.***" And Jesus Himself said, "The ***words that I have spoken to you*** are spirit and are life."[98]

Why have we strayed to our own words? For 1,500 years in practice, and 400 years in written form, we have taken a different course than the one He laid out for us. (More on this can be found in 'Appendix: A Brief History of King James Version Mistranslation and the Establishment of 'Church' Culture.') An illustration will help us calculate the toll of straying even a little. Suppose you were to take off from an airport at the equator, intending to circumnavigate the globe, but your course was off by just one degree. By the time you return to the same longitude, making one total circuit of Earth, that tiny one-degree error will have thrown you off course by almost 500 miles. Whether the distance you are traveling is a matter of miles or time, degrees matter. Spiritually speaking, degrees can equal destiny. Are we on target, or off course?

In *Their Finest Hour,* the second volume of Winston Churchill's grand recounting of World War II, the story is told of how Hitler's German High Command developed a new "split beam" radar. This radar was guaranteed to conduct the Luftwaffe bombers to precise London targets. However, scientists at Number Ten Downing Street figured out a way to throw off one of the Nazi's beams by the tiniest, undetectable amount. Soon, volleys of German bombs were exploding to no effect in remote areas. Furthermore, the pilots were disoriented. The Prime Minister took fierce pleasure telling of one German bomber who confidently landed in Devonshire, thinking he was in France.[99]

Because we are fallen creatures, human error is inevitable, even with divine things.[100] But with knowledge comes grace to repent and change course. Let's form up, man up and line up, cooperating with His Word as never before, rather than pretending church and ekklesia are the same thing. In the coming darkness of the last days, sloppy devotion to Scripture will not merely be negligent, it will be dangerous. If Jesus says we are the ekklesia, then it is high time we start thinking and acting like ekklesia!

### Becoming Ekklesia

The word ekklesia combines two Greek words: *ek,* 'out of,' and *klesis,* 'a calling' (from *kaleo,* 'to call')." The morphology of the word (i.e. the structure and form it takes) has been used by many preachers to suggest that "the church" is meant to be "called out, separated, holy." While this is certainly a true statement with regards to holiness, as numerous verses attest, it's highly doubtful that this is what ekklesia meant to those who heard it.[101] For example, many words are a combination of other, recognizable words, such as blackmail and butterfly. Yet over time, the words take on their own identity. Nobody thinks of whipped milk fat soaring through the air when we say butterfly. Instead, you picture the beautiful, winged insect, right? Why? Because etymological roots are not always sufficient. Some words have a clear cultural and/or historical context that greatly illuminates their meaning and usage. Ekklesia is such a word.

Ekklesia is used 115 times in the New Testament. Of these, it is improperly translated church in all but three verses. The three remaining occurrences more accurately read as congregation or assembly, for that is what ekklesia generally, literally means: "assembly."[102]

Case closed, right? Church, assembly, congregation...it's all the same. Not so fast. It is a general truism that many Bible words do not have definitions so much as histories. Such is the case when, centuries later, we reduce the fullness of ekklesia to the rather flat "assembly."

Bear in mind, Jesus could have employed a number of worthy alternatives. He could have told Peter He would build His family, bride, temple, army, kingdom. Likewise, if Jesus had merely meant an assembly, He could have used other words such as the verb *sunago,* which denotes the action of assembling, with its noun form, *sunagoge,* which denotes the meeting place in which they assembled.[103] This is the Synagogue of Jesus's day, and it enjoyed high usage. It was by no means exclusively Jewish or religious, just as ekklesia was not. It was simply a useful word that over time came to be identified exclusively with the Jewish culture and religion. In the common Greek of the day, sunagoge clearly rivaled ekklesia as a generic term for assembly if that is what Jesus wanted. But He didn't pick that word.

Why? I believe it relates to the *function* of this particular assembly—the ekklesia—which was practically, linguistically and culturally intrinsic to the word, though these ideas are not conveyed by the literal interpretation. You see, the ekklesia was not just an assembly, *it was a ruling assembly.* It was governmental. By the time of Christ, having been used in this sense for approximately 500 years, ekklesia had specific, well-acknowledged connotations. According to Oskar Seyffert's *Dictionary of Classical Antiquities,* ekklesia was originally used to describe "the assembly of the people, which in Greek cities had the power of final decision in public affairs."[104] It was the principal assembly of the Athenian government, which eventually became the model of government for city-states throughout the hellenized world. Eventually, as Roman culture both supplanted and incorporated Greek culture, this included the Roman world of Judea.

Ekklesia has both a Greek and Hebrew background. We know this because the Greek translation, called the Septuagint, helps us.[105] This translation was widely used in New Testament times, and is quoted word-for-word by a number of the New Testament writers.[106] From that fact alone, Christ's disciples would have been familiar with the word. By comparing, we see that the idea of ekklesia was common to the Hebrew mind due to the various times and places God assembled the nation of Israel, such as in the giving of the Law at Sinai.[107] The following verse sets the stage by which the Septuagint translates the Old Testament equivalent of ekklesia.

> "Remember the day you stood before the Lord your God at Horeb, when the Lord said to me, 'Assemble the people to Me, that I may let them hear My words so they may learn to fear Me all the days they live on the earth, and that they may teach their children'" (Deut. 4:10).

Later, in Deuteronomy 9:10 and 18:16 this is called "the day of the assembly ('*qahal*' in Hebrew)" or in the Greek Septuagint, *"the day of the ekklesia."* So, at the gathering of Sinai, we witness the first ekklesia in Israel's history. Utilizing the Principle of First Occurrence, we see that the Hebrew qahal and Greek ekklesia refer to a summoned people, assembling together to receive God's law and act upon it. While we can homiletically apply this to the idea of personal discipleship, the later understanding of ekklesia's governmental function forces different conclusions.

- The "ekklesia in the wilderness" (Acts 7:38) was led by Moses, the Law-Giver
- The ekklesia of grace is led by Christ, the Law-Fulfiller
- The Old Covenant ekklesia first assembled around Mt. Sinai to receive the Law of God, thereby forming a covenantal identity
- The New Covenant ekklesia first assembled around Christ, and from Him received the commission to carry His rulership into the earth as a covenantal community
- The Old Covenant ekklesia was summoned by the voice of thunder and trumpets
- The New Covenant ekklesia was summoned by the voice of Christ

As William Barclay notes, "The Septuagint...translates the Hebrew word *qahal,* which again comes from a root which means 'to summon.' It is regularly used for the 'assembly' or 'congregation' of Israel...In the Hebrew sense it, therefore, means God's people, called together by God, in order **to listen to** or **act for God.**" For this reason, Barclay observes, "In a certain sense the word 'congregation' loses a certain amount of the essential meaning" because qahal and ekklesia are both, clearly, *summoned together* for a purpose, rather than merely "assembling because they have chosen to come together."[108]

### The form of ekklesia in the Greek-speaking world

A large body of secular references to the ekklesia help us understand what the term meant. Remember, it wasn't a specifically religious word. Far from it. Rather, the participants of the ekklesia were:

- Male citizens over the age of 18
- Up to 6,000 in number (comprising a quorum)

And the functions of the ekklesia were:

- To actively participate in legislation
- Election of officials, including *strategoi* (military generals) and others, such as *archons* (chief magistrates of the city-state)
- The banishment of citizens
- Judicial decisions (in limited cases)

Seyffert says, "In legal co-operation with the senate, the Ekklesia had the final decision in all matters affecting the supreme interests of the state, as war, peace, alliances, treaties, the regulation of army and navy, finances, loans, tributes, duties, prohibition of exports or imports, the introduction of new religious rites and festivals, the awarding of honours and rewards, and the conferring of the citizenship."[109]

In other words, the secular ekklesia had expansive authority in determining the affairs of their cities and territories. To adequately manage these affairs, the ruling council typically met three to four times a month. The ordinary assembly, *Ekklesia kuriai,* was generally pre-scheduled and covered routine business of state. Special assemblies were called *ekklesia sugklrtoi* as needed for emergencies or other pressing concerns. All qualified persons were expected to participate. In comparing the secular application of ekklesia to the ruling council which Jesus convened, Barclay observes, "The summons was not to any selected few; it was a summons from the State to every man to come and to shoulder his responsibilities; it was a summons from God to every man to come and to listen to and to act on the word of God."[110]

The responsibilities shouldered by each member came with real and collective power to enforce the will of the ekklesia within the community. In the *Apology of Socrates*, Plato refers to an incident in which the ekklesia decided to make a group of naval commanders stand trial in one group. Though each of the men had the right to be tried individually, the ekklesia decided otherwise. The commanders were condemned, and some, executed. This incident serves to reveal how the ekklesia was, in a certain sense, all-powerful in the Athenian democratic system. "Apart from the fact that its decisions must conform to the laws of the State, its powers were to all intents and purposes *unlimited* (emphasis mine)."[111]

While it is beyond the scope of this work to fully defend what follows, the theological and linguistic contortions that must be performed to adopt church into a Christian worldview are sizable and humorous. Because we are using a false word, we have to add on numerous modifiers to make sure people understand what Jesus meant. So we speak of the "local...visible...true...militant" church. It would be nonsensical to speak of these things with reference to the ekklesia, because each of these concepts is either explicitly embedded or, at the very least, already familiar in the usage.

Furthermore, the Apostle Paul was very skilled in the Greek of his day. If he felt another word might have added to our understanding, he could have replaced ekklesia with another word. Instead, he repeatedly used the same word, because "as a wise master builder"

(1 Cor. 3:10) he sought to build on the true foundation of Christ. He used the word because Jesus used the word. Jesus used the word *because it meant something very specific to those who heard it.* Likewise, the writer of Hebrews, and the apostles James and John employed the same word, over and over and over again.

Contrasting the common view of church with what has been presented thus far will likely produce one of three reactions among readers:

1.  You are unimpressed. In this view, it all sounds synonymous. Since we understand one meaning of church to be "congregation," isn't this all just mincing words, i.e. "Church, assembly, what's the difference? We all know what we mean. Let's not major on minors."

2.  You are frustrated/angry. In this view, it all sounds dangerously disrespectful to the institution of the church. Our traditional language is fine, thank you very much. Or perhaps a different cause for anger is the feeling of been tricked or misled. Whatever the cause, you're getting a little uncomfortable with where all this is going.

3.  You're intrigued. It sounds like perhaps we're saying the whole system is wrong, and while you don't have all the facts yet, you cherish the details of the Word above your traditions, so you sincerely want to understand more.

Over the course of my investigation, I fell into the second category. I felt a bit duped. Why haven't we ever been taught this stuff? For me, personally, the fact that the words church (kyriakon) and assembly (ekklesia) are superficially synonymous is not good enough. Not even close! Meaning and usage are too different in this case. From where I sit, the system appears fundamentally flawed, being built on a known falsehood. Regardless of how much we cherish our notions of church, I can only conclude that we are long overdue to get this right. Many important things are at stake, including the integrity of divine revelation. "The words of the Lord are pure words; as silver tried in a furnace on the earth, refined seven times" (Psa. 12:6). I want a pure Word without bias rather than "invalidating the word of God by your tradition" (Mark 7:13). The whole Bible is inspired, but ekklesia is in red letters. Jesus was the first person to introduce the term in the New Testament, and I believe He was intentional in His selection of words. Let us not pretend to be wiser than our Master.

---

## The ekklesia was by definition a governmental assembly.

---

In summary, the ekklesia was by definition a governmental assembly. Therefore, the authority and function of the assembly is fundamental to properly understanding what Jesus inaugurated in Matthew 16:18. If this chapter is true, the thought of willfully continuing to play church rather than "shouldering our responsibilities" as duly summoned representatives of God's ruling council must become abhorrent to us. Let us repent, and cooperate with God in the administration of His kingdom on planet Earth.

If you are uncomfortable, so am I. Believe me, my sensitivities are heightened. I realize the position this puts me in, but I assure you, I have no axe to grind and no desire to launch a diatribe against church. I simply want to discern and reclaim the original intentions of Jesus. If you are with me, then in a spirit of humility and boldness, let's press ahead.

# 9

## EKKLESIA: GOING DEEPER

A curious event coincidentally precedes Peter's confession of Christ in Matthew 16. Under the inspiration of the Holy Spirit, Matthew informs us of an encounter with the Pharisees and Sadducees which, at least in the narrative, immediately precedes the Caesarea Philippi episode. Gleaning these insights may be compared to scraping crumbs off a large banquet table. At the end, you realize your crumbs have become a whole other meal. In Matthew 16:1-5 we are told:

> "The Pharisees and Sadducees came up, and testing Him asked Him to show them a sign from heaven. But He answered and said to them, 'When it is evening, you say, 'It will be fair weather, for the sky is red.' And in the morning, 'There will be a storm today, for the sky is red and threatening.' Do you know how to discern the appearance of the sky, but cannot discern the signs of the times? An evil and adulterous generation seeks after a sign; and a sign will not be given it, *except the sign of Jonah*'" (Mat. 16:1-6).

Okay, hit pause. Let's review. Just a few verses later in this chapter, Jesus will call Peter, "Simon Barjona," which means Simon the "son of Jonah." Note: though Andrew is Peter's brother, he is never called son of Jonah, and though James and John are often called the "sons of Zebedee," Peter and Andrew are never called the sons of

Jonah. Remembering the tradition of wordplay in Jesus's exchange with Peter, I think it is possible that Jesus is intentionally imbedding one more layer of meaning which the Holy Spirit will highlight later in the construction of Matthew 16:13-19. Could it be that we are meant to understand that Simon's life or confession shares certain characteristics with Jonah's? Matthew 16 starts with Jesus pointing out that the ultimate recognition of who He really is will be the sign of Jonah, then when Peter actually recognizes Him, Jesus points us back to the only sign He pledged to give the Pharisees. Interesting, huh? So the pun frames Peter as a sort of "spiritual son." Indeed, when later tested, Peter, like Jonah, would flee his responsibility— not only denying Jesus, but also walking away from the call and returning to being a fisherman. Or perhaps Simon is like Jonah in being the first to carry good news to the Gentiles (Acts 10), just as Jonah was used to bring salvation through repentance (albeit via a word of judgment) to the Gentiles at Nineveh.

But I think there may be something deeper. Jesus tells Simon Barjona four things:

- Your name is Peter
- I will build My ekklesia
- The gates of Hades will not prevail
- Keys will be given for binding and loosing

What is the connection to Jonah? When asked to prove that He was the Messiah, Jesus said the great sign of Jonah was the only proof He would give to that generation.

> "For just as Jonah was three days and three nights in the belly of the sea monster, so shall the Son of Man be three days and three nights in the heart of the earth. The men of Nineveh shall stand up with this generation at the judgment, and shall condemn it because they repented at the preaching of Jonah;

and behold, something greater than Jonah is here" (Mat. 12:40-41).

If you read Jonah's little book, the prophet's prayer in the belly of the fish connects him directly to this exchange between Jesus and Peter. Jesus describes Jonah's three-day experience as a foreshadowing of His own harrowing journey to Hades as the ransom fee for humanity, where He would lie in the depths of darkness, dead. Only one other person had ever known something comparable and lived to tell about it: Jonah. Can you imagine the psychological and physical horror of being trapped in a huge, acidic stomach hundreds of feet under the ocean in total darkness...for three days? Now multiply that manyfold with the understanding that Jesus *actually died and went to Hades.* For three days, He was confined to the underworld.

Yet He did not stay in the tomb, nor remain in the darkness of Sheol.

He arose, triumphing over death and the grave.

"Therefore it says, 'When He ascended on high, He led captive a host of captives, and He gave gifts to men.' (Now this expression, 'He ascended,' what does it mean except that He also had descended into the lower parts of the earth? He who descended is Himself also He who ascended far above all the heavens, that He might fill all things)" (Eph. 4:8-10).

From the depths of Hades, Jesus triumphed. Brothers and sisters, it is important that we reclaim the fearless heart of our King. He is not afraid of anything, least of all Hades. "When He had disarmed the rulers and authorities, He made a public display of them, having triumphed over them through Him" (Col. 2:14-15).

Jesus was the point of the spear in a massive, triumphant assault against Satan's dominion of Earth. The mission was a success. The sting of death and sin was removed when Jesus burst forth from the tomb, liberating all mankind from death's grip with resurrection power.[112] In the construction of Matthew 16, the Holy Spirit is nudging us to read between the lines. Christ is King and Messiah, He who was anointed, and He who anoints. Simon is typecast as the son of Jonah so that we understand that radical acts of intercession from the depths of the earth—even from the prison of Hades itself—bring forth a sound by which an entire city is captured for God.

> "I cried for help from the **depth of Sheol**...I descended to the roots of the mountains. **The earth with its bars** was around me forever, but You have brought up my life from the pit, O Lord my God...and **my prayer came to You,** into Your holy temple" (Jonah 2:2, 6-7).

Jonah is telling us that:

- From the belly of Sheol (Gr: 'Hades'), which was like a prison
- Prayer arises (because prayer is effective even in the hardest, most hellish places)
- Which is heard in the temple of Heaven
- Releasing the word of God with resurrection power to people trapped in darkness
- So that entire cities are delivered

Peter, son of Jonah, *this* is the mission of the ekklesia. Reader, should you choose to accept your ekklesial identity, this is your mission, too. Be a catalyst for spiritual change in your territory. Take your outpost seriously. Take your commission seriously. Cause prayer to rise from the hardest, darkest places in the earth. Where death and hell currently possess men's souls, contend for the rulership of Christ instead. Advance the kingdom. Do not let circumstance dictate your action. No stronghold is too great, no sin too vile, no darkness too black, no injustice is too entrenched to withstand Lord Sabaoth's army, or the King's government of righteousness.

# Ekklesia Rising

In *The Barbarian Way,* Erwin McManus recounts a compelling insight he received into the history of the Douglas clan while visiting Scotland. The story begins with Robert the Bruce, the Scottish noble who famously betrayed William Wallace, as immortalized by Mel Gibson in the movie *Braveheart*. Later, Robert the Bruce rose up to lead Scotland to freedom after Wallace's execution.

> "Before his death in 1329, Robert requested that when he died, his heart would be removed and travel into battle with a worthy knight during the crusades. One of his closest friends, James Douglas, honored the request. The heart of Robert the Bruce was embalmed, placed in a small container, and carried around Douglas's neck. In every battle he fought, Douglas literally carried the heart of his king into the fight. In a campaign against the Moors in Granada, Spain, Douglas was surrounded by enemies. Knowing his death was imminent, he took the heart of Robert the Bruce from around his neck and flung it into the midst of the enemy forces, shouting, 'Fight for the heart of your king!' One historian quotes Douglas as saying, 'Forward, brave heart, as ever thou were wont to do! And Douglas will follow his king or die!' To this day, the motto of the Douglas clan is simply, 'Forward.'"[113]

In Matthew 16, Jesus declared that His clan, above all other people, should carry His heart forward. By virtue of its function, the *ekklesia* clearly has been given the task of governance, justice, and the overcoming of evil. By contrast, the *kyriakos oikia* has none except to gather together. It is no accident that the unifying theme of the messages to the seven churches in Revelation 2-3 follows a similar pattern to Matthew 16:16-19. We see 1) deeper revelation of Christ, followed by 2) the call to overcome.

I'll provide two samples, but read all seven for yourself.

- "To the (messenger) of the (ekklesia) in Ephesus write: The One who holds the seven stars in His right hand, the One who walks among the seven golden lampstands, says this...'To him who over-comes, I will grant to eat of the tree of life, which is in the Paradise of God'" (Rev. 2:1, 7).

- "And to the (messenger) of the (ekklesia) in Smyrna write: The first and the last, who was dead, and has come to life, says this...'He who overcomes shall not be hurt by the second death'" (Rev. 2:8, 11), etc.

In the great upheavals of the closing of this age, the ekklesia will finally rise to the privilege bestowed upon Adam, which is also the challenge Jesus put forth to His disciples: to rule and reign on Earth.

---

**Implicit in Christ's words, "My ekklesia," is a threat to every corrupt human government and demonic principality.**

---

Now that you have a grid that ekklesia means far more than just an assembly of people, let's have a "he who has ears to hear" moment. Hear the statement Jesus made as the disciples would have heard it. When the Lord declared, "Upon this rock I will build *My* ekklesia," He is clearly inviting contrast with *other* ekklesia. "Every city has a ruling assembly, an ekklesia. I, Jesus, am now forming *my* ekklesia." A new president doesn't utilize the old president's cabinet. He installs his own. A new king brings his own council! In Matthew 16:18, God installed another regime on planet Earth, a government that would be responsible and loyal to Him above all others. Implicit in Christ's words, "My ekklesia," is a threat to every corrupt human government and demonic principality. The disciples understood this, but that is not enough. We must understand it. Like never before, we must take up an orbital position around this mission.

For this reason, the Petrine Revelation of Matthew 16 should be understood as a Preamble to the Great Commission: "And Jesus came up and spoke to them, saying, 'All authority has been given to Me in heaven and on earth. Go therefore and make disciples of all the nations.... and these signs will accompany those who have believed: in My name they will cast out demons, they will speak with new tongues, they will pick up serpents, and if they drink any deadly poison, it shall not hurt them; they will lay hands on the sick, and they will recover" (Mat. 28:18, 19; Mark 16:17-18).

We've tried to do this with a church mindset, haven't we? Does anyone doubt that we've tried? Not me. The people of God have been so sincere for so long—generations and centuries. Over that time, how many books have been written describing the inadequacies and failures of the church to accomplish the Great Commission? How many new proposals have been written basically saying, if only the church would do this, or that, then we would succeed? May I simply say, unless you get the question right, the answer will always be wrong. Did Jesus promise to build a church or an ekklesia, *that's* the question. The Great Commission was never given to a *kuriakon* or *chirch*. It doesn't have the tools, nor the DNA.

No, the mission of Christ uniquely requires the ekklesia to arise.

## The best defense is a strong offense

A number of times over the course of my life, the Holy Spirit has clearly spoken to me through the agency of dreams. Of course, many are meaningless "bad pizza dreams" while others are full of soulish angst. But a few have been providentially and spiritually instructive. One such dream came several years ago. In that dream, my high school basketball coach (who always represents the Holy Spirit in my dreams) gave me written instructions and sent me to a destination. Though I was in my thirties at the time, in the dream

I thought I was being sent as a player, yet when I arrived I realized that coach had sent me to coach this team in his stead. They were behind and there wasn't much time left on the clock. Upon arriving, I finally looked at the instructions he had given me. The note simply read: "Defense 12-29." I knew this was critical, but I didn't understand it. Then I awoke.

I must tell you, I played basketball in high school. I was pretty good. And as any basketball fan knows, there is no such thing as a 12-29 defense. It's a nonsensical instruction. So I puzzled over this dream for more than a decade before, quite by chance, I realized that there was a well-known 12-29 in the Bible that answered the riddle. This passage perfectly captures the common coaching adage that "the best defense is a good offense." With new eyes, I read Matthew 12:29: "Or how can anyone enter the strong man's house and carry off his property, unless he first binds the strong man? And then he will plunder his house."

When you are behind, you don't put points on the board with defense. You have to shift to an offensive mindset. When a strong man holds a territory, you get a stronger man to break in.

Sir Winston Churchill knew a thing or two about offense and defense. Churchill was a leader born for formidable times and given a daunting task. By October 1941, London had become a bombed wasteland and the people's nerves were frayed. Paris had already fallen. Hitler seemed unstoppable. But Churchill was unbowed. Faced with Hitler's ruthless advance, and overwhelmed by the German war machine, Churchill nevertheless turned his attention to attack. As a great soldier statesman, Churchill understood something fundamental to war: a primarily defensive posture will *always lose ground* over time. If new territory is not taken, old territory will be lost. If you do not rule with a rod of iron, the enemy will place a yoke of iron on your neck.[114]

In Churchill's memoirs, we see the "Lion of Britain" realizing the strategic urgency of taking the battle to the enemy, and scaling for a full offensive. It was not enough for London to weather the bombs, nor for the English to keep a stiff upper lip. They had to attack.

> "Small-scale raids by the Commandos paved the way for greater things, and not only gave us confidence and experience, but showed the world that although beset on all sides we were not content with passive defence...
>
> (When) Admiral Keyes was succeeded by Captain Lord Louis Mountbatten, we were still hard-pressed, and our only ally, Russia, seemed near to defeat. Nevertheless, I had resolved to prepare for an invasion of the Continent when the tide should turn. First, we had to increase the intensity and scope of our raids, and then translate all this experience into something much more massive. To mount a successful invasion from the United Kingdom, new engines of war must be contrived and developed, the three fighting services must be trained to plan and fight as one team, supported by the industry of the nation, and the whole island converted into an armed camp for launching the greatest seaborne assault of all time.
>
> When Mountbatten visited me at Chequers before taking up his new duties, I told him, according to his account, *'You are to plan for the offensive. In your Headquarters you will never think defensively.'* This governed his actions."[115]

Question: what governs *your* actions? Clearly, the ekklesia Jesus has committed to build is meant to have devastating impact on the enemy's kingdom. His language plays offense as clearly as Churchill's. Go assault the gates. Go into all the world! Leave no dark stone unturned until "the kingdom of the world has become the kingdom of our Lord, and of His Christ; and He will reign forever and ever" (Rev. 11:15). This is why the revelation of Christ must come first, not only for Peter, but for you and me, as well. It is only at the point where fallen man grasps the enormity and totality of Jesus's leadership over all of history and human affairs that he is ready to enlist in the body by which Jesus intends to execute His will and extend His reign over the planet.

The consistent witness of Scripture could be compared to a huge connect-the-dots picture. In Matthew 16, Peter finally connects the dots, perhaps in a way which even John the Baptist missed. To John, Jesus was both the Lamb of God and He who would baptize in the spirit and fire. But as Christ stands before His disciples, saying, "Who am I?" in a burst of divine inspiration, Peter connects the dots. "You're that guy! The ruler above all rulers! The promised King." It is no accident that Jesus seizes *that* moment to announce His takeover plans. What are they? To diffuse His rule into an assembly of brethren. "You're right, Peter! And because I am that ruler, I say *you* are." The formation of the ekklesia was entirely dependent on this revelation of Jesus as the Christ. Thus convened the first New Covenant, governmental assembly of Heaven on Earth, the ekklesia of Christ.

Here we see one of the premiere types and shadows, nay, even replications, in all of Scripture. Just as the angelic *bene elohim* prefigured Adam as a human son of God, it is the witness of Scripture that man is a type and shadow of God Himself. Isn't that what God said, that we are created in His image? And though that divine spark may have dimmed in the Fall, yet in Christ, the firstborn of many brethren, doesn't the New Covenant assembly actually form a new *bene elohim*—a company of born again, mortal sons? Thus, we see that Jesus assembles the ekklesia *on Earth as they are in Heaven*. Angels in His council in Heaven, who traffic on Earth, and men on Earth, with access through Christ to His council in Heaven. In this, Lord Sabaoth is revealed as the stronger man, binding Satan's authority over planet Earth, who then commissions an earthly council to execute His merciful justice and extend His rule, with the full availability of the heavenly council/army at their disposal.

"Occupy till I come," He told us in Luke 19:13. The word occupy means, "carry on My business."

---

## While we exist in the world, the ekklesia is actually convened out of Heaven.

---

Ekklesial language helps us better understand what it means to be in, but not of, the world. "If you were of the world, the world would love its own; but because you are not of the world, but I chose you out of the world, therefore the world hates you" (John 15:19). While we exist in the world, the ekklesia is actually convened out of Heaven. The ekklesia is the heavenly, eschatological, New Covenant congregation that Paul has in mind when he refers to Jesus as "the head of the body, the ekklesia" (Col. 1:18). Though he uses the old, unfortunate word church, Peter O'Brien rightly argues that the ekklesia is nothing less than the full manifestation in space and time of the one, true, heavenly, eschatological, New Covenant assembly.[116] Every ekklesial gathering, denoted by Jesus as being "in My name" (Mat. 18:20) should see themselves as outposts of Heaven on the lawless frontier of Earth. We are not only types of "the Jerusalem that is above," but literal colonies by which a corporate and visible expression of "the glorious freedom of the children of God"[117] is made manifest and tangible.

If we have eyes to see it, this is precisely what the writer of Hebrews shows us in the comparison of Sinai and Zion. Just as the assembly at Sinai receives their sacred identity as being covenantally bound by Law to their King, so too does the assembly at Zion become covenantally bound to the rulership of Christ and the extension of His rule. This is central to our New Covenant identity.[118]

"But you have come to Mount Zion and to the city of the living God, the heavenly Jerusalem, and to myriads of angels, to the general assembly and *ekklesia* of the first-born who are enrolled in heaven, and to God..." (Heb. 12:22-23).

Get this, it's vital: *You* have come to Mt. Zion. You are there, *now.* You have approached the unapproachable light of God (1 Tim. 6:16). You are seated with Christ in heavenly places (Eph. 2:6). You are assembled before the throne right now, amongst the myriads of angels. Though you stand on Earth as a human being, your name, your identity is "written in Heaven" (Heb. 12:23, NIV). Wow!

*My ekklesia,* Jesus said. A new divine council comprised of the mortal redeemed, endued with the authority of His name to get the business of Heaven done on Earth. Let's look at a few other verses to round out our understanding of ekklesia. Obviously, I can't quote all 115 occurrences in the New Testament, much less 115 more in the Old Testament. But a sampling will help.

- "And He put all things under His feet, and gave Him to be head over all things to the *ekklesia,* which is His body, the fullness of Him who fills all in all" (Eph. 1:22-23).
- "And He is before all things, and in Him all things consist. And He is the head of the body, the *ekklesia,* who is the beginning, the firstborn from the dead, that in all things He may have the preeminence" (Col 1:17-18).
- "Blow a trumpet in Zion, consecrate a fast, proclaim a solemn *ekklesia.* Gather the people, sanctify the *ekklesia;* assemble the elders" (Joel 2:15-16, *Septuagint*).

In light of Matthew 16, plus this short sampling of verses, we realize:

1.  Jesus has all authority. He established the ekklesia and serves as its federal head.
2.  The ekklesia is built on divine revelation, not human intellect.
3.  Demonized systems of death cannot prevail against the ekklesia.
4.  The ekklesia are given keys by which they forbid or permit in localities on Earth.
5.  The ekklesia is the living embodiment of Christ on Earth. Therefore, Christ fills the ekklesia with the fullness of who He is.
6.  By virtue of their intimate connection to Christ, the ekklesia express His rule on Earth.
7.  Finally, in Joel 2, the ekklesia intervene as intercessory arbiters of national crisis.

In the midst of crisis, God's kingdom draws near. Jesus said, "the kingdom of heaven is at hand" (Mat. 4:17). For Jesus to announce that the kingdom had come could mean nothing other than that the King had come, for there is no kingdom without a King. But if the King has returned to Heaven "until the restoration of all things" (Acts 3:21), how shall the kingdom persist on Earth, except that He leave His government intact? And so He did, represented in tens of thousands of representative assemblies, governmental outposts, which take seriously His command to occupy, proclaim and prayerfully enforce His rulership "until He comes" (Luke 19:13). Ask yourself, when you assemble in "church," do you think like:

1.  Ambassadors in a foreign land, representing the will and character of your king?

2. The high command of an invasion force during wartime, plotting strategies to take your region?
3. Spiritual senators, legislating in prayer the higher law to which criminal demonic activity and false ideologies must yield?

Chances are, the answer is no. And to be fair, these pictures are incomplete. Yet they help to illustrate the deficit in our current view of *why* we assemble.

**What does church do?**

Every Sunday, "church" must battle the navel-gazing, inward-focused gravity of its own narcissistic identity. That may sound harsh, but a poll of honest, weary pastors would likely bring to light that all too often, the agenda of the flock is Me with a capital 'M!' How does worship make *me* feel? Did the sermon strike *me*? Did the Sunday School program help *my* kids? Why didn't the Pastor say hello to *me*? While this is certainly the product of human nature, and not entirely the fault of the word church, the fact is that the construction and history of the term lends itself to such an identity.

In this respect, the public perception of church is often well-deserved. Church culture is typically an insular, closed system—conservative in action and small in vision—as opposed to demonstrating the bold apostolic and prophetic witness which characterized first century believers. The *kyriakos oikia* meet 2-3 times a week mainly to reinforce and edify a local group of people by tending almost exclusively to pastoral concerns, preaching sermons, and growing the Christian family. While this is a vital, thoroughly biblical aspect of body life, it hardly represents the fullness of governmental rulership. However, the drift makes sense. Viewed from a certain vantage point, the church has actually done a fantastic job of building what it *thinks* Jesus committed to, i.e. if we understand

Jesus to be building a *church,* our energies should naturally focus on tending to those who gather regularly to the Lord's house. A church can evangelize, feed the poor, build the family and run a great Sunday School program, but it takes an ekklesia to act with senatorial spiritual authority across their region. That's why the ekklesia is founded on apostles and prophets (Eph. 1:22, 23, 2:20). The mindset of "sent ones" and "council visionaries" is different than pastors and teachers. Though all are equally important, the chief concern is to rightly prioritize the ekklesial charter.

When the charter is misaligned, the agenda of God stalls, similar to legislation on Capitol Hill that never reaches the president's desk. But how can this be? I'll tell you, we need an identity transplant. Actually, it's waiting for us if we'll take it. In the brilliant scheme of God, each ruling assembly is characterized by Christ actually *dwelling inside each representative* via the Holy Spirit. This could be properly compared to a future president, to assure that his administration's agenda is completely fulfilled, having every member of Congress and the Supreme Court undergo a full brain transplant with genetically cloned duplicates of his own mind. Then he does the same with his cabinet. In fact, not only is his brain cloned and surgically inserted, but also his personality and values. Do you know that this is what we are promised?

"But you have the mind of Christ" (1 Cor. 2:16). Oh my friends, do you see?

Obviously, the formation of the personality and values of the King within us is as crucial as His agenda for justice. In other words, a rulership mindset is not the only component of "life together" as Dietrich Bonhoeffer put it. The communal nature of the ekklesia requires patient pastoral care for the soul. Wounds need tending. Relationships need mending. Truth must be taught. Disciples must be made. Since we fellowship, worship and pray *together,* shepherding is vital. This isn't about choosing sides, it's about order.

Furthermore, the church has done much good, acting tangibly as salt and light in the world. Even factoring in major historic transgressions, such as the Inquisition and slave ownership in the American south, the church has generally been a moral force for good, and has been used to boldly proclaim the gospel throughout every generation since the time of Christ. The church has invested hundreds of billions of dollars over the last 2,000 years to reach every culture with the message of redemption and grace. Pastors and preachers within the church system often serve as faithful, underpaid, overworked witnesses in proclaiming the truth of the Word. People have given heart and soul to serving and building their local church. So to put forth the idea that we are reclaiming something lost (ekklesia) is really a difficult, delicate thing, especially when the replacement (church) is so dear to our hearts. I was raised in the church, and in writing this book, do not wish to sound like Don Quixote tilting at the windmills of "church." Rather, I joyfully recognize that God is sovereign over all, even mistranslations. History is not a mistake, it is His story. It is said that Martin Luther, reflecting on his own use as the great reformational vessel of God, proclaimed, "God can build even with the warped board and plow with the lame horse."

Vance Havner rightly adds, "God uses broken things. It takes a broken soil to produce a crop, broken clouds to give rain, broken grain to give bread, broken bread to give strength. It is the broken alabaster box that gives forth perfume…it is Peter, weeping bitterly, who returns to greater power than ever."[119]

In humility, we enter the flow of grace, but this does not mean we should continue offering God lame horses. Is church a broken word? A broken system? I simply contend that it is the wrong word, and therefore cannot impart other than a wrong identity and mission as compared to ekklesia. Chief values for the typical church are numerical growth and bigger buildings, rather than advancing a mission. A local ekklesia definitely needs strong pastoral leadership, but it is considerably more difficult to harvest a culture of ruling prayer from a traditional church than it is to integrate pastoral care into a praying ekklesia.

"My house ('oikos') shall be called a house of prayer for all nations," Jesus said in Mark 11:17.

---

**Prayer is fundamental. It's the baseline. How can we be His house if we aren't characterized by a culture of prayer?**

---

Get this: it's not just a house of believers. In other words, not just an assembly. Nor is it a house of worthy causes and much activity. Not a house of programs and outreach, however good those may be. No, His house is a house of *prayer*. Prayer is fundamental. It's the baseline. How can we be His house if we aren't characterized by a culture of prayer? Prayer is the way the ekklesia legislates for change. We see a stronghold such as abortion. In response, we weep, we cry. We take action. But above all, we pray. Prayer is the power of God. Prayer channels divine energy toward Earth. Prayer represents the great weakness in which the strength of God is best revealed—the hand stretched forth to His garment's hem—for when we spend our time in prayer, we are admitting to God that His answer is better than all the energy we could be pouring into any other sort of human response. For whom do we pray? Me? Sometimes, yes. That's part of it. But the inward focus of church must be radically balanced by the outward mission of ekklesia. Jesus could not be plainer: this is prayer for the nations.

Quite often, a well-intentioned reformist within his local fellowship or even a well-known pastor will offer a critique of the Body of Christ, something like, "We need to quit playing games and *be the church*." Their zeal is sincere, but their diagnosis is entirely inaccurate. The problem is, we've been the church for hundreds of years! *We need to be the ekklesia.*

Robert Lightner offered the following definition of a local church: "1) purpose is the public worship of God, edification of the saints, and spread of the gospel. 2) organization: planned meetings (Acts 20:7), corporate discipline (I Cor. 5), money raising projects (II Cor. 8-9), recognized leaders such as pastor, elders, deacons (Heb. 13:7, 17). 3) ordinances practiced."[120] It should be noted, this was not a critique, merely a statement. We could quibble over details, but I think most people would feel this to be an accurate and fair assessment. However, it is almost unrecognizable compared to what Jesus *the Christ* said He would build: a ruling assembly to assault the gates of Hades and use keys of the kingdom to bind and loose.

We have lost the clarity of our commission and the confidence of our command.

Historian Stephen Ambrose provides a fitting picture of our situation in his recounting of how the Allies won World War II. For our purposes, the beachhead of Normandy could be compared to any strongly fortified gate of Hades. It was a strategic place, and had to be taken, so on "D-Day," the largest amphibious invasion of all time commenced. Five thousand ships delivered over 160,000 troops to shore. This bloody, heroic enterprise was famously captured in movies such as *The Longest Day* and *Saving Private Ryan*. As the Allies overcame fierce German resistance, they broadened the beachhead, which eventually allowed them to overrun Normandy, then France, then drive all the way to the German border. It was perhaps the most decisive turning point in the entire European campaign.

On June 7, 1944, along the "plateau above the bluff at Omaha," we are introduced to Brigadier General Norman "Dutch" Cota. General Cota finds a group of infantry pinned down by some Germans in a farmhouse. Ambrose tells us "in the hedgerows...German sniper fire came from all directions. The Norman farm homes and barns, made of stone and surrounded by stone walls, made excellent fortresses." What follows is almost a perfect parable, told in modern language, to understand what Jesus was doing with His disciples in Caesarea Philippi.

"Well, I'll tell you what, captain," said Cota, unbuckling two grenades from his jacket. "You and your men start shooting at them. I'll take a squad of men and you and your men watch carefully. I'll show you how to take a house with Germans in it."

Cota led his squad around a hedge to get as close as possible to the house. Suddenly, he gave a whoop and raced forward, the squad following, yelling like wild men. As they tossed grenades into the windows, Cota and another man kicked in the front door, tossed a couple of grenades inside, waited for the explosions, then dashed into the house. The surviving Germans inside were streaming out the back door, running for their lives.

Cota returned to the captain. "You've seen how to take a house," said the general, still out of breath. "Do you understand? Do you know how to do it now?"

"Yes, sir."[121]

### Soldier statesmen

Where are the great statesmen of prayer for this generation? Where are those who will steadfastly contend for justice in the assembly? Where are the noble orators of the Holy Spirit who fast and pray, and declare the oracles of God, who will not bow their knees to idols, who stay steadfast until the most cruel and immovable gates of Hades yield to the glory of Christ?

During World War II, the motto of the 447th Bomb Group of the Eighth Air Force was *Fiat justitia ruat coelum*: "May justice be done though the heavens fall." Dark times may arise, the skies may fall, but *Heaven will stand forever*. Justice and righteousness are the foundations of God's throne.[122] Even so, we can echo the trepidations of the psalmist who cried out, "if the foundations are destroyed, what can the righteous do?" (Psa. 11:3). We live in an age of great shaking. Foundations of nations are trembling. Meanwhile, our best plan to engage and motivate our youth is to schedule more exciting Xbox nights. With more pizza. Lord, help us!

Again I ask, where are the great statesmen of prayer?

The military references in this book are not accidental, nor are they incongruous with the model of the ruling council of prayer. Several historic models of worldly rulership are available to us, including the Philosopher King, the Benevolent Dictator, the Despot and the Republic. But perhaps the greatest champions have been Soldier Statesmen. Throughout history, these statesmen heroes have left their mark in every generation, from Imperial China to Mongolia, Athens, Rome, Jerusalem, India, England, South America, Russia and the USA.

It would be a grave mistake to divorce the soldier from the statesmen, for it is often the experience of battle that molds the character necessary to lead a nation to peace. Consider a sampling of familiar names: King David, China's Duke of Zhou, Julius Caesar, Charlemagne, the Duke of Wellington, Simon Bolivar, Theodore Roosevelt, Churchill, Eisenhower. The list could go on. America's revolution produced many world-class statesmen—Thomas Jefferson, John Adams, Patrick Henry, Benjamin Franklin, Thomas Paine and others—but it is no accident that George Washington, our first president and the one called "The Father of our Nation," was also the commander-in-chief of the Continental Armies. When I first read the placard on the bronze statue of the statesman patriot, Samuel Adams, outside Faneuil Hall on Congress Street in Boston, I was gripped. It said, "A statesman, incorruptible and fearless."

Incorruptible...and fearless! What spiritual legacy will I pass on to my children? If you and I were to be given monuments by future generations formed by the Holy Spirit, what would be stamped on our placard?

---

**Assemble purposefully *with an ekklesia mindset*. Govern in His name. We need men and women of character, husbands and housewives, who will serve quietly and peaceably through the mundane grace of normal life, but when they assemble, they *roar*.**

---

With this book, I hope to issue a summons for legacy-worthy soldier-statesmen to form ranks in the kingdom. Men and women who know the will of God, who stand in His council, hear His voice and walk in intimate fellowship with Him. Do this: assemble purposefully *with an ekklesia mindset*. Govern in His name. We need men and women of character, husbands and housewives, who will serve quietly and peaceably through the mundane grace of normal life, but when they assemble, they *roar*. A generation is rising that will discard their preference for lesser pleasures driven by expediency, comfort and self-gratification. These champions of discipline, wisdom, and selflessness will rally to the mission of the Christ because they are enthralled with revelation of His glory. They will form loving communities. Of authority and power. And heaven-rattling prayer.

### Why not *sunedrion*?

An astute reader of Greek may raise the question: if the emphasis of ekklesia supposedly carries the notion of legislation and rulership— if the idea of a council of judges was intended—why didn't Jesus use the word '*sunedrion*', the judicial organ of hellenic city-states (and in Jewish practice, translated Sanhedrin)? Good question. Every community in Israel had a Lesser Sanhedrin, comprised of 23 judges. Rabbinic tradition holds that the Sanhedrin began with seventy elders, headed by Moses, for a total of seventy-one. So the

Great Sanhedrin in Jerusalem, the ruling council which governed the religious affairs of Judea, was comprised of 71 scribes, Pharisees and Sadducees. It was this body, headed by the High Priest, Caiaphas, which tried and convicted Jesus.

Indeed, why not sunedrion? I suspect the answer is rather straightforward. Both the sunagoge and sunedrion maintained exclusive memberships. For the sunagoge, one must be Jewish. For the sunedrion, one must be a rabbi or Torah sage. By contrast, the ekklesia summoned *all* male citizens to join and take part. Common man, blue collar man and scholar alike.

The astute reader may further ask, but isn't "male" also exclusive? Good point. We'll address the masculine nature of the ekklesia in Chapter 13. For now, we must turn our attention to other pressing matters.

Our world groans under the weight of evil. What shall be done? If revelation of Christ produces rulership, then rulership should produce results. This won't happen without a fight.

Quite naturally, then, we come to the gates of hell.

# MY NOTES

_____

_____

_____

_____

_____

_____

_____

_____

_____

_____

_____

_____

_____

_____

_____

# RESULTS

---

*"The gates of Hades shall not overpower it...
and whatever you shall bind on earth
shall be bound in heaven"*

---

"And though this world, with devils filled,
should threaten to undo us,
we will not fear, for God hath willed
His truth to triumph through us.
The Prince of Darkness grim,
we tremble not for him;
his rage we can endure,
for lo, his doom is sure;
one little word shall fell him."

Verse 3: *A Mighty Fortress is Our God*
– **Martin Luther**

# 10

## WHAT ARE THE GATES OF DEATH?

First, let's clarify the difference between hell and Hades, which are theologically distinct entities. Up until this point, I have tried to maintain the language of ekklesial dominion specifically in relation to Hades, because Jesus said "the gates of *Hades* shall not prevail." I must confess, I've occasionally borrowed "gates of hell" as a matter of poetic license due to common usage (as in the closing lines of the last chapter). The fact is, we have no charter against hell, which is the Bible's designation for Satan's eternal penitentiary, where he will be confined and punished forever.[123] Hell is not Satan's domain, as we popularly use the term, nor is it the seat of his kingdom. Satan was cast down from Heaven and confined to Earth. He doesn't rule Earth from hell, but will one day be sentenced to hell (which is synonymous with the lake of fire).

The next couple of paragraphs get a little technical, but it helps to fine-tune our discussion. In the Greek, the word properly translated hell is Gehenna, a literal reference to the "Valley of Hinnom," which served as a garbage dump for all of Jerusalem. As the city's local incinerator, it was well known as a place of perpetual burning. In this sense, Jesus used it to symbolize a destination of eternal torment created for Satan and his demons, to which the resurrected wicked would also be assigned after the final judgment. Historically, it was also the site of heinous idol worship where children were sacrificed to the demon god, Molech.[124]

Contrast Gehenna with Hades, which is roughly the Greek equivalent of the Hebrew Sheol.[125] Hades and Sheol merely represent the underworld, or the abode of the spirits of the dead. It is thought of as a place situated below ground,[126] in a place of dark, silent forgetfulness.[127]

Prior to Christ, Sheol referred to the state of both righteous and wicked dead, since both wound up there eventually. This is the place to which the spirit of Jesus was assigned after the crucifixion,[128] when He "descended into the lower parts" (Eph. 4:9) and "preached even to those who are dead" (1 Pet. 3:18-19, 4:5-6). For this reason, Jesus, as victor and Lord of all, proclaims, "I was dead, and behold, I am alive forevermore, *and I have the keys of death and of Hades*" (Rev. 1:18). This link between death and Hades is common to the book of Revelation.[129]

In modern usage, Hades and hell have unfortunately become synonymous thanks to the influence of the King James Version. Modern translations such as the New International Version and New American Standard properly distinguish the two, labeling the Sheol concept as Hades and the Gehenna concept as hell. So the admonition to "fear Him who is able to destroy both soul and body in hell" (Mat. 10:28) is accurate because the Greek says Gehenna, whereas Matthew 16:18 actually says "the gates of Hades," not "the gates of hell." The language of the King James does not offer these distinctions; both are simply rendered hell.[130]

Two other facts should be noted regarding Hades. First, Hades was not only a destination, it was also a false god. In fact, in Greek mythology, he was the third member of the high triumvirate, which included Zeus (sky god and ruler of Mt. Olympus), Poseidon (ruler of waters) and Hades (ruler of the underworld). This is more than trivial.

Second, as a location, and as the form of a god, Hades was the embodiment of death. He/It was euphemistically used for death and dying. In this sense, Hades is more properly the domain of Satan than hell, for all things that contribute to death are part of Satan's kingdom. Hades, therefore, represents the kingdom of darkness, with death as the ultimate wage of every sin, claiming every soul at birth until the kingdom of light breaks through and Christ is confessed as Lord and Savior. That Hades, not hell, is actually the nearest and truer symbol of Satan's influence, obviously, is also important.

---

**Hades, not hell, is actually the nearest and truer symbol of Satan's influence**

---

Why? Because Jesus committed His ekklesia to contend with Hades.

### Gates and keys

First, what are gates? In Israel, gates served a variety of functions. Not only were they defensive structures, they were legal and cultural transaction centers. Gates were the place where the business of the land was done. Justice, judgment and commerce were achieved in the gates. Each day, the elders of the city would gather there to bear witness to business transactions between men. Also, after listening to accusations, as well as appeals from the accused, elders would decide the case. All of this happened as they sat at the city gates.

Metaphorically, gates are access points, by which one transitions into or out of something. A gate is both an exit and an entry. We understand this intuitively so much that we don't really think about it. If a friend comes over to visit and you are in your fenced backyard pulling weeds from your garden, your friend must enter through the gate to see you. If the gate has a lock, you must go unlatch it. When you are done conversing, your friend must leave through the same gate. Thus, the single gate becomes the means by which a thing is either allowed or refused. The point of entry is also the point of departure.

Many virtues are described in relation to gates: Heaven (Gen. 28:17), righteousness (Psa. 118:19; Prov. 14:19), praise (Psa. 9:14, 100:4; Isa. 60:18), the King's presence (Psa. 24:7, 9), wisdom (Prov. 1:21, 8:3), security (Psa. 147:12-14) and salvation (Mat. 7:13-14).

Because elders sat in the gates in biblical times,[131] Scripture describes a variety of highly symbolic activities occurring there. For example: gates of homes and cities were to be marked with the Law and the love of God (Deut. 6:4-9); idolatry was punished and removed by trial at the gates (Deut. 17:2-5); disobedience and rebellion of sons was judged at gates (Deut. 21:18-19); likewise, at the gates a daughter's sexual purity was defended (Deut. 22:15); adulterers were stoned at the gate (Deut. 22:23-24); fraternal neglect was tried at the gate (Deut. 25:7); 'redeemer' privileges were invoked at the gate (Ruth 4:1); rebellion against the king was plotted at the gate (2 Sam. 15:2); 'High Places' of idol worship were set up at the gates (2 Kings 23:8); weeping and mourning for judgment took place at the gates (Isa 3:26, 14:31); gates were the place of prophetic words, including calls to repentance and justice (Jer. 7:1-7, 17:19-23); ruined gates served as evidence of God's judgment (Lam. 2:9, 4:12; Hos. 11:5-6); a lack of elders in the gates was emblematic of a city's lack of rulership (Lam. 5:14); restoration of gates was fundamental to prophetic renewal (Ezek. 40); justice and injustice were settled at the gates (Amos 5:10-15); damnation and destruction is associated with gates (Mat. 7:13). Finally, the gates of death (Sheol) is also a common phrase (Job 17:13-16, 38:16-17; Psa. 107:18-19).

From this great collage of literal and symbolic functionality, a number of insights can be drawn:

*1. Gates Are Primarily Defensive.* A gate is stationary, not mobile. Gates are part of a defensive system. Gates don't attack, they protect. Furthermore, within that defensive system, the gate is actually the *weakest* point in the wall. In Matthew 16, Jesus said the gates of Hades were to be assaulted. To assure us that they would not prevail does not describe the gates as failing in their attack against us—this is nonsensical—but as failing to resist the determined assault of the ekklesia.[132] For this reason, in the spirit, as in the natural, a gate is a focal point for enemy resources.

The plural form, gates, should not be thought of merely as a set of double doors, but also as a sequence of gates, especially for heavily fortified compounds. The Philistine stronghold of Keilah was "a city with double gates and bars" (1 Sam. 23:7). Other cities were notably more impressive, including Jericho. Recent excavations on the monumental city gate complex at the city of Dan reveal how critical it was for cities to bolster their gates. The website of the Israeli Ministry of Foreign Affairs describes the scene thus:

> "The gate complex...is composed of an outer and an inner gate, both built of large basalt stones. Beyond these gates, a magnificent processional road winds its way up the slope to the city. The inner gate is the best preserved and is a good example of Israelite city gates during biblical times. It consisted of four guard rooms, two on each side of a paved passageway. The threshold, made of a large basalt stone, includes the door-stop and hinge-sockets which once supported the massive wooden doors."[133]

Four guard towers, likely housing dozens of men, guarding two separate gates. This was what you had to penetrate to capture the idolatrous city of Dan. Do you see? The great battles of the age will not be easy. Death is deeply entrenched in our culture. We will not simply be granted entry, yet enter we must. In other words, you may have to penetrate multiple obstacles to gain the victory. You may have to learn to pray differently. You may need more of the Word inside you. But be assured, the promise of dominion over the enemy's gates was included early in God's covenant with His people. In Genesis 22:17, God told Abraham, "Indeed I will greatly bless you...and *your seed shall possess the gate of their enemies.*" Galatians 3:29 assures us this is our promise, too: "If you belong to Christ, *then you are Abraham's offspring*, heirs according to promise."

*2. Gates Are Secondarily Offensive.* A gate is indirectly offensive in that it represents the establishment of a stronghold; therefore the aggregation of force within. Though gates don't attack, they do *release.* Behind a gate lies the will of whatever ruler dwells inside, as well as the resources of that ruler. Gates are used to channel armies from within to do the ruler's bidding.

The human body also has gates. They are called the five senses, though perhaps the mouth most clearly functions in the dual capacities of giving and receiving. The mouth consumes food, but also vomits sickness. Likewise, demonic gates are strategic assets by which the enemy vomits sickness into a region, a nation, or even the planet. Racism is an example of a ruling spirit that influences the entire planet. Some strongholds can be geographically identified. Hollywood is a powerful example of a gate that is vomiting lies and perversion across the whole earth. When this happens, bastions of righteousness are assaulted, not directly from the gates, but from whatever epicenter of immorality those particular gates defend. How much sexual immorality has spewed out of Hollywood?

We must become more strategic and united in how we stand against such evil. In Isaiah 28 it says, "in that day the *Lord of hosts* will become a *beautiful crown* and a glorious diadem to the remnant of His people; a *spirit of justice* for him who sits in judgment, *a strength to those who repel the onslaught at the gate*" (vs. 5-6). Again we see Lord Sabaoth, commander of armies. He is beautiful and glorious in His kingship (the *crown* and the *diadem*), which is a picture of Christ the King. He will also render justice and strength "at the gate." The Lord of hosts will "repel the onslaught *at the gate.*" In this scenario, it appears that God's covenant people have become so defensive that they must be rescued by their King because invading armies of darkness are storming the strongholds of righteousness.

A bold, crusading spirit is vital to the ekklesia. We must be people of action, sacrifice and war. Just as the feminine heart of the Bride is necessary for *intimacy* with our King, so also the masculine soul of the ekklesia is the way we *represent* His Kingship (see Chapter 13). Contending prayer must become part of the DNA of God's people around the globe. The tables must turn. If we cut the enemy off at his gates, demonic supply lines will be interrupted. When that happens—when we take the battle to dark powers—those access points from which evil and vomit are currently unleashed will dry up. We have much to learn.

> "Questions flood our minds. How do these spiritual powers exert their influence in society? Where do they get in? Is there a distinctive modus operandi that would help us identify them? What can or what should we be doing to control and prevent their intrusion? Since God is sovereign and omnipotent, is it not our place to let him deal with these supernatural powers in his own time and way?
>
> The Bible must have answers to these questions, and it does. But the terrifying fact of a hostile world of evil and malicious spirits paralyzes many Christians into inactivity and unwillingness to seek out biblical answers and to apply them. Edith Schaeffer says that 'there is a deafness, a blindness, an insensitivity among many Christians, for they refuse to recognize the war in which they are involved. They are letting the enemy attack and score victories without resistance.'"[134]

Ekklesia, this must not stand! Rulership is your inheritance. "Ask of me, and I will surely give the nations as Your inheritance" (Psa. 2:8). The bunker mentality of church must be abandoned, for if you are "in Christ," His inheritance is also yours.[135] Our nations, communities and homes are under assault in a massive, Psalm 2-style rebellion against every divine constraint. The kings of the earth are taking counsel together in the spirit of antichrist. The Body of Christ, the Anointed One—that's us!—is being reviled. Marriage is under assault. Legislation is being drafted in the halls of human power, crafting clever hate-speech laws so as to render the proclamation of biblical truth illegal. The spirit of lawlessness is being codified into law and defended in our courts. Perversion and the occult is rampant. A radical homosexual agenda, funded by some of the wealthiest men in the world, is demanding that the governments of the earth openly support their cause. Most shocking of all, the governments of the earth are bowing to these threats! Wave after wave of economic crises are being manipulated to stir mass hysteria, forcing the fearful masses to forfeit their authority and independence to the State in exchange for security and protection. Illegal wars are routine. Cultures of death abound in human trafficking, abortion, drug violence and gang wars. The infrastructure of our cities is crumbling. We live in an age of gross darkness, among those "who call evil good, and good evil; who substitute darkness for light and light for darkness" (Isa. 5:20).

In the midst of it all, our hearts are tempted to faint. We feel powerless to respond. Church-thinking has dulled our instinct for war, turning us into polite, domesticated, timid little people. The scale of corruption around us is so disheartening, we just sag our shoulders, admit defeat, visit the buffet, maybe catch a movie. Play Xbox. Facebook for an hour or two. Drown ourselves in distraction and creature comforts. If we're particularly inspired, we might write a Letter to the Editor, so we can at least feel like we've done our civic duty. Meanwhile, the agenda of God stalls across the nations of the earth. Having failed to grasp both the truth of His government and our place in it, we fiddle while Rome burns. We legislate nothing in prayer. Is it any wonder that the culture of hell prevails on Earth? We hide in steepled bunkers preaching wealth and singing feel-good songs, or worse, simply hoping Jesus comes back soon enough to save us from this mess. Having no iron in our souls, it is no accident that we wield no rod of rulership in our prayers. We live small lives, think small thoughts, assault nothing and, no surprise, achieve nothing.

---

**Church-thinking has dulled our instinct for war, turning us into polite, domesticated, timid little people.**

---

As a result, the gates of Hades stand largely unchallenged. Mind you, Satan is not nearly so timid. He is on the prowl. His vomit will continue until we realize it is our job to make it stop.

> The Lord of hosts...says, "You are My war-club, My weapon of war; and with you I shatter nations, and with you I destroy kingdoms" (Jer. 51:19-20).

Are you His war-club, or aren't you? Will you shatter nations (dark powers), or not?

Oh sure, we may weep and moan. Who in their right mind wouldn't? The horrors happening around the planet certainly merit outrage. At the same time, moral indignation is insufficient. It must turn into motion, energy, prayer, sacrifice. Do not stay stuck in the emotion of defeat. Many feel inept to challenge the rising tide. We do not understand our authority.

This is why revelation is crucial. We must first see *Christ*, to whom *all* authority has been given. Do you see Him like that, the possessor of all authority? If not, you must keep looking until you see Him that way!

> "The Lord will go forth like a warrior, He will arouse His zeal like a man of war. He will utter a shout, yes, He will raise a war cry. He will prevail against His enemies" (Isa. 42:13).

This is imperative. Yes, you are small, but He is great. And because He is great, He has invested great authority in "two or three." That's all it takes to rule against gates of death (more on this in Chapter 14). Enlarge your bull's-eye. Wherever darkness may be found, that is ground zero. You are commissioned in the spirit of Christ to "rule *in the midst* of Your enemies" (Psa. 110:2).

Jesus travelled to Caesarea Philippi to make this very point, that we must take the battle to the enemy's camp. Are we His ekklesia or not?

*3. Gates Symbolize Imprisonment.* Psalm 107 describes the misery of those who dwell "in darkness and in the shadow of death" as "prisoners in misery and chains." The reason for their misery is Psalm 2: "They had rebelled against the words of God, and spurned the counsel of the Most High." Later in this passage, both rebellion and iniquity are described as the cause of those who draw "near to the gates of death." In Psalm 107, however, instead of continuing in their sin, the people repent. They humble themselves and "(cry) out to the Lord in their trouble." In His mercy, God responds. He saved them out of their distresses. He "broke their bands apart...shattered gates of bronze, and cut bars of iron asunder" (Psa. 107:10-18).[136]

Gates of death (remember, this is Old Testament language for gates of Hades) represent not only demonic barriers over cities or regions, but forms of personal imprisonment. These gates are like bronze, in a prison of iron. A prison is a place of torment, a dark hole where you feel alone, malnourished, forgotten. The action of

Jesus, Lord Sabaoth, is to "proclaim liberty to captives, and freedom to prisoners" (Isa. 61:2).

Quite literally, the armies of Lord Sabaoth deliver His people from prison, as in the case of Peter, when "an angel of the Lord during the night opened the gates of the prison, and (took) them out" (Acts 5:19).

It is no accident that the action which brought release from prison in Psalm 107 and Acts 5 was prayer. So now that we understand the power and influence of the gates of death that tower above our culture, what are we supposed to do? I'm glad you asked. Read on!

# 11

## EITHER UNLOCK THE GATES, OR SHATTER THEM

**G**ates are tricky. They aren't just closed, forming a barrier. They are locked, forming a puzzle. Spiritual gates form a spiritual puzzle. Fortunately, the ekklesia are promised keys. Keys create rights of access. Keys are manifestations of authority.[137] Keys bestow divine favor.

> "I will give you the keys of the kingdom of heaven" (Mat. 16:19).

Heaven authorizes gate-busting endeavors. Heaven authorizes the dismantling of strongholds, the shattering of high places. When you commit to contending prayer, Heaven backs you up. You get keys. If you are never engaged in this process, you will never receive keys. Why? Because you have no need of them. A key is only for someone who is in the process of unlocking things. The only time you pull out your keys is when you approach your home or your car, and find out it is locked. You don't wave your keys at the grocer or the plumber and expect any reaction, nor do you receive keys from them. However, if you go to the bank and request access to your safety deposit box locked in the bank's vault, they supply a key.

In general, the key which unlocks a particular gate is customized to that gate's lock. Keys are not generic in their design. If keys were commonly available and generically shaped—one size fits all—then the security of the gate would be pointless. For this reason, gates *and their unique keys* are always closely guarded. Jesus repeats these ideas in Matthew 16. After pointing His ekklesia to the gates of Hades, He immediately promises to supply them with keys. With these keys they will bind and loose, which, in its given context, should probably be viewed synonymously with gaining access or denying access to the gate itself.

Opening a gate with a key is relatively easy. Once you have the key, the gate is (mostly) yours. *Obtaining* the key, however, may be quite difficult. So the question before us is simple: how do you get keys?

*1. Keys Are Knowledge.* In many respects, the battle for the key is greater than the battle for the gate. Jesus rebuked the lawyers of His day for binding or "hindering" the people by locking them up and keeping the keys. "You have taken away the key of knowledge; you did not enter in yourselves, and those who were entering in you hindered" (Luke 11:52).

In other words, the absence of knowledge prevented entry into the ways of God.

And so it is. If you want to go to college, a High School diploma represents acquired knowledge that opens a door to the next level of education. If you want to decrypt an encoded email transmission, you need a key in the form of knowledge, a password, to unlock the file. If you lose your car keys, you call a locksmith. He brings knowledge with him, to create the specific key you need.

Spiritual keys are specific, timely, divine revelation. Once again, revelation lies at the heart and soul of rulership. We must see Christ first. Then we must see our mission in light of His. Furthermore, we must perceive the invisible gates as real, tangible and consequential. But we must also see the keys that unlock them.

Every unchallenged stronghold will persist, and increase—the rules of pornography, abortion, corruption, warmongering, racism and profiteering—if the ekklesia does not accurately discern thrones and dominions at work, protected by gates of death, and then commit to their destruction.

---

## Spiritual keys are specific, timely, divine revelation.

---

When Elisha prayed for his servant in Dothan, he did not simply ask for a confirming miracle, but that his servant would literally see into another dimension. The vision he gained revealed a reality that was present and active *before* he ever saw it. In other words, seeing didn't make it so. It simply allowed him to understand what had been there all along. What would our homes, cities and nations look like, if we saw with such eyes? Even so, it is not enough to perceive the gates.[138] We must also see the form and shape of what is truly at work. We must understand *what* binds if we are to effectively loose. Sometimes the shape and meaning of the key is our means to comprehend the nature of the lock. For example, a plastic credit card with a magnetic strip is the right key at the gas pump, but it is the wrong key to pop the cap off a bottle of root beer. Likewise, the beeper for your car won't open your house, and the little metal shape jangling in your pocket won't check out a book at the library. Yet if I showed you each of these, you would immediately know what they "open" based on their shape. Thus, "key knowledge" is fundamental to discerning the specific power of the gates at work.

Such knowledge is both a divine right and a divine process. To rule effectively, the ekklesia must get comfortable with *divine process*. This is why council access, dreams and divine revelation are so important. Keys are typically not bestowed quickly, nor flipped on like a light switch. Daniel waged a prayer battle just to get some answers. He fasted and prayed for 21 days. While it's clear in Daniel

10:12 that he was heard from the moment he prayed, a great conflict arose to prevent him from receiving the answer. Revelation is highly toxic to the enemy! He wants to prevent it at any cost! The conflict was eventually resolved only through the intervention of the great angelic prince, Michael. Interestingly, the revelation Daniel received involved both answers to previous revelation (from an earlier vision), as well as new comprehension regarding the future. The point is threefold: Firstly, keys must be contended for, they are not automatically granted. Contending includes fasting, repentance and diligent, unrelenting prayer. Secondly, prayer is the means of releasing the key.[139] Thirdly, revelation may include a download of past, present and/or future knowledge. This knowledge has specific contours and details for unlocking, rendering powerless, and crippling the defenses of gates of death.

Follow the progression of images and thoughts in the following verses.

- **Keys on the shoulder**: "Then I will set *the key* of the house of David *on his shoulder*, when he *opens no one will shut*, when he *shuts no one will open*" (Isa. 22:22). The keys of authority rest on the shoulders. The keys grant rights to opening and closing in a manner which cannot be abrogated.
- **Government on the shoulder**: Likewise, "the *government* will rest *on His shoulders*" (Isa. 9:6). The parallel language sets up a direct correlation. Keys relate to governmental authority.
- **Jesus has the keys**: Jesus described Himself as "He who is holy, who is true, who has *the key of David*, who *opens and no one will shut*, and who *shuts and no one opens*" (Rev. 3:7).

- **Jesus gives the keys:** After forming His government among men, calling them "My ruling council (ekklesia)," the same Lord and Christ promised to share His keys for the same purpose, that common men and women like you and me could open, close, bind and loose. "I will give you the *keys of the kingdom of heaven*; and whatever YOU shall *bind on earth shall be bound in heaven*, and whatever YOU shall *loose on earth shall be loosed in heaven*" (Mat. 16:19).

Multiple occasions throughout Scripture indicate the importance of keys. Typically, if Israel exerted themselves in their own strength, they failed. On the other hand, when they received and obeyed divine counsel, no matter how strange the "key" might be, success was assured. Note in each of the following how entire regions and multitudes of people were threatened with destruction. In most cases, prayer was offered. In every case, divine communication provided a stratagem which had to be followed to avoid calamity. Though we know these stories by heart, we don't often think of how they prefigure keys by which the ekklesia bring life instead of death.

| CRISIS FACED | KEY GIVEN |
|---|---|
| Noah and a global flood | Build a boat |
| Joseph and famine | Interpret dream, build storehouses |
| Moses and death of firstborn | Mark doors with lamb's blood |
| Joshua and Jericho | Surround the city in silence, shout on seventh day |

| Gideon and Midianites | Trim army to 300, use pots, torches and trumpets |
| David and Philistines | Listen for sound in mulberries |
| Jehoshaphat and Ammon/ Moab | Position singers before army, praise |
| Hezekiah and Assyria | Wait and trust |

Gideon's strategy wouldn't have helped Hezekiah. Joseph's dream was not a solution for David with the Philistines. Our job is not even to win the battle. It is simply to contend for the keys which unlock the Lord's victory.[140] Practically speaking, this revelation could manifest in understanding how "key" people or the alignment of "key" circumstances might open a closed gate and thereby produce victory. Other keys might involve the promotion or demotion of certain leaders, or the public exposure of a certain falsehood, or the failure of immoral legislation, or the triumph of righteousness in the courts, or specific repentance for traumatic, sinful events in the history of a region.

"Key revelation" isn't typically a mysterious oracle that nobody understands. While it might start that way, symbolism seeks incarnation. In some form or fashion, God will permit the answers to manifest if we seek them. The challenge isn't getting Him to speak, it is that the process of filtering Heaven's language into human comprehension takes time, study and attention. A listening ear and a tender heart. Since humility and patience confound the enemy, God's brilliance is evident in the difficulty of the process. Why? Just as the Allies relied on the Navajo language to form an unbreakable code for safely transmitting war plans during World War II, symbolism encodes divine strategies, leaving the enemy no opportunity to counter. When the Holy Spirit breathes on a particular passage, or releases dreams or prophetic revelation—captured and bathed in the slow, steady process of listening to God—it create buffers of anointing for the ekklesia to comprehend God's mind and the keys He is releasing, giving the enemy no recourse. Keys unveiled in this manner leave the enemy exposed and clueless as to how to defend his gates. So you see, the symbolism is not an end unto itself. As a mysterious process, it is meant to draw us to more intimately pursue the mind and beauty of God. But make no mistake, though God's battle plans may seem like divine Morse code, the results will be real and devastating to the gates of death.

*2. Force Also Shatters Gates.* Not all gates have keys. In Bible times, a city's defenses were "walls and towers, gates and bars" (2 Chron. 14:7). There are only two ways to enter. If it is locked, unlock it. Failing that, *break it down!* Gates need keys (revelation) to unlock, or force (authority) to shatter.

This is both practical and reassuring, because we all see dimly. Some revelation simply exceeds our grasp. The reasons are varied. For one, we're human. Sometimes our resources, gifting or faith may simply be too small for the particular gate being challenged. Or maybe the purposes of the Lord are yet unfathomed for that particular engagement. In His sovereignty, the key is withheld. Perhaps the enemy retains legal access that exceeds further discernment and inquiry by the ekklesia. Whatever the case may be, if a key is missing, do not despair of victory. Countless invading armies throughout history have faced the same challenges. In response they retreated to nearby forests, emerging days later with heavy, tree-trunk battering rams with which they began to bludgeon the gates of their foes. In those instances, the gates weren't opened, they were *shattered.* Keys definitely open gates, but in their absence, battering rams of prayer will do the same. In either event, gates of Hades crumble, spoils are taken, captives go free and darkness retreats.

We see this play out with the Persian King, Cyrus. Cyrus was commissioned as the human agent through which God would open gates.

> "Thus says the Lord to Cyrus His anointed, whom I have taken by the right hand, to **subdue nations** before him, and to **loose** the loins of kings; to **open doors** before him **so that gates will not be shut**: 'I will go before you and make the rough places smooth; **I will shatter the doors of bronze, and cut through their iron bars**'" (Isa. 45:1-2).

This is a curious passage, but take note. The Lord, the Anointed One, *anointed a man* named Cyrus to do four things:

- Subdue nations (bind)
- Loose the loins of kings (loose)
- Open doors/gates
- Shatter doors and cut the iron bars

As you can see, the way Cyrus opens is not with keys, but with force. He shatters the doors and cuts the bars. Sometimes, the spiritual equivalent of brute force is required.[141]

### Gates of darkness are not moral abstractions

From our previous discussion of types and shadows in Chapter 7, we know that symbols help us understand higher realities. A symbol does not diminish the reality, it confirms it. In like manner, high places were not merely symbolic locations in Israel. They were the means by which invisible, evil beings influenced the land, gaining greater access and authority over human affairs for the purpose of incurring the judgment of God, and thereby inflicting harm. The gods of the land literally contended with Yahweh in the gates.

"New gods were chosen; then war was in the gates" (Judges 5:8).

Demonology is a fact of our existence. It's ugly, brutal and certainly merits no undue fascination, but we are hardly served by pretending demons are not real. Some make too much of it, but on the whole, the church makes far too little. While this is permissible for church, it is not for the ekklesia. We must not be cowed by those who belittle demonology as superstitious mumbo-jumbo. Revelation 16:14 says "spirits of demons, performing signs...go out to the kings of the whole world, to gather them together for the war of the great day of God." John confirms that demonic influence over every strata of society is actually persuading human kings to one day take up arms against the returning Lord Jesus. If demons have no real influence, this is a baffling, nearly illogical thought, yet we see the prophecy unfolding before our very eyes.

---

**An invisible realm of evil prevails upon the visible realm of men. Unless it is challenged by Lord Sabaoth's heavenly council convened on Earth, it will triumph.**

---

An invisible realm of evil prevails upon the visible realm of men. Unless it is challenged by Lord Sabaoth's heavenly council convened on Earth, it will triumph. For this reason, the "manifold wisdom of God" is meant to "now be made known *through the ekklesia* to the rulers and the authorities in the heavenly places" (Eph 3:10). You thought that verse said "made known through the *church*," didn't you? Wrong.

Paul warned the Corinthians not to "become sharers in demons" (1 Cor. 10:20). One must ask, if the possibility of evil defilement and demonic influence is as small as many today wish for us to believe, why give the warning? No, there are not demons behind every bush. Such ridiculous assertions discredit divine realities, keeping people trapped in the belief that nothing is expected from them, least of all the need to challenge legitimate, invisible evil powers. But Jesus could not have been more plain about the fundamental conviction that governed His earthly ministry. He said, "How can anyone enter the strong man's house and carry off his property, unless **he first binds the strong man**? And *then* he will plunder his house" (Mat. 12:29).

Notice the word, *then*. After the strong man is bound, then comes the plunder.

*After* evil is recognized, *after* revelation is gained in the spirit, *after* Christ is revealed, *after* the ekklesia take their place, *after* the battering ram of prayer...then! My friends, we need some *thens*!

Demons may not lurk behind every bush, but they are highly insinuated into every facet of human interaction. It is inevitable. Whatever touches humans as the prized creation of God—or said another way, whatever humans touch—is marked in the spirit for demonic defilement and control. Business, government, media, arts and entertainment, education, the family and religion are the seven primary spheres of human interaction. Bill Bright, founder of Campus Crusade for Christ, and Loren Cunningham, founder of Youth With A Mission, identified these as the "Seven Mountains" of influence in the earth. In olden times, high places were built on mountains for a reason, to demonstrate the preeminence of the god of that mountain. The god of the high place was higher and greater, dominating the land below it. Do not kid yourself: not one of these mountains will ever enjoy the enemy's neglect. He is fixed on them, targeting both humans and the systems around which humans relate and depend. He is invested in every source of pleasure, comfort, justice, beauty and truth, for these form the human experience. They are all on his calendar, his evil to-do list. He has sophisticated strategies for controlling and further corrupting each one, in hopes of totally enslaving humanity and scheduling the earth for God's wrath.

Now look at these seven mountains as seven huge gates. The high places of evil must be confronted. High places were to be torn down *because* they were gates; not only because worship and human immorality occurred there, but because they were sources of spiritual defilement for the land. "They sacrificed to demons who were not God, to gods whom they have not known, new gods who came lately, whom your fathers did not dread" (Deut. 32:17). Archaeological digs have revealed evidence of idols literally being placed inside a city's gates, right at the entrance, such as in the case of the city of Dan, near Mt. Hermon.[142]

Is it any wonder that in the account of King Josiah's powerful work of restoration, we read, "he broke down **the high places of the gates**" (2 Kings 23:8)? Read the whole chapter. Josiah was relentless in destroying every vestige of idolatry, and there was a lot to destroy!

It is imperative that we realize that sins such as sexual immorality, murder and idolatry do not exist unto themselves. They have a blast radius. Like radioactive fallout, they defile the land in which they are committed. If this were not so, the land would not need to be cleansed. After spending the entire chapter of Leviticus 18 describing forbidden sexual acts such as incest, homosexuality, adultery and bestiality, along with sacrificing children to idols, murder, and idol worship, we are told:

> "Do not defile yourselves by any of these things; for by all these the nations which I am casting out before you have become defiled. *For the land has become defiled*...for the men of the land who have been before you have done all these abominations, *and the land has become defiled*" (Lev. 18:24-27).

Commenting on Israel's moral compromise in the land of promise, Scripture says,

> "They even sacrificed their sons and their daughters to the demons, and shed innocent blood, the blood of their sons and

their daughters, whom they sacrificed to the idols of Canaan; *and the land was polluted with the blood*" (Psa. 106:36-38).

While horrific, we must not be tempted to dismiss these accounts as evidence of primitive culture. Children were literally offered to demons through the agency of the idol.[143] We are not so different. Legalized abortion continues to pollute the land with blood sacrifices to Molech draped in the freewill idol of "pro-choice." We must not kid ourselves regarding the lure of the high places, nor their power. No less a man than Solomon the Wise, after building the temple of God, eventually embraced idolatry. God describes these false gods as "abominations" and "detestable."[144] These high places provoke the Lord's anger. They "aroused His jealousy with their graven images" (Psa. 78:58).[145]

Allowing high places, bloodshed and immorality to pollute the land prevents fruitfulness and dominion.

> "You have become guilty by the blood which you have shed, and defiled by your idols which you have made...You rely on your sword, you commit abominations, and each of you defiles his neighbor's wife. *Should you then possess the land?*" (Eze. 22:4, 33:26).

It is no accident that the adulteress positions herself "at the doorway (i.e. 'gate')...by the high places of the city" (Prov. 9:14). Even so, dominion is promised to God's people to "tread upon their high places" (Deut. 33:29), to "destroy all their figured stones, and destroy all their molten images and demolish all their high places" (Num. 33:52).

### Samson as a picture of our anointing

In closing this chapter, let's take a moment to understand how the anointing of Christ in Matthew 16 is prefigured in the story of Samson. Samson was all too human. He was a man of weak character, but he made a Nazirite's vow. As long as he maintained his Nazirite consecration, he operated in the anointing of God. Interestingly, Samson's is a story of bindings and loosings. The enemy repeatedly tried to bind him, but repeatedly "the Spirit of the Lord came upon him mightily so that the ropes that were on his arms were as flax that is burned with fire, and his bonds dropped from his hands" (Judges 15:14).

The Nazirite vow is a spirit of 1) consecration 2) unto dominion. It is an Old Testament picture of the ekklesia. What does this most famously anointed Nazirite do? Well, of course...he breaks gates.

> "Now Samson lay until midnight, and *at midnight he arose and took hold of the doors of the city gate and the two posts and pulled them up* along with the bars; then he *put them on his shoulders* and carried them up to the top of the mountain which is opposite Hebron" (Judges 16:3).

The hour of midnight has come to the earth and countless gates have been raised by Hades, god of death. Left unchallenged, the culture of death has ruled from the high places of Earth. But in this dark hour, Samson, the Nazirite, arises. Anointed by God, he dismantles the gate and, with governmental authority, carries it away on his shoulders.

He that has ears, let him hear.

# 12

## BINDING AND LOOSING

At the beginning of this book it was stated that the principles of ekklesia are not intended as a treatise on spiritual warfare in the conventional sense. However, to the degree that rulership, prophetic moral clarity and governmental prayer necessarily expose evil, draw battle lines and invoke images of war, we must be prepared to accept that life is a battleground. A.W. Tozer said,

> "The idea that this world is a playground instead of a battleground has now been accepted in practice by the vast majority of Christians...The 'worship' growing out of such a view of life is as far off center as the view itself—a sort of sanctified nightclub without the champagne and the dressed-up drunks."[146]

We are most certainly in a war. It doesn't help that revelatory intercession often attracts flakey people. War does not equal weird! Yet in the mysterious union of symbolism and prayer, some people find a vehicle to justify their weirdness. Intercessors are often sincere, passionate, beautiful, wounded souls, who dearly love God and want to serve Him. They have a vision for prayer, and pour out their lives in the closet on their knees. They are dear to God, but their concerns don't fit easily into the normal rhythm of "church life." They often feel like outcasts. They use strange words and often seem fixated with strange ideas. Sometimes, when they are rejected, they get even weirder, like a cry for attention, in hopes that the strangeness they display will translate into prophetic legitimacy in the eyes of others.

This is tricky, since the process of revelation is rarely linear or logical. (It is also an indictment against the foreignness of prayer within our churches.) As outlined in the preceding chapters, the ways of God are often offensive to the natural mind, with rules of engagement that seem highly subject to change from one battle to the next. The offensiveness and unpredictability of God's ways are used by flakey people to shield themselves from otherwise reasonable pastoral guidance and biblical scrutiny. It would be impossible to capture all the possible flavors of this, but the line of defense often goes something like, "Just like Elisha told King Joash to strike the ground with arrows for victory over Aram, God told me to crush these ice cubes to break the power of this winter storm!" And then they might smash the bag of ice on the ground and dance upon it, "binding the foul demon of winter." Worse, they ask others to join the dance. Meanwhile, everyone else just feels...weird. The horror stories of prophets and intercessors run amok is enough to make any reasonable pastor want to ban the words "bind" and "loose" from his flock's vocabulary.

---

**Needless to say, much of what passes for "warfare," involving "binding and loosing," is the result of presumption and silliness more than genuine prophetic authority.**

---

Needless to say, much of what passes for "warfare," involving "binding and loosing," is the result of presumption and silliness more than genuine prophetic authority. First and foremost, we must wisely bind ourselves to Scripture if we are to make sense of all this. On the one hand, we do not want to neglect the tools of rulership Christ obviously intends for us to possess. How do humans wield a supernatural scepter of iron? It's an important question. On the other, we do not wish to behave like children with toys, brandishing our weapons in the flesh, bringing derision to their intended purpose.

### Already forbidden, already allowed

Binding and loosing were common to the language of rabbis both before and after Christ. When the rabbis bound something, they "forbade" it, and when they loosed something, they "permitted" it. A. T. Robertson, a well-regarded 20th century Greek scholar, wrote: "To 'bind' in rabbinical language is to forbid; to 'loose' is to permit."[147] Clarke agrees, writing: "It is as plain as the sun, by what occurs in numberless places...that binding signified, and was commonly understood by the Jews at that time to be, a declaration that any thing was unlawful to be done; and loosing signified, on the contrary, a declaration that any thing may be lawfully done."[148]

In his commentary on Matthew, John Lightfoot devoted several pages to this topic. "To bind and loose, a very usual phrase in the Jewish schools, was spoken of things, not of persons...One might produce thousands of examples out of their writings...first, that it is used in doctrine, and in judgments, concerning things allowed or not allowed in the law. Secondly, that 'to bind' is the same with to forbid, or to declare forbidden...Hence (the Apostles) bound, that is, forbade, circumcision to the believers...They loosed, that is, allowed, purification to Paul and to four other brethren for the shunning of a scandal (Acts 21:24)."[149]

Most versions render the phrase as something similar to, "whatever you bind will be bound in Heaven," which sounds a lot like a big, fat blank check for us to spend on our pleasure. Thus, I glibly bind fever blisters, the color puce and D-minor on my piano, because all of those make me sad, and I don't want to be sad. What can Heaven do but bow to my will? Since I have bound these things,

Heaven must ratify my decision, right? But the Greek phrasing does not possess the simple future tense, as "will be" implies. The verbs 'bind' and 'loose' are passive in the Greek text. The NASB gets close to right, but a lesser known translation by Charles Williams might be the best of all.[150]

> "I solemnly say to you, whatever you forbid on earth *must be already forbidden in heaven,* and whatever you permit on earth must be already permitted in heaven" (Mat. 18:18, Williams Translation).

Some feel this greatly confines our binding and loosing, since the periphrastic, past tense phrasing suggests that what is bound on Earth merely documents decisions already made in Heaven. But does it? Is that what we are meant to understand? Before we explore this further, two other passages are immediately relevant. The first is Matthew 18.

> "Truly I say to you, whatever you shall bind on earth shall be bound in heaven; and whatever you loose on earth shall be loosed in heaven" (Mat. 18:18-19).

The language of Matthew 18 is identical to chapter 16, yet in context it seems highly associated with the act of forgiveness, along with a procedure that has come to be understood as "church discipline." John 20:23 confirms the association of binding and loosing with forgiveness. "If you forgive the sins of any, their sins have been forgiven them; if you retain the sins of any, they have been retained." Forgiveness releases or retains, similar to binding and loosing.

We will examine both these latter passages in more detail next chapter. For now, suffice it to say that binding and loosing can be interpreted in several ways, as forbidding certain behaviors, laying down rules, forgiving or retaining sins, and imposing or lifting excommunications.

**What are the ties that bind?**

Generally speaking, humans can be bound:

- by and/or to demons (Luke 11:27, 13:16; Mat. 8:16)
- in covenant (to God, or other humans, as in marriage; Rom. 7:2; 1 Sam. 18:3)
- to a purpose or destiny (Col. 4:3; Acts 20:22)
- in falsehood (2 Cor. 10:4-5; Eph. 4:17-18)

Thus, anything that can be bound to a human can be loosed from a human. *Any prevailing idea, sin or spirit that binds humans across an entire region can be loosed from humans across that entire region.* Each person still must exercise free will. But controlling authority can be broken.

Some imagine that the past tense phrasing of Matthew 16:19 places rather tight limits on what we can or cannot bind. In fact, it is equally possible to find this construction liberating and empowering in the context of governmental rulership. If we view our mandate through the lens of the constitution and character of Heaven, then anything that does not exist *there* should ultimately be viewed as illegal *here,* on Earth. Every manifestation or operation of death is thus subject to binding. Matthew 18 makes it clear that, at least in part, binding is the work of prayer.

> "Prayer is at the cutting edge of any work for God. It is not a supplemental spiritual rocket to get some well-meaning effort off the ground. Prayer is the work and the working power in any spiritual ministry. It should be the central thrust. The spiritual history of a mission or church is written in its prayer life. The expression of corporate life is not measured in statistics, but in prayer depth...
>
> Prayers that have blunted edges have no power of penetration...As it takes a sharp edge to inflict wounds, our best endeavors ought to be concentrating on preserving a razor-sharp cutting edge."[151]

If this is true, small prayers might be the greatest sin of all. We must learn to pray with confidence and great faith! Remember, Jesus has already told His disciples, "Pray, then, in this way..."***Thy will be done, on earth as it is in heaven***"(Mat. 6:9-10). Shortly after teaching them to pray like this, He took them to Caesarea Philippi and expanded their prayer license. The previous parameters were simple: make Earth like Heaven. Okay, good. Rabbi, how do we do that? Jesus responds with a question: Who am I? First, know that I am Christ. Second, accept your identity inside My mission. You are my ekklesia, My government. Third, use the keys I will continually give to dismantle the gates of Hades in all the hard, dark places of Earth. With these keys, begin to *bind* and *loose.*

No, we are not allowed to arbitrarily and proactively bind, then expect Heaven to salute and make it happen. Yet we are permitted—and expected!—to reactively bind and proactively loose. Some would say only a passive reaction is permitted. Others would say this primarily relates to church governance, but if church and all that it implies is a blatant mistranslation, this only begs the question. I contend our reaction should never be passive, but aggressive in the Spirit, tearing down high places and prevailing against the gates of Hades.

Instead, what do we do? I say this gently, but gravely: we attend church.

The problem with being the church is nothing more or less than *refusing to act like ekklesia.* What do you do with a government that refuses to govern? In the United States, if our nation ails, do politicians' poll numbers go up? Of course not! Why? Because there is a direct connection between the prosperity of our land and the actions of our rulers. We voted them into a position of authority to actively solve problems. If they refuse to get involved, why are they there? Why are *we* seated with Christ on a throne, if we refuse to rule? Our passivity is actually rebellion, perhaps sedition, for it undermines His government. God forgive us!

Ask yourself. Does death, sickness, poverty, gambling, alcoholism, child abuse, sex trafficking, drug lords or pornography *have any legitimate voice or influence in Heaven?* No, those are "already forbidden in heaven." As the ekklesia, we must start acting upon our charter. You have been given latitude to band together with others and rule in prayer. We are authorized, nay, commanded to forbid those things on Earth, "To execute vengeance on the nations, and punishment on the peoples; *to bind their kings with chains,* and their nobles with fetters of iron; to execute on them the judgment written; this is an honor for all His godly ones. Praise the Lord!" (Psa. 149:7-9).

---

**As the ekklesia, we must start acting upon our charter. You have been given latitude to band together with others and rule in prayer.**

---

In Psalm 149, the binding of kings is symbolic of spiritual powers. Colossians 1:16 clearly says there are invisible thrones, dominions, rulers and authorities. Let me be clear; we don't bind *people,* we bind powers. Binding people is witchcraft. Binding powers is "an honor for all His godly ones."

If you bind a king, you shift a nation, right? Does your faith accommodate the possibility of influencing an entire nation? Why not? It's built into your identity. "In the Septuagint (ekklesia) is used to designate the 'gathering' of Israel, summoned for any definite purpose, or a 'gathering' regarded as *representative of the whole nation.*"[152]

In acts of binding and loosing, the ekklesia is authorized to shift an entire nation in prayer. It also requires that we get comfortable with the masculine side of our faith, and wielding a spiritual form of humble, godly, masculine strength.

# 13

## THE BALANCE OF MASCULINE AND FEMININE

Years ago, President George W. Bush was famously lampooned by his critics for declaring, "I'm the decider." While some may question his policy decisions, the duty of a leader to lead *by deciding* can hardly be challenged. In fact, the Hebrew root word for father is *ab*, as in Abraham, father of many. Do you know the root meaning of *ab*?

It is: "He who decides."[153]

This is what fathers do. This is what leaders do. This is what the ekklesia, with its masculine characterization, is meant to do.

---

**While the "Bride of Christ" is a critical biblical revelation, it's important not to downplay the ekklesia's essentially masculine aspect.**

---

While the "Bride of Christ" is a critical biblical revelation, it's important not to downplay the ekklesia's essentially masculine aspect. Masculine strength is fundamental to a fruitful, righteous, ordered society. In his book, *The Abolition of Man*, C. S. Lewis said, "In a sort of ghastly simplicity we remove the (male) organ and demand the function. We make men without chests and expect of them virtue and enterprise. We laugh at honor and are shocked to find traitors in our midst. We castrate and then bid the geldings to be fruitful."[154]

Think that's bold and gruesome? The Septuagint goes even further. "No one who is emasculated, or has his male organ cut off, shall enter the *ekklesia* of the Lord" (Deut. 23:1).

Contrary to conventional wisdom, the masculine spirit is a gift to humanity. It is a source of great courage, honor, wisdom and strength. The headship of God, revealed as Father who decides, assures us that everything is under control.

Let me make a clear distinction at this point. This isn't a question of gender. Obviously, *human males* cannot and should not claim exclusive rights to the virtues of courage and bravery. Every time a child is born, I am reminded how small the population would be if childbirth were left to men! Women are champions in their own right, not only in rearing and defending their children, but also facing down injustice and enduring hardship for the sake of those they love. Women can demonstrate grit, humor, and a spirit of adventure equal to men in every respect, often surpassing them. This isn't about placing limits on women, but recognizing the unique distinctions within God's design. It is only as we *understand and value both the masculine and feminine* that we gain the proper perspective. Likewise, females are not the only gender capable of nurturing, compassion and gentleness. Stereotypes are never wholly accurate, but the general traits of both genders inform us of higher things. Why? Because humanity itself is a type and symbol. An image of God. In a sense, the likeness of God is preserved in the human body. So let's pause for a minute and gain insight into the masculine and feminine soul. Again, this isn't about gender or physical plumbing, it's about *identity*.

**"Once upon a time..."**

That's how every good story begins, right? This once upon a time begins in the Garden. Adam was created *outside* of paradise, then transferred into paradise. Have you ever considered that? Notice the order of things.

> "Then the Lord God formed man of dust from the ground, and breathed into his nostrils the breath of life; and man became a living being. And the Lord God planted a garden toward the east, in Eden; and there He placed the man whom He had formed...the Lord God took the man and **put him into the garden of Eden** to cultivate it and keep it" (Gen. 2:6-7, 15).

By contrast, Eve drew her first breath *inside* paradise. Man was born in the wild, woman was born in Eden.[155] Man was the refinement of Earth and "the glory of God", created from the dust. Woman was the refinement of man, "the glory of man" (1 Cor. 11:7-8), for from man she came forth. In Genesis 2, God assigned man the duty of taking care of the earth. In labor and rulership, man discovered meaning and joy. Because of her creation in response to man's loneliness, the implication is that a woman's principal joy would be found in relationship, in taking care of man. But the circle continues, for as man took care of the earth, he also took care of woman. In the beautiful, politically incorrect environment of Eden, Eve awoke every day in the stable, secure environment provided by Adam's labor on her behalf, which protected and enriched her life. She in turn found herself adored and recognized as utterly necessary to his existence—"Bone of my bones and flesh of my flesh" (Gen. 2:23). These two souls, male and female, were mutually dependent upon one another and mutually valuable to one another,[156] though for entirely different reasons. Adam cleaved to his wife. Eve rested in Adam's strength. Take a secret poll of 100 women with no social pressures placed upon them, and you will likely find this to be a good description of a nearly perfect marriage.

Though the description above is hardly complete, the rabbit trail was necessary to demonstrate how the core of the masculine soul is *un*domesticated, and this is a good thing, while the core of the feminine soul is domesticated, which is equally good. In *Wild at Heart*, John Eldredge summed up three primary masculine needs. For a rich and meaningful life, men need:

1. A battle to fight
2. An adventure to live
3. A beauty to rescue[157]

If Adam was made in God's image, then in limited fashion, when we understand man's original design, we also better understand God. Who is God? Jesus said, when you pray, pray this way: our *Father.* The Father is Protector, Provider, Ruler, Life-Giver. He is also "The Decider." Adam was supposed to decide what happened in the garden and what didn't. He was supposed to permit some things and forbid others. He was supposed to bind and loose. The snake was never supposed to have voice or a place. God gave rulership to Adam *to decide these things*! He should have crushed the serpent's head the moment it dared to speak to his wife!

Similarly, we are given a picture of the Garden of Eden as a prototype. Eden occupied a finite section of Earth's total real estate. Eden did not fill the whole earth...yet. This suggests that Adam's commission, along with Eve and their offspring, was to reproduce paradise everywhere. In other words, make the whole earth like Eden![158]

In Christ, our original commission is restored. Listen again to how we were taught to pray: "On earth as it is in heaven." Wow! The ekklesia are authorized to expand the kingdom across the planet.

## The problem of mixed metaphors

As was discussed in Chapters 8-9, by function and constitution, the Greek ekklesia was a male entity. A male body, if you will. The legislative and executive authority of the quorum was not only limited to men, but exerted masculine authority for the good of their city. Hopefully, this makes more sense now, for while the cultural milieu has certainly changed, the masculine nature of the ekklesia remains the metaphorical counterpoint to the feminine nature of the Bride. In fact, as Paul makes clear to the Ephesians, just as Eve came out of Adam, the Bride is formed out of the ekklesia.[159] So sexuality is not the issue, but rather, masculine and feminine traits. The language of "Bridal Paradigm" has been so helpful in recent years to give us a framework to grow in relational zeal and passion. The Bride of Christ is not only a literal reality, it is also the feminine template by which we understand our relationship to the Heavenly Bridegroom. God, who "is above and beyond all things, is so masculine that we are all feminine in relation to (Him)."[160]

Understand Eve's importance to Adam and you gain a smidgen of understanding for the ravished heart of Christ for His bride. The Bridal Paradigm is important doctrine because it gives us language to understand the eternal motivations of God and the tender affections of His heart. More than a mode of thought, a Bridal lifestyle is crucial to rightly posturing ourselves at the close of the age. Almost without exception, Bridal verses relate to intimacy, moral purity, and our state of preparedness related to the Lord's return. They tell us how we should think and feel toward the Lord. For our purposes, however, we must note that *not a single verse directly associates the Bride with dominion.* We have been led to believe that the Bride will "rule and reign" with Christ, because "church" has become a popular, catch-all phrase, so that the Bride is basically another synonym for church. Since a number of symbolisms are employed by Scripture to describe us as heirs of faith and grace, we think "the church" is also a flock or sheepfold,[161] God's building or temple,[162] salt and light,[163] and sons.[164] But with only one exception, the references given above do not compare the "church" to those things. Rather, they are stand-alone metaphors. It is the "saints" or "you" or "them that believe" who embody those symbols. Each description is true of all Christ-followers.

Once we disentangle ekklesia from this wrong associative habit, we will see that it is not a metaphorical catch-all, as we have allowed its substitute word, church, to become. The whole point of this book is that words matter, because the Word of God matters! So the ekklesia is not primarily a flock, nor a Bride, though each of those adequately explains a part of our life before God. I do not advocate viewing these as different groups, i.e. some people are the ekklesia, and some are the Bride. Not at all! Both metaphors reference the same people, but the Bride (mostly) emphasizes those qualities that are feminine in the body of Christ, while the ekklesia (mostly) emphasizes those qualities which are masculine.

Consider my claim in this light. Scripture employs a certain economy of language by which the Holy Spirit emphasizes certain concepts. If we homogenize all the metaphors, we actually hinder whatever insight the metaphor is meant to afford. For example, light doesn't prevent decay or add flavor, but *salt* does. Likewise, salt doesn't illuminate a path or expose what is hidden in darkness, but *light* does. So it is that the flock *follows* and *feeds*; the salt *seasons* and *preserves*; the body *connects* and *incarnates*; the temple offers *holy sacrifice,* that it might be *indwelt by God's presence*; the Bride *loves, prepares for* and *tenderly communes* with her Bridegroom; while the ekklesia *rules, binds* and *looses.* Similarly, the flock needs a *Shepherd,* a body needs a *Head,* the temple needs a *High Priest,* the Bride needs *a Groom,* a kingdom needs a *King,* and the ekklesia needs a *Christ.* These oversimplifications confirm the larger point, that we must let each metaphor stand on its own if it is to have any inner logic or meaning.

So, while most commentators have generically applied dominion verses in the book of Revelation to the Bride, this is actually inaccurate, making this glorious book an ultra-pasteurized, ultra-homogenized, milk-of-the-Word diet. "The church is the Bride and that's who Jesus is coming for so it's all the same. Close enough." Respectfully, no. Passages that speak of the people of God in a position of ruling their circumstance are overwhelmingly masculine, either described as ekklesia (who are challenged to be "overcomers" seven times in chapters 2-3), a "male child...to rule all the nations with a rod of iron" (Rev. 12:5), kings and priest (Rev. 5:10, 20:6), or "my son" (Rev. 21:7).[165] There is not a single allusion to the Bride as ruler. As the feminine response to the masculine Divine, the Bride is filled with adoration, passion, purity, devotion, Proverbs 31-styled "good works" and holy anticipation. The Heavenly Bridegroom expresses His desire for love through the response of a Bride, but Christ expresses His rule through masculine, not feminine means.

It is sons who inherit a father's kingdom. It is sons who rule. Jesus, the Son of God, sits on His throne,[166] while "the anxious longing of the creation waits eagerly for the revealing of the sons of God" (Rom. 8:19).

Obviously, rulership does not always mean triumph or success. We don't always "win" according to conventional definitions. Rather, rulership should be eschatologically defined as faithfully expressing the victory of Christ even to the point of death (see Chapter 16). The point is simply that we must not mash these compelling and distinct realities into a generic, meaningless blob.

## Divine math

This is not to say that there are not clear pair bonds. As indicated earlier, key verses serve as connective tissue for us to understand that, yes, the Bride *is* the ekklesia: "Husbands, love your wives, just as Christ also loved the ekklesia" (Eph. 5:25). There is no contradiction here. Paul conceives of Christ's intimate oneness with His bride in Genesis language that explicitly draws comparison to the union of husband and wife.

> "In the image of God He created him (singular); male and female He created them (plural)" (Gen. 1:27).

Look closely and you will see that in God's math, 1+1=1. Alone, Adam insufficiently represents the image of God. Only together do male and female form a complete divine image. In this singular passage (made notable not only for its beauty and mystery, but also for being the lone deviation), Paul connects the Bride to the ekklesia, but by doing so he creates an important connection in our minds. It requires both the male and female of the Spirit, the feminine Bride and masculine ekklesia, to accurately represent God's image on earth. *Thus, the people of the Bride understand their rulership not as a Bride, but because they are also the ekklesia, and likewise, the ekklesia understand the critical need for intimacy not as a function of their rulership, but because they are also the Bride.*

They are two sides of one coin, but they are *two* sides.

The debilitating "gender confusion" that plagues this generation has, in effect, plagued God's people for nearly 400 years. While this will be a controversial statement, if *church* is synonymous with the *Bride*, as we've been taught, then two essentially female portraits have been made to represent God's purpose for His people. Eve + Eve. Where then is Adam's Genesis commission to be located in the Body of Christ? If it's there at all, we say it is the "warring Bride's" job! Huh? Is it any wonder men are bored with church?[167]

Church is amply capable of generating enthusiasm for relationship, but fails outright to generate enthusiasm for war. Castration and feminization are inherent to the labels we've chosen. Rather than letting Scripture inform our thoughts and summon us to the councils of Heaven for rulership, we've been summoned to Fifth and Main for another fine, 10:30 AM social sing-along. I'm perhaps overdramatizing for effect, and forgive the sarcasm, but this much is plain: men want to break things, fix things, and blow things up. Men sign up for war. Where is the war? We're told about it all the time, but no one lets us fight! Only when we fully express the soul of masculine *and* feminine faith will we mature as "members of His body" wherein "the two shall become one flesh." Indeed, as Paul said, it is a great mystery. But lest there be any doubt, "I am speaking with reference to Christ and the ekklesia" (Eph. 5:30-32).

If we must assign priority, it is telling that bridal references occur about 30 times in the New Testament, while ekklesia is mentioned 115 times.

### The agency of Christological dominion

Whereas the Bride is comprised of beneficiaries of unconditional love—we who receive and respond to love, and are therefore *counterpoints* of the masculine Divine—the ekklesia is actually *emblematic* of the masculine Divine. As ekklesia, we do not primarily demonstrate God's emotion, but His rulership. If the Bride is a revelation of the First Commandment, the ekklesia is the agency of Christological dominion. As a male entity, it is an aggressor in service of righteousness. It conveys headship and militancy. In the natural, maleness is defined by a penetrating organ. Our culture feels uncomfortable with this sort of language, because strong men do many bad things. "The vocabulary of attack is not popular today. Many of the Lord's eagles have been influenced by the mood of the world and assumed the character of doves."[168]

But this is nonsense, as the point is often missed that it takes strong, *good* men in every generation to stop strong, *bad* men. It is a liberal fantasy to think that masculinity is the root issue, or that neutering male strength will somehow balance the books. Rather, doing so will only give free reign to evil men who blatantly refuse to be anything other than men.

So, if the feminine right of the Bride is to be governed by the impulse of love, then in similar fashion it is the right of the ekklesia to be governed by the impulse of rulership. If it takes a Bride to love Jesus as He deserves, the DNA of Matthew 16 reveals that it takes an ekklesia to conquer Hades. The popular charismatic notion of the "Bridal Army" is, in a sense, a myth (likewise, the "victorious church"), to the degree that it pictures a feminine spirit storming the front lines at the end of the age. This is not God's design! Judge for yourself: historically, culturally, sociologically, physically and emotionally, does the feminine personality typically relish the cold realities of battle and bloodshed—mud, grime, sweat, rain, foxholes, hunger, stenches, death, bullets, bombs, deprivation, hardship, etc.? Similarly, not until recent times have armies been thought of as anything but exclusively male. Yes, we must embrace our bridal identity, but no less our ekklesial mandate.[169] The masculine call to governance must begin to grip us. War should stir our blood and rouse our passions—men and women alike. The *bene elohim* of the covenant of grace must begin to convene in invisible halls of power. With statesmanlike authority, they must petition, command and release God's will onto Earth.

There's a lot of material in this chapter, so the following table will help to compare and summarize key points regarding the Bride, the ekklesia, and church.

| | Bride | Ekklesia | Church (Kyriakon) |
|---|---|---|---|
| Definition | "Betrothed woman" | "A called out assembly" | "Of the Lord's" |
| Meaning | Beloved companion and soul mate | Ruling council | People that meet and/or the property wherein they meet |
| Purpose | Intimacy, fellowship with God, holiness, surrender, discipleship, zeal | Unity, legislation, governmental decrees, war, judgment, binding, loosing | Community life, pastoral care, doctrinal conformity, perpetuity of local assembly, evangelism |
| Key Passage | Rev. 19: 7-8 "Let us rejoice and be glad and give the glory to Him, for the marriage of the Lamb has come and His bride has made herself ready. And it was given to her to clothe herself in fine linen, bright and clean; for the fine linen is the righteous acts of the saints." | Mat. 16:18-19 "...Upon this rock I will build My ekklesia; and the gates of Hades shall not overpower it. I will give you the keys of the kingdom of heaven; and whatever you shall bind on earth shall be bound in heaven, and whatever you shall loose on earth shall be loosed in heaven." | Non-existent |

| | **Bride** | **Ekklesia** | **Church (Kyriakon)** |
|---|---|---|---|
| Number of occurrences in New Testament | 31 | 115 | None |
| Themes | The beauty of the Lord, refinement of the human heart, fullness of love and devotion | Expansion of the kingdom of God, revelation of Christ, rulership in prayer, justice | Bible teaching, worship, fellowship, possibly evangelism, traditions |
| Typified by | Feminine / Shulamite | Masculine / Nazirite | Considered synonymous with Bride, so feminine by default. |
| Necessity of Prayer and Fasting | Yes | Yes | No |
| Impact | To know and be known. Hearts that are alive, unoffended, and prepared. "Spirit and the Bride say, 'Come!'" (Rev. 22:17) | Authority to challenge corrupt natural and supernatural powers, imposition of Heaven's government on Earth | Favorable, but limited social continuity. Dullness, boredom; tends to replace obedience with obligation. |
| Public perception | ? | ? | Increasingly out of touch, judgmental, detached, isolationist |

## Strength for a purpose

Even with the many qualifiers I've sprinkled throughout, all this manly, military talk can lead to wrong conclusions, so let me clarify once more: the ekklesia is *not* an earthly militia or political body. Furthermore, it not gender exclusive, but inclusive. Both genders form the universal Bride of Christ. Likewise, men and women equally form the ekklesia. The *soul* of the ekklesia is what is at stake. I'm not advocating a physical army nor a spiritual Boy's Only club. We can lay that to bed now, right? My hermeneutic lens is focused on the character of ekklesia, who love a Bridegroom, but follow a Christ.

## Going after the big dogs

First we have to unlearn bad masculinity, as the two primary modern conceptions of masculinity are both wrong. Men are viewed as either politely feminized creatures, or bloodthirsty, napalm-wielding tyrants pulled straight out of the violent video game culture. The Word clearly states that the Body of Christ on Earth should be peaceful citizens, upholding the law, submitted to authority, acting as salt and light to withhold lawlessness.[170] We are not renegades on Earth, we are convened out of Heaven. Therefore, we must think spiritual thoughts.

> "For the weapons of our warfare are not of the flesh, but divinely powerful for the destruction of fortresses. We are destroying speculations and every lofty thing raised up against the knowledge of God, and we are taking every thought captive to the obedience of Christ" (2 Cor. 10:4-5).

In this passage, Paul is describing the intensely personal mental battles that result from false ideologies waging war upon humanity. Ideas may be veiled to the eyes, but they are neither static, nor powerless. History bears witness to these invisible titans. Ideas have sparked the fires of revolution, bankrupted nations, launched ships to war, set kings on thrones and thrones on fire, and amassed great wealth for the innovators who could successfully turn their clever ideas into real products for hungry markets. Tides of history shift, sometimes monumentally, every time one idea supplants another in the public mind. Ideas carry the language of either truth or deception to the faculties of the mind and from there, into the very soul of entire people groups.

In Ephesians 6, Paul reveals the power base behind these "fortresses" and "lofty things." Instead of "weapons of warfare," now we're wrestling, but not with flesh and blood. Battles may play out to certain conclusions in the carnal, physical realm, but they are decided in heavenly places. This is why the arena of true ekklesial conflict must be properly configured against "principalities, against powers, against the rulers of the darkness of this world, against spiritual wickedness in high places" (v. 12), because human philosophies do not exist independent of the defilements and control of evil spiritual forces. Over time, worldviews become fortresses inhabitable by demons. Unintended cooperation between human enterprise and spiritual wickedness in high places extends the rule of darkness around the world. As we have demonstrated repeatedly in this book, the spiritual realm directly affects the natural. Mathew's depiction of society some 30 years ago is even more terrifyingly true today.

> "'Principalities and powers in heavenly places' have mustered their unseen array, rigged their Trojan horse, infiltrated society, and opened the gates for a flood of evil to take over."[171]

If this is true of *evil* powers, then a *holy* ekklesia must learn to wrestle and prevail. What demonic fortresses exist in the earth? Take your pick. Abortion, sex trafficking, drug cartels, the radical homosexual agenda, policies of poverty and oppression, the deviant perversions of Hollywood, and more.

To overturn these, legislative protocols of the ekklesia could roughly be compared to the way laws are written in Washington, D.C. Senatorial *filibusters* wear down the will of their opponents. One way the ekklesia does this is by fasting. Fasting is designed to stall and thwart the desires of the flesh with its urges for instant gratification. In this way, we expand our authority over the carnal impulses which empower so many strongholds. We also *censure* and *impeach* demonic rulers through acts of binding and loosing. We *make motions* on policy and law in acts of prayer, and then form *majorities* and *quorums* to drive the legislation through by agreeing with others in His name (more on the "power of agreement" in the next chapter).

---

**Fasting is designed to stall and thwart the desires of the flesh with its urges for instant gratification**

---

**Go ahead, pick a fight**

The masculine soul contemplates such challenges with a spirit of eagerness and vigor. While admitting that chauvinistic cultures have prevented many women from occupying positions of leadership, it remains an historic fact that the governing bodies of the world have always been overwhelmingly male.

The masculine soul is crafted for governance, the masculine temperament for conflict. Likewise, the male body is sculpted by God for penetration. *This itself is a form of revelation*, so I'll close the chapter with this: sometimes it's not enough to resist a stronghold. In a world full of hard, dark, scary places, nested with demons like a viper pit, what do we do? Do we say, "Well, I guess Christ won't rule there!" No, no. Precisely there, the ekklesia must rise. Precisely there, the strong man must be bound. Sometimes, retaliation is too late. We need to pick a fight.

In military terms, this is called infiltration.

As a veteran of World War II, R. Arthur Mathews is also a man committed to prayer. According to Mathews, "*infiltration* is now accepted as standard procedure and universally practiced" in modern warfare. As part of Force 136, Mathews participated in the strategy of infiltration pioneered by Major General Orde Wingate, who formed the Long-Range Penetration Group (LRP), and "organized an expedition to penetrate behind the enemy lines and operate there as a part of the main offensive. With their special training and equipment, and relying on supply drops from the air, these brigades were to ambush the enemy's support columns, blow up his supply dumps, and strangle his lifeline to the front-line troops."

LRP actually helped turn the tide in the Pacific Theater. As a result, Mathews interprets the effect in spiritual terms. "Victory can be hastened and casualties lessened by infiltrating the enemy's vulnerable control zone, where plans for attack are conceived and from which the orders are issued. This area is not marked on our atlases as a geographic point, but that does not make it any less real...The temerity of this aspect of prayer warfare appalls many and, because the results are not easily measured, is often put to one side. But it is a way of victory."[172]

I believe this is why Jesus picked Caesarea Philippi. He didn't need another conversation, He needed to make a deep impression—one that would stick. It worked. After Pentecost, the disciples journeyed through great peril to "repugnantly degenerate places, where God is not even known...that make Caesarea Philippi look tame... places in Asia Minor and the ends of the earth, where 'gods' were worshipped in unspeakably awful manners and where Christians would be persecuted in horrific manner, and they gave their lives doing exactly what they were told to do by their Rabbi."[173]

# 14

## THE SYMPHONY OF PRAYER

Like the many different instruments in an orchestra, a great harmony of themes has come together. Now it's time to get practical. Very simply, ekklesia must be a 1) *community* 2) *of prayer* 3) *in holiness and love* or it cannot be an ekklesia. It is not peopled with Lone Rangers who demand Heaven's enforcement of their carnal whims. In Matthew 18, only two chapters after the discourse at Caesarea Philippi, Jesus described the same, powerful binding and loosing process, only this time He did it in the context of our interaction with one another. As the only other ekklesia reference in the four Gospels, these communal insights are vital. Thus, the following passage in Matthew 18 greatly illuminates Matthew 16 by defining the corporate health and process of interaction for communities that pray. Not surprisingly, it builds the power of prayer around wholeness and agreement, by which we are assured that Jesus is in our midst.

> "And if your brother sins, go and reprove him in private; if he listens to you, you have won your brother. But if he does not listen to you, take one or two more with you, so that 'by the mouth of two or three witnesses every fact may be confirmed.' And if he refuses to listen to them, tell it to the **ekklesia;** and if he refuses to listen even to the **ekklesia,** let him be to you as a Gentile and a tax-gatherer. Truly I say to you, whatever you shall **bind on earth shall be bound in heaven;** and whatever

you *loose on earth shall be loosed in heaven.* Again I say to you, that *if two of you agree on earth about anything that they may ask,* it shall be done for them by My Father who is in heaven. For *where two or three have gathered together* in My name, there I am in their midst" (Mat. 18:15-20).

The key portions of Matthew chapters 16 and 18 reveal not only the authority of Christ in His ekklesia, but healthy modes of interaction necessary to sustain the mandate of prayer. In other words, Jesus is hardly naive about human nature. If there are people, there is a people dynamic! As a result, He decides to answer some basic questions even before they're asked. Ekklesia is a simple idea, but it takes work: two or three who live holy, love well, and by virtue of their forgiving and praying together, bind and loose.

While prayer may be the most obvious beginning, it is by no means the end. The extraordinary power of agreement must be added. This means that you have to love me and I have to love you at a gritty, practical, life-level, as well as in the context of corporate prayer. People dynamics can tear groups apart, which is why binding and loosing in love and forgiveness has to be as much a part of the focus internally as externally. When Jesus said, "If two of you *agree* on earth about anything...it shall be done for them," the word translated 'agree' is the Greek word *sumphaneo,* a word that shares the same root from which we get our word, 'symphony.' The root means harmonious. Which leads us to six instruments in the symphony of prayer.

### 1. The symphony of unity

Think about a symphony. What do you have? Many instruments follow the lead of a single conductor, and a string of notes on a page. The unique tonal qualities of each creates layered strands of melody and harmony, eventually becoming a single unity of music. So the ekklesia are many voices, many perspectives, many prayers, conducted by the Spirit of Christ, blended into a governmental sound that commands the earth into alignment with His will. Interestingly, Jesus used the same word in the context of the importance of new wine being put into new wineskins. He described the problem of sewing a patch of new cloth onto an old garment. The "new will not match the old" (Luke 5:36). Actually, it says "the new will not *sumphaneo* the old," meaning they will not agree, or connect, or relate well, and so the garment will be torn.

---

**The ekklesia are many voices, many perspectives, many prayers, conducted by the Spirit of Christ, blended into a governmental sound that commands the earth into alignment with His will.**

---

Love between the brethren is vital. Our personal relationships as brothers and sisters must be closely guarded. We must deal gently and patiently with one another. Flutes and trombones and drums can easily clash because they are such different instruments. Wounds and miscommunication are inevitable. The point of Matthew 18 is that forgiveness must be routine to the covenantal community. Hearts are better positioned in prayer when they are clean and whole. How can we seek to rule in prayer if we hate our brother? Instead, we are to relate to one another "with all humility and gentleness, with patience, showing forbearance to one another in love" (Eph. 4:2). Hundreds of years before Paul, Isaiah described the answers to prayer that come when we do this.

> "*Then* you will call, and the Lord will answer; you will cry, and He will say, 'Here I am.' *If* you remove the yoke from your midst, the pointing of the finger, and speaking wickedness" (Isa. 58:9).

Paul complained to the believers at Corinth, "When you come together as an ekklesia, I hear that there are divisions among you"

(1 Cor. 11:18). He exhorted them "by the name of our Lord Jesus Christ, that you all agree, and there be no divisions among you, but you be made complete in the same mind" (1 Cor. 1:10). Agreement is vital not only for harmonious interpersonal relationships, demonstrating the love of Christ to one another, but also because the ekklesia are involved in rendering judgments on Earth. "Can two walk together, except they be agreed?" (Amos 3:3).

> "For I am afraid that perhaps when I come I may find...strife, jealousy, angry tempers, disputes, slanders, gossip, arrogance, disturbances" (2 Cor. 12:20).

Unfortunately, evil agreement is also possible. In Acts 5:9, Peter confronts Sapphira, the wife of lying Ananias, "Why is it that you have agreed ('*sumphaneo*') together to put the Spirit of the Lord to the test? Behold, the feet of those who have buried your husband are at the door, and they shall carry you out as well."

Both Ananias and Sapphira were struck dead by the Lord. Why? The very question is lacking in revelation of the Christ. We must understand, *Jesus presides over the ekklesia.* After the judgment of God, we are told that "great fear came upon the whole ekklesia, and upon all who heard of these things" (v. 11). Compare this to the way the Secret Service thoroughly vets people and locations before the president arrives. No threat or hidden agenda is allowed. Snipers lie in wait to take out anyone who demonstrates dangerous intentions. The ekklesial security measures of Matthew 18 are not meant to intimidate us, but to create a secure environment, so that we can have confidence our prayers are in alignment with His will.

But if sumphaneo includes the idea of unity, it also transcends it. When we agree together, we stand in covenant, and covenant releases favor. But don't worry! Covenant is not cookie-cutter conformity. Though we share a common purpose, our unity is not so timid and flaccid as to demand monotone, flavorless prayer. When we mark a target for our intercession, each heart and voice still prays out of the revelation they have received, while also supporting and receiving from the revelation others have received. In a symphony, the trumpet does not follow the clarinet, nor the clarinet the violin, as a matter of preeminence. Each plays their part, and the conductor weaves every note into a sum that is definitely greater and more beautiful than its parts.

## 2. The symphony of purity

The tremendous authority God willingly entrusts to fallible humans, though shockingly unfettered, does not come without safeguards. Rightly so, for war is a sober thing. Rulership amidst the council of God is a high and holy privilege, and the lives of those who would seek such an office should be characterized by brokenness, humility and submission to the Lord, grieved to think they might grieve the Holy Spirit, quick to relinquish sin, and growing in holiness. According to Longman and Reid, "Since at the heart of holy war is God's presence with the army, Israel had to be as spiritually prepared to go to battle as they would be to approach the sanctuary."[174] The Apostle John tells us that the children of God and the children of the devil are obvious both in the practice of righteousness and the love of the brethren.[175]

Even endowed with true authority, if we do not persist in the practice of righteousness and love we are empty vessels, echoes with no voice. As such, our impact will be diminished. How can the children of the devil bind the devil? It will not happen.

Thus, in Matthew 18, we see that it is not only the substance of our prayer, but the constitution of our community that matters to the Lord. The group dynamic must operate with integrity and wholeness. Constituents of the ruling body are expected to demonstrate lives of genuine holiness, not merely outward facades of good behavior. Sin is expected to be challenged, though perhaps the notion of "church discipline" here has been misunderstood. The point seems not so much to reprove and expunge the sinner from their midst, as to insure the quality, authority and unity of their prayers. If someone is lacking in covenant devotion with the Lord, tolerating sin, and/or persisting in flagrant, damaging behavior, *and* he shows no outward concern or signs of repentance, then how can he be allowed to participate in enforcing the moral judgements of the ekklesia in prayer? This is a matter of integrity. The authority invested in the ekklesia is not to be trifled with, for the promise is that God hears and responds to what we ask.

> "And this is the confidence which we have before Him, that, if we ask anything according to His will, He hears us. And if we know that He hears us in whatever we ask, we know that we have the requests which we have asked from Him" (1 John 5:14).

Even today, in America, felons are not allowed to vote. Nearly every state places some kind of limitation on prisoner voting rights. Why? Their moral behavior excludes them from participation in the government. It taints the high ideals of the process.

> "So when you spread out your hands in prayer, I will hide My eyes from you, Yes, even though you multiply prayers, I will not listen. Your hands are covered with blood" (Isa. 1:15).

Binding and loosing—forbidding and permitting—therefore directly relate to the community within, not just the prayers without. This cleansing activity is foreshadowed in Leviticus 13, where the priest looked upon the leper and either pronounced him clean, and therefore permitted to rejoin the assembly, or unclean and disallowed. We are mutually required to distinguish between the clean and the unclean, those fit or unfit for a place at the table of *ruling* prayer. This is very different than excommunication merely for sin, for excommunication has no larger purpose than confirming the consequence of sin to the minds of both sinner and the general assembly. As it pertains to dominion, such difficult choices fuse both ideal and pragmatic holiness into the purposeful recognition that ekklesia cannot truly rule if they are compromised from within.

### 3. The symphony of two or three

I spent part of my early childhood in a town called Tahlequah, Oklahoma. Tahlequah is the setting of the book, *Where the Red Fern Grows,* by Wilson Rawls, and also the termination point of the brutal forced march of the Cherokees called the Trail of Tears. Local legend says three Cherokee elders were supposed to meet at that location to determine the Cherokee Nation's new, permanent capital. After two elders arrived and waited for the third, dusk approached. Finally, one said to the other, *'Ta'ligwu,'* which means "Two is enough." The meeting would continue with just two.

Jesus said the same. Just two or three, that's all that's needed to get something done.

Practically speaking, the most liberating, dangerous revelation is not that Jesus is the Christ, nor that we are His ekklesia. Nor furthermore, is it that gates will fall before us as we bind and loose. No, the most liberating (for us) and dangerous fact (for the enemy) is that this authority is invested in groups as small as two or three! If we understand that the authority of the group derives both from Christ and the covenantal integrity of the members, we are free, within the Holy Spirit's guidance, to pick a fight. Pick a gate, and attack.

This is devastating news for the ranks of darkness.

Jesus quoted Deuteronomy 17:6 when He mentioned the smallness of the group. In this passage of the Torah, Moses is putting safeguards on accusations made against one another, and the judgments to be rendered. He said, "On the evidence of two witnesses or three witnesses, he who is to die shall be put to death; he shall not be put to death on the evidence of one witness."

The principle of two or three is a baseline, and it is as small of a baseline as can humanly exist. One more than one. It is fascinating that Jesus did not pick another holy number, like seven or twelve. He lowered the limit as low as it could go and still possess integrity. In this, two or three is like a safeguard; it's C-SPAN for prayer. No one exerts council rulership alone. We are required to judge each other's words. There is a public dimension to ruling prayer. Agreement brings power. Since every word is confirmed in the mouth of two or three witnesses, integrity is assured, as another brother can disagree if needed.

Ezekiel reveals that even one faithful intercessor can avert disaster. When God tells the prophet that he looked for a man to "stand in the gap" but found none, the picture is similar to that of a broken gate. There is a hole in the wall that must be filled with prayer. Even one intercessor could have accepted this role. "Stand... before me *for* (on behalf of)" is clearly intercession. There is so much power in prayer! Yet while one can stem the tide of judgment, one is insufficient for rulership.

However, an ekklesial understanding of authority only requires *one more than one* to form a "body" of legislators capable of dominion. In the ekklesial paradigm, small is the new big. Immediately, this should unleash faith across thousands of small prayer gatherings. Take a deep breath, rejoice...it all counts! You aren't ineffective, you aren't too small. You're ekklesia and He is Christ, so your prayers matter. Three chapters—Matthew 16, 18 and Joel 2—form an interpretive grid, a cord of three strands that is not easily broken, connecting ekklesial binding and loosing (Mat. 16) to prayer and prophetic decrees (Mat. 18), after which the summons in Joel 2 extends the ekklesia's legislative protocols to include fasting and repentance. When this happens, tectonic shifts in society are possible.

The principle of "two or three" is as fundamental to the ekklesia as it is foreign to church. Daniel and three young Hebrews set up an ekklesia in the dark heart of pagan Babylon, and you know what? They ruled! Mighty Babylon bent around their courage and their prayers. Mega-numbers were not necessary to shift the nation, they simply needed faith, perseverance, fasting and prayer. You know the story. Nebuchadnezzar has a troubling dream, but he is sick of meddling, incompetent advisors. So he declares that unless one of his conjurers or magicians can both reveal and interpret his dream, with no prior knowledge allowed, he will tear them limb from limb and reduce their houses to rubbish. Nebuchadnezzar finally sees through the machinations of his court's power brokers. "You have agreed together to speak lying and corrupt words before me," he tells them. Unfortunately, Daniel, Shadrach, Meshach and Abednego are guilty by association. When Arioch, the captain of the king's guard shows up at Daniel's house to kill them, what did they do?

> "Then Daniel went **to his house** and informed **his friends,** Hananiah, Mishael and Azariah, about the matter, in order that they might **request compassion from the God** of heaven **concerning this mystery,** so that Daniel and his friends might not be destroyed with the rest of the wise men of Babylon. **Then the mystery was revealed** to Daniel in a **night vision.** Then Daniel blessed the God of heaven...Then Arioch hurriedly brought Daniel into the king's presence" (Dan. 2:17-19, 25).

This tiny little intercessory prayer group numbered a whopping four. Four people against big, bad Babylon. In every natural respect, they were powerless. They were young. They were exiles in a foreign land, presumably orphans. Their captors were pagans who worshipped demons. Yet in the midst of this dark and oppressive circumstance, God prepared a table before them in the midst of their enemies. Properly understood from God's perspective, two or three or four is practically an unfair fight! We've got to shake loose of our small, "pity me" attitude. Together, we are armed and dangerous.

---

**Properly understood from God's perspective, two or three or four is practically an unfair fight!**

---

So Daniel and his friends begin to extend a rod of rulership. Previous verses have already demonstrated that these young men are committed to purity, prayer and fasting. As crisis looms, we see them assemble. They are small in number, but they pray. They ask for secrets. Keys. Just as Matthew 16 promised, God grants them. What began as a crisis ends in a promotion. Though many other tests lay ahead, by the end of the tale, these four Hebrew boys will have faced down the entire nation, refused to bow to idols, literally come through a raging fire, prophesied to kings, overseen "changes (in) the times and the epochs" as God removed kings and established other kings (v. 21), ultimately serving as receptacle for one of the most staggering visions of the Christ ever recorded in Scripture.[176]

The ekklesia of Babylon was very small. Four guys. True to form, that's all it took.

How does this affect the global prayer movement? For one, it authorizes and unleashes countless little houses of prayer and home prayer assemblies to believe their prayers matter! No longer are they some strange arm of the church, the crazy pray-ers, always seeking greater numbers for their prayer meeting and feeling impotent when no one shows up. No, two or three or four, that's all it takes. Beloved, be released to believe! You are not the church of man's design, you are the ekklesia of Christ's.

It should hardly surprise us that Jesus structured His initial outreach plan around His own model, sending His disciples out two by two.[177] There were many good reasons for this—accountability, support, encouragement. More to the point, after the mission wrapped, there were now thirty-five ekklesias who had now seen for themselves, "It works! All we need is two!"

## 4. The symphony of decrees

The greatest instrument of all is the human voice. As image bearers of the One who spoke and "worlds were prepared by the word of God, so that what is seen was not made out of things which are visible" (Heb. 11:3), so we too must express our authority in what is spoken aloud, not what is hidden within. It is not enough to think your prayers inside your head. Release them from your mouth!

> "But having the same spirit of faith, according to what is written, 'I believed, therefore I spoke,' we also believe, *therefore also we speak*" (2 Cor 4:13).

As if anticipating how His disciples will struggle with the implications of the Lord's Prayer and also the ekklesial mandate, only a few verses later we find Jesus telling them: "if you have faith… you shall *say* to this mountain, 'Move from here to there,' and it shall move; and nothing shall be impossible to you" (Mat. 17:20).

Speaking is one of the works of faith. If you want to rule in prayer, you must not only petition, but at times, decree. When is the right time for this? Every situation will be different. Not all gates are the same, nor the keys that unlock them. Practically speaking, the battering ram phase of the assault might continue for an extended period (hours, days, weeks…months?), but eventually there may come a time when sufficient revelation has unfolded to produce a gift of faith. This gift is typically deposited into the community at large as the mind of God becomes clear to all under the direction of the Holy Spirit. Typically, one will speak it out and everyone will sense the strength of it in the Lord's heart. At this point, "prayers" are done.

It is time to decree.

As a legislative act, this could be compared to the roll call of votes in Parliament. A time comes, after the legislation has been debated, argued, written and rewritten as much as it can. It is now in final form, and there is a spirit of agreement, but it must be ratified. Once revelation is crafted to the point of enactment, vote upon it in prayer. These are prophetic acts of decree, by which the ruling council, having faithfully sought and contended for the will of God, now begins to boldly declare it.

As you declare it, take strength knowing that your voice is your address on planet Earth. It is the means by which you represent your sanctified will to the community of faith, joining them as you decree the enforcement of God's plan. It is both your trumpet and drum. Your vote in prayer is a holy thing.

This sort of power demands not only *sumphaneo* by first testing any piece of legislation in the mouths of two or three witnesses, but also the expansion of a communal voice via the principle of multiplication. A single voice has power. A single man or woman anointed of God "puts to flight a thousand, for the Lord your God is He who fights for you" (Josh. 23:10). Yet as powerful as a single voice can be, a choir resounds. A trumpet signals, but a symphony declares. And so Scripture helps us understand the power of multiplication, where one can chase a thousand, but two can put ten thousand to flight.[178] This reveals a tenfold increase in the effectiveness going from one to two—the increase is exponential, not linear. Thus, "The Lord will cause your enemies who rise up against you to be defeated before you; they shall come out against you one way and shall flee before you seven ways" (Deut. 28:7).

## 5. The symphony of generations

If family is central to church, it is even more central to ekklesia. The covenant of family is the blueprint for building the kingdom of Heaven on the earth. As previously inferred, every marriage is a mysterious window into the unity and passion of Christ for His bride. Every father and mother reflect both the strength and tenderness of God's heart for His children, how He provides for them, nurtures them and protects them. Every sibling relationship demonstrates the topsy-turvy, cantankerous, glorious possibilities of *koinonia,* the communion and fellowship of the saints. So it should come as no surprise that families form their own ekklesia, and the ekklesia is also formed of families.

Time does not limit this equation. The ekklesia also spans generations, each one looking out for and honoring the other. A good example is seen in the history of the Picts. When these primitive forebears of modern Scotland would form in battle array, the men stood with their wives and children behind them on the battlefield, and everyone fought, including the women. The blue-painted Picts were greatly feared by Rome's armies and legendary for their ferociousness. Do you know why? Because when a man faces a foe knowing his wife and children are right behind him, naked to the enemy's swords, he fights with the intensity and zeal of a madman. He will do whatever he must to assure their survival. A Pict's wife and children were not safely tucked away at home; in war, "safely tucked away" is an illusion, for if the battle is lost, the home will eventually be overrun anyway.

As with the Picts, we need to see our family on the battlefield with us. How might that affect your zeal and focus in prayer? Will you continue to be soft and quiet, or will a Pictish roar bellow from your lungs? Will you poke your sword aimlessly, or will you thunder and prophesy the word of God, realizing you wield something "living and active and sharper than any two-edged sword" (Heb. 4:12)?

## 6. The symphony of contending

There are many types of prayer and all of them are valuable and enriching, but contending prayer is a contact sport. It is not dull and dreary and soft and quiet. Passion and discipline are vital. If we wish to do more than speak vain, flaccid words to God, we must learn to have a contending spirit. Zeal causes us to persevere. Zeal brings boldness and conviction to our words. Remember, though Abraham was the friend of God, and Isaac was a type of Christ, the entire nation was named after Jacob, the one who wrestled with God and prevailed.[179] Your spiritual DNA is not only faith, as Abraham's seed, nor the promise of atonement, as Isaac's. It is the contending spirit of Jacob, whose name was changed to Israel, meaning, "He Who Wrestles with God and Prevails!"

> "In his (Jacob's) maturity he contended with God. Yes, he wrestled with the angel and prevailed; He wept and sought His favor. He found Him at Bethel...even the Lord, the God of hosts (Lord Sabaoth)" (Hos. 12:3-5).

Jacob wrestled and wept. His emotion showed he was invested. The outcome mattered to him. Do you pray like the outcome matters? Emotion is part of the human experience, therefore how can it not be part of prayer? A symphony produces emotion. The music may be heavy or buoyant, sorrowful or joyful, despairing or triumphant. Sometimes it is peaceful, or warring, or exuberant with praise. But if *no* emotion is felt, the musicians have likely failed. Let's look at these emotions.

*1. Sometimes tears are needed.* Dick Eastman, noting that C.H. Spurgeon called tears "liquid prayer," lists six types of tears in

Scripture: "Tears of sorrow or suffering (2 Kings 20:5); tears of joy (Gen. 33:4); tears of compassion (John 11:35); tears of desperation ( Est. 4:1-3); tears of travail (Isa. 42:14); tears of repentance (Joel 2:12-13)."[180]

*2. Sometimes a vehement, righteous indignation is needed.* Anything less would be to dishonor the Lord and the gravity of the injustice that is being addressed in prayer. This is the spirit that came on Phinehas when Balaak sent Moabite women to tempt the men and thus brought defilement into Israel's camp. (Here again we see the need for the purity of the covenant community if they wish to persist in rulership.) As judgment came near, Phinehas was possessed with a spirit of jealousy for the Lord, so he took a spear and killed the Israelite man and Moabite woman who were openly fornicating in the midst of the camp. Though 24,000 died, the plague stopped, for God was moved by Phinehas' zeal as much as his deed. He said Phinehas "was jealous with My jealousy among them" (Num. 25:11).

When we see apostasy, gross immorality, the destruction of our children's souls and a turning to antichrist, this is not a time for timid prayer. We must be jealous as unto the Lord for transformation and breakthrough.

*3. Discipline and consistency are needed.* In the parable of the widow with the unjust judge in Luke 18, Jesus makes it clear that we are meant to ask and keep asking until mastery is gained and governance established. The ruling council does not pray to pray, but, in one sense, to wear down opposition. A well-ordered, consistent prayer strategy requires watchful vigilance. The diligent searching of Jeremiah 29:12-13 matches the groaning, early morning prayers and eager watching of David in Psalm 5:1-3. When David says he will "order my prayer to Thee," the word 'order' is elsewhere used to describe the careful arrangements and preparation of items in the sanctuary, but also the precise formations of an army, "a strong people set in battle *array*" (Joel 2:5).

---

**The ruling council does not pray to pray, but, in one sense, to wear down opposition. A well-ordered, consistent prayer strategy requires watchful vigilance.**

---

Spiritual battles are not won instantly, nor with sloppy, inconsistent prayers. An army doesn't storm the castle after a single stroke of the battering ram against the enemy's locked gate. No, the archers are marshaled, the foot soldiers take the ram and shield-bearers surround the troops to deflect enemy fire, all while the trebuchets, catapults and cannons release mortars over the walls into the heart of darkness. Precise, diligent strategy is required.

What if the believers had failed to contend all night for Peter, locked inside his prison gates? "So Peter was kept in the prison, but prayer for him was being made fervently by the *ekklesia* to God" (Acts 12:5).

*4. Sometimes a shout is needed.* Obviously, prayer is not about volume, per se. Prayer is about walking in stride with the Holy Spirit. But the Holy Spirit not only reveals His strategies, He also conveys His moods. Prayer should be viewed more holistically than the words we speak. We should be in sync with the larger rhythms of our divine supply. The idea of integrity in prayer as a matter of cooperation with God means that we stay ultra-sensitive to what He is doing. Sometimes He is quiet. Sometimes He is laughing (as in Psalm 2), but war often brings a shout, and to deny the moment is to deny the power and the victory of the sound of Heaven. We see this both with Gideon's trumpets and Jehoshaphat's worshippers. A loud and raucous noise is sometimes a high and holy thing, which only self-righteous pretensions would deny. In Numbers 10:1-10 the assembly (Heb: 'qahal'; Gr: 'ekklesia') was both summoned with a trumpet, and also commissioned to war by the alarm of the trumpets. It was this noise by which the Lord promised to remember them and "be saved from your enemies" (v. 9). War trumpets are not blown softly.

So while prayer is not about shouting, sometimes shouting is necessary. Thus we come to Jericho, perhaps one of the clearest examples of contending prayer in the Bible.

Jericho, we are told, was "tightly shut...no one went out and no one came in." This heavily fortified city was locked down. No one was getting through those gates, or over those walls. How will Israel triumph? After Joshua meets with Lord Sabaoth, he is given the key to victory.

- "March around the city, all the men of war circling the city once...for six days."
- "Also seven priests shall carry seven trumpets of rams' horns before the ark."
- "On the seventh day you shall march around the city seven times, and the priests shall blow the trumpets. And it shall be that when they make a long blast with the ram's horn, and when you hear the sound of the trumpet, all the people shall shout with a great shout, and the wall of the city will fall down flat."

This is lunacy! This is a crazy battle plan! And yet, it is so unusually specific. Do you believe that the Lord would give such clear revelation today? If not, why not? Are our gates any easier than Jericho's? Is He the same yesterday, today and forever...or not? Most importantly, did the plan work? By contrast, are our clever, sane and respectable plans working?

You know the story. Israel surrounds this heavily fortified city, carving a path of daily, obedient prayer until rulership is gained and the day of trumpets comes, the shout—Luther's "one little word will fell him"—by which the walls fall.

But make no mistake, they *had* to shout. Victory was not assured without it. If a moment of prayer calls for a barbaric cry, and you continue to speak your eloquent supplication in soft tones, it doesn't matter how right your words, the prayer is void. Yet it is equally mistaken to think contending prayer *is* the shout. Too many intercessors spend all their time shouting, thinking they are contending. Jericho shows us that the final word is actually simple if we've done the steady business of surrounding, contending prayer. The shout was brief. The walls fell.

Victory.

# 15

## PUTTING IT ALL TOGETHER

C.S. Lewis said, "Christianity is the story of how the rightful King has landed, you might say in disguise, and is calling us all to take part in His great campaign of sabotage."[181]

In war or sabotage, it is imperative to know four things:

- Who you are (and therefore, which side you are on)?
- Who is the enemy?
- What is your part?
- What resources are at your disposal?

A restatement of the above would be: in war, as in life, identity is crucial. Jesus said, "I know where I came from, and where I am going" (John 8:14).

A person's identity also represents *value*. Today, identity theft is rampant. In the United States, ten million people are victims of identity-based fraud schemes annually, including illegally obtained information from credit cards, utilities, bank, employment, loan and government sources. The repercussions include being stripped of their savings and credit ratings, thrown into disputes with lenders, stockbrokers and even law enforcement. All because their identities had been stolen and put to criminal use.

When 32-year-old former dishwasher, Abraham Abdallah, pleaded guilty in a New York court to masterminding an identity theft scheme, his crime was valued at $80 million. Abdallah had taken 800 fake credit cards, as well as 20,000 credit card blanks. He had managed to steal the identities of Steven Spielberg and Paul Allen and gained credit records for Warren Buffett, George Lucas and Oprah Winfrey.[182] For Abdallah and his wealthy victims, identity translated directly to dollars and power.

Identity also equals *privilege.* In the military, rank is everything. You salute every rank ahead of you, and are in turn saluted by every rank under you. We know our law enforcement and civil servants according to their identity. We know the difference between police officers, senators, governors, and diplomats. Yet each of these identities comes with a certain rank, which could be understood as the ability to commit to a plan of action, draw upon necessary resources, engage others, and achieve results.

This section has been all about achieving results. The ekklesia is meant to produce results for the kingdom of God in the earth, but results are contingent on proper identity. We must know we are the ekklesia if we are to act like the ekklesia. That is why it is such a big deal that something has gotten lost in translation. Literally.

Church. Assembly. Congregation. Ekklesia. It's all the same, right?

PTA. Town Hall. Police Academy. Congress. It's all the same, right?

Clearly, no. C.S. Lewis put it this way, "All mortals tend to turn into the thing they are pretending to be."

Are you pretending to be a church member, or a member of God's parliament? When a typical Sunday morning dawns, do you wake up thinking: "I'm going to church this morning" or "I'm about to take my place in the Divine Senate"? The difference could be compared to a man in Revolutionary France saying to his wife, "I'm off to my book club, dear," or "Honey, I've just joined the Resistance!" Where might the ekklesia be today if, instead of thinking like "the church" for the last four centuries, they thought like a "ruling council"? Every single time "two or three have gathered together in My name" a Conclave of Righteous Decrees has convened. An Executive Council, a Territorial Tribunal, a Dominion Caucus....a Parliament of War Statesmen! You cannot read the resulting impact of the convening of the ekklesia—hell assaulted, binding and loosing, etc.— and not see the heroic actions of people taking their stand as agents of the will of God on earth. When we assemble, we become the Son of David's "Mighty Men."

---

**When a typical Sunday morning dawns, do you wake up thinking: "I'm going to church this morning" or "I'm about to take my place in the Divine Senate"?**

---

Several decades ago, the phrase "The spirit is willing but the flesh is weak" was given to a translation machine to be rendered into Japanese word for word. The result in English: "There is some good whiskey, but the roast beef is mediocre." A similar story is told of an American preacher, ministering in Korea. When he said to his audience, "I'm tickled to death to be here." The confused translator, who did not understand the English phrase, told the audience, "I scratch and scratch until I die."

What's the point? *If we don't translate ekklesia correctly, nothing makes sense.* Our own job description becomes a muddled mess. And so we must close as we began, needing true revelation. A recognition of Christ, properly conceived by the Spirit and birthed in us, will always produces a reciprocal revelation of ourselves. When Peter recognized Jesus as the Christ, Jesus recognized Peter as a rock. He didn't just give Peter a new name, He gave a job description.

Hebrew linguist Benjamin Lee Whorf said, "Language shapes the way we think, and determines what we can think about." What do you *think* about when you identify yourself as a "church member?"

If the evidence of this book is true, then confront yourself with this question: is your "church member" identity the right identity? It's not enough to say, "I'm not a church member, I'm a Christian." No, if you are in Christ, you are part of the ekklesia. Does your thinking reflect the goals and aims of Christ? If Whorf is right, our language has not only shaped us, it has perhaps also deformed us. If I have made the case well and rightly, then the first step is to repent of allowing our mission to be defined by the wrong word, for the wrong word produces wrong understanding. The fact that "church life" is now so culturally engrained that we cannot fathom how to change it is not an excuse to stay in the this rut. But what can be done?

### Shifting culture one little word at a time

I am crying out for a new reformation. With Luther's great hymn, I posit that "one little word will fell him." I assure you, Satan is terrified of the ekklesia. If we truly become governmentally organized around the mission of Christ, Satan knows his gates are doomed. By contrast, he has no reason to fear the church, because *Jesus never promised to prevail against the gates of Hades with church.* One little word makes all the difference! The Big Word, of course, is *always* Christ. But the little word that can revolutionize our thinking, galvanize our will and more dynamically mobilize our assembling is *ekklesia.*

How is that we call Him Lord and King, but refuse to use the Word as He spoke it, especially in light of Jesus's own warning in Mat. 7:24-25, which describes a wise building as hearing His word and acting upon *that* Word? Before you read this book, ignorance was an acceptable excuse. After reading, you are responsible for the truth you understand. We must not refuse to correct our use of the word *church*. We need to shed our old identity and radically align ourselves with the ruling council inaugurated in Matthew 16. Fear of man and love of tradition must not cause us to basically say, "C'mon, Jesus, is it that big of a deal? Did you really mean what you said, because, frankly, it doesn't seem important enough to matter. We're doing just fine with our substitute word and substitute system, thank you very much!"

Don't kid yourself. We are not doing fine with our substitute word.

Everywhere we turn in our post-Christian culture, we hear desperate calls for moral leadership to stem the rising tide. Justice and hope are rare, prized commodities. The world is searching for answers like never before. Those answers will not be found in Washington, London or Beijing. They will not be found in more money for education, or in fixing Social Security. The vitriol and polarization of our public debate, along with the profound interconnectedness of the new global society, make true and genuine reform almost unachievable from a purely human standpoint. Our leaders are simply not wise enough to untangle this mess. Add in the wild cards of rogue nations and demonized international leaders, the bizarre trends in weather, economic volatility, plus shocking levels of immorality increasingly being written into law, and you have a toxic recipe for disaster on every front.

In other words, the gates of Hades loom large. What can be done? Pray, yes. But who and how and why? The "praying church" is a misnomer. For countless generations, this has been attempted with only nominal success. The necessity of prayer is deeply woven into the typology and function of both the ekklesia and the Bride, but it is rather incidental to church, which is why the church rolls without it. Churchianity simply does not see prayer as fundamental to its mission. Perhaps this is why a true, praying church has been so hard to develop and sustain. Meanwhile, prayer *is indispensable to the ekklesia.* The ekklesia could no more abandon prayer than a Senator could do his job without voting. Prayer that changes history is fundamental to our DNA.

Are we fated to doom? G.K. Chesterton said, "I do not believe in a fate that falls on men however they act; but I do believe in a fate that falls on them *unless* they act."

Faith, prayer and action germinate into destiny. Some like to think that destiny is a river you ride and it carries you where it will, i.e. fate. But if fate is a river, then free will is a paddle to guide our vessel, and prayer is a miracle power to change the course of the river itself.

In Disney's *The Lion King,* though the young cub Simba was born to be king, a mistake caused him to end up living a "Hakuna Matata" life, with no worries, no responsibilities. Everything changed when he received a vision of his father telling him, "Remember who you are!" What happened? He deposed the false king. He started to rule.

According to Matthew 16, you *cannot receive a revelation of Christ and remain the church.* You must become who He says you are. You have been summoned to deliberate, legislate, and exert the will of God against demonic systems, injustice and false ideologies.

Ekklesia, remember who you are!

## A charter for the new mindset

Let's say you're redecorating your home. As part of the renovations, you decide to enlarge the painting hung over your mantle, or your bed. You get a new picture. When this happens, you can't fit the newly enlarged picture into the frame of your old picture. *You have to get a new frame.* For this entire book to be meaningful, we have to get a new frame of mind.

I would like to propose the following *Ten Commandments of Ekklesia.* The Ten "C's" aren't really commandments, per se, but instead represent the governing values for those who sign up to begin governing in prayer. To be consistent with Biblical guidance, the ekklesia must be:

1. **Corporate:** Two or three, or more, but not one.
2. **Covenantal:** Bonded in unity of voice, purpose and love for one another. Pastoral care and sacramental elements remain vital to "body life." Five-fold ministry remains vital to ekklesial well-being.
3. **Clean:** Pure in heart, maturing in union with Christ, divorced from sinful habits, established in the word of righteousness. Growing in sanctification and the fruit of the Spirt, washed by sound teaching of the Word.
4. **Christ-centered:** Revelation of Jesus is preeminent. Worship is central. Also, to be Christ-centered means we are not concerned with personal status, while "programs" are valued only to the degree they increase effectiveness of Body life, Bridal love, or Council strength.
5. **Contextual:** Meetings are geographically local, with a clear and consistent prayer charter typically focused on regional issues.
6. **Compassionate:** Invested emotionally and financially in the people and mission of their region for the sake of justice, restoration and love.
7. **Consecrated:** Members are set apart, called out, with a clear sense of duty and responsibility. They faithfully "show up" when the council meets. They are committed.

**8. Controlled by Spirit:** Dependent on the Holy Spirit and committed to obedience; also, developing an active spirit of listening, including dreams, discernment, prophetic unction, and other divine revelation.

**9. Clear purpose:** Clear moral objectives are met with targeted intercession (i.e. abortion, drug trafficking, government corruption, etc.)

**10. Contending spirit:** Manifested through disciplined prayer, fasting and sacrifice. Will not yield to setback, delay or frustration.

**Wanted: Thousands of Small Gideon Bands**

Perhaps no story is more fitting to end with than that of Gideon. Gideon is a study in the power of divine revelation, authority to bind and loose, the reality of evil, and the power of small, courageous bands of faith. Read the story in Judges 6, then follow with me as I outline a trail of themes below:

First, Gideon was told to physically "pull down the altar of Baal which belongs to your father, and cut down the Asherah that is beside it." Obviously, evil is real. Territorial demonic control centers are real. Gideon was not battling a symbol. He was not told to persuade the locals to "change their mind," or "replace the Baal metaphor with a new Yahweh metaphor." Before any victory over the felt oppression of Midian could occur socially, politically or economically, Gideon had to demonstrate fidelity and repentance within his own home over the entrenched, invisible principality, Baal. We are told that Israel did what was evil in the sight of the Lord, for which the Lord "gave them into the hands of Midian...and the power of Midian prevailed." Baal worship was a gate by which Midian prevailed.

# Ekklesia Rising

Before Gideon could break Midian, he had to break the gate of idol worship. By prevailing upon this gate in his own life, he was positioned for the authority necessary to bring wholesale deliverance to the nation. The process for Gideon begins with revelation (it always does!), when the Lord sends a prophet to remind them of God's power and to reveal their apostasy. After this, the angel of the Lord brings direct instruction to Gideon. This was the first of several "keys" of revelation leading to total victory.

On this topic, it is very interesting to me that the angel of the Lord came to Gideon as he was secretly threshing wheat in a wine press in order to save it from Midianite raiders. Several months before I began laboring on this book, I had a dream in which Lou Engle asked me to produce an album for a band called Iron and Wine. I understood in the dream that there was a sound being prepared, that musicians were coming, but that my job was to add the ministry of the Word to the music. Now, as you may remember from Chapter 8, the ekklesia of Old Testament Israel was called *qahal* in Hebrew. They were summoned by music, the sound of trumpets. In the Greek city-states, the ekklesia were summoned by a trumpet or a town crier. The ekklesia of Christ is summoned by the voice of the Holy Spirit. In my dream, a summons had gone out out, but I was supposed to put words to it. Months after this dream, I began to investigate Matthew 16 in earnest. As a former pastor, I was familiar with the Greek word, ekklesia, having taught on it as "church" just like everyone else. I had never done a proper word study. Like most pastors, I assumed the standard line of interpretation which I myself had been taught by others. I had no idea how clearly an *iron* rod of rulership would emerge from my study. Yet here in Judges 6, Gideon is hiding in a *wine vat* when the angel of the Lord summons him to rule Midian with Lord Saboath's rod of iron. This is not accidental. Movements of the Holy Spirit are often compared to things like fire, water, wind and wine. The wine is the sweetness of His name, the pleasure of His presence. It is rightly intoxicating in the most holy fashion. But that is not enough. Iron must be added to the wine if we are to advance the kingdom.

> "And the Lord looked at him and said, "Go in this your strength and deliver Israel from the hand of Midian. Have I not sent you?" (v. 14).

As the governing arm of Christ, the ekklesia are called to band together in prayer. As an invasion force they are sent. As previously stated, Matthew 16 must be understood as the Preamble to the Great Commission. The Lord says to Gideon, "Have I not sent you?"

Gideon responds with typical reservations based on size, influence and numbers.

> "O Lord, how shall I deliver Israel? Behold, my family is the least in Manasseh, and I am the youngest in my father's house" (v. 15).

Hundreds and thousands of home prayer groups exist in every nation of the earth. The majority of these little Gideon bands feel disconnected from any larger sense of purpose. Many feel *uncom-missioned*, or powerless. They are not! As God will soon confirm to Gideon, He doesn't need or want great numbers. In fact, the opposite appears more true, in that He often prefers small companies to great armies.[183] When Gideon amasses 30,000 men, God immediately begins trimming their numbers to a fraction of that total. Human strength is never going to win the battles of our day. Relative to the 30,000 men he had, and the "120,000 swordsmen"[184] he faced, Gideon's final 300 was basically a company of "two or three" in comparison their foe. But they had something going for them. Actually, two things: the presence of Lord Sabaoth, and an extraordinary spirit of unity among that small band.

But the Lord said to him, "Surely I will be with you, and you shall defeat Midian *as one man*" (v. 24)

In battle, in prayer, we are one army. We operate with one mind, the mind of Christ. We speak with one voice. Israel was often called to battle as twelve tribes acting in harmony...in *symphony*! This is the power of agreement. But what happens when some don't join the fight? How many Gideon bands are just muddling along with respectable little prayer meetings, doing nothing to shake the heavens and change the earth? How many prayer meetings end up spending more time on how Aunt Mabel stubbed her big toe than wielding a rod of authority? Some might say, well, it's all in God's hands, we can't really change it. Since He is sovereign, prayer is for personal communion, not for shaping the outcome of moral conflicts or toppling systems of injustice. But when Deborah sang her song in Judges 5, as she recounts the heroic deeds of several tribes, she also complains about those who chose to sit on the sidelines. She said that Gilead remained across the Jordan, Dan stayed in ships, and Asher sat at the seashore. In the end, a terrifying pronouncement is made.

> "'Curse Meroz,' said the angel of the Lord, 'Utterly curse its inhabitants; *because they did not come to the help of the Lord,* to the help of the Lord against the warriors.'" (Judges 5:23).

Meroz did not come to the help of the Lord against His enemies. Now, does the Lord *need* help? Of course not. Nevertheless, does He want us to engage, join our brothers, and learn rulership? Yes! It is not without purpose that He "trains my hands for war, and my fingers for battle" (Psa. 144:1). Deborah said the Lord is blessed when "the leaders lead and the people follow."[185] Take your place, join together, and fight!

Now when Gideon was told to pull down the altar of Baal and cut down the Asherah beside it, he was given a key piece of revelation—a gate-breaking assignment. His later mission against the Midainite army was pointless if he did not first prevail against the gate within his own community. This Baal idol was so big and heavy it required yoking two bulls to topple the demonic structure. The Asherah pole was basically a tree that had been whittled into into the shape of a fertility goddess. Because of their construction, Asherah poles *had roots into the land.* Deeply rooted demonic structures must be uprooted.

We know the local power of this idol because the men of the city demanded that Gideon's father, Joash, surrender his son to be put to death as a result of his actions. The village elders were terrified that Gideon had brought a curse on them because he had torn down the altar of their false god, when in fact Gideon was launching a full-frontal assault to deliver them from that very curse. Though he was delivering them, they hated him for it. *Gates have control over the thoughts and emotions of those within their sphere of influence.* Again, Baal's idol was not a symbol. When Joash challenged the men to let Baal defend himself "because someone has *torn down his altar*" (v.31), he was confirming that the idol was *the physical property of a demonic spirit.* This "god" exerted power over the minds of the men of Israel, and caused them to resist the true God's efforts to save them.

Thus, it was not enough to uproot the idols. *It is never enough to uproot idols.* Though you begin with repentance, you must conclude with dominion. Something must replace what you have destroyed or spirits seven times worse will fill the void.[186] Years ago, Lou Engle was given a vision of Christian houses of prayer contending with every other false house of prayer in the earth: Buddhism, Islam, Wicca, etc. Every victory we achieve must be matched with a house of prayer that continues to occupy that ground. Likewise, Gideon was instructed to:

> "**Build an altar to the Lord your God on the top of this stronghold** in an orderly manner, and take a second bull and offer a burnt offering with the wood of the Asherah which you shall cut down" (v. 29).

To build atop a false idol requires blood, sweat and tears. It requires sacrifice. It will cost us to demonstrate the dominion of Christ. Oh, but what joy! This is our challenge, our great privilege, our delight, to be be *His* ekklesia, scattered around the face of the planet, challenging gross darkness and monumental foes until the light of dawn breaks forth.

Though Gideon's task was barely begun, in a sense, it was also already won, having dethroned the principal idol and raising an altar to the Lord in its place. Of course, he still had significant tests ahead and more keys to acquire, i.e. let the fearful depart, release those who lap the water like dogs, use a torch and a pot. Crazy stuff. Intercessory weirdness. More faith challenges. It wasn't easy. A tenacious spirit is part of your ekklesial job description. But eventually, that small band of two or three (hundred) brought about a huge victory for the people of God, and a massive humiliation for the enemy.

"*Upon this rock I will build my ekklesia, and the gates of Hades shall not prevail.*"

As Derek Prince said, "If, at times, our position with Christ on the throne seems remote or unreal, the reason is simple: we have not received the revelation that the Holy Spirit, through the Scriptures, makes available to us. Without this revelation, we can neither understand nor enjoy the benefits of our heavenly citizenship. Instead of reigning as kings, we find ourselves still toiling as slaves...

Until Gideon got a revelation, Israel lived as slaves under the rule of Midian. So while all Christians look forward to the day when

Christ's enemies will be completely subdued—and the Bible promises that day will come—we must not let that promised, future glory blind us to our responsibility. In the face of all the forces of evil, it falls to us to demonstrate that Christ is already *"Lord of lords, and King of kings"* (Rev. 17:14).[187]

In light of this, a paraphrase of Matthew 16 might help. Imagine Jesus speaking the following directly to you:

> **"Upon the revelation of My true identity and anointing for rulership, I am now convening outposts of divine legislation that will continue to advance My kingdom until I return. These gatherings will be consumed by My zeal to bring justice and peace to the earth. Because I am the Christ, My executive assemblies shall possess an inherently offensive capacity and disposition, enough that death itself cannot resist My glorious plan. With your eyes fixed on Me, you will utilize the authority I grant to open and shut upon earth as if I myself were opening and shutting in heaven. And thus My Kingdom come, My will be done. Thus, together, in unity, you are my ekklesia."**

Amen! Brothers and sisters, let's get to it.

# MY NOTES

_____

_____

_____

_____

_____

_____

_____

_____

_____

_____

_____

_____

_____

_____

_____

_____

_____

_____

# REALITY
# CHECK

---

*"From that time Jesus Christ began to show His disciples that He must go to Jerusalem, and suffer many things."*

---

"That word above all earthly powers,
no thanks to them, abideth;
the Spirit and the gifts are ours,
thru him who with us sideth.
Let goods and kindred go,
this mortal life also;
the body they may kill;
God's truth abideth still;
his kingdom is forever."

Verse 4: *A Mighty Fortress is Our God*
– **Martin Luther**

# 16

## A CAUTION AGAINST TRIUMPHALISM

**C**hrist, the Anointed One, *always* overpowers the strong man. Two thousand years ago, in a devastating showdown on a Roman gibbet, they met in climactic battle. Threatened with brutal torment, Lord Sabaoth did not blink. He endured the Cross, descended into Hades, and burst forth three days later, alive forever more. Since the Cross is a finished work, His triumph is now forever complete. No more can be added to it, nor can anything be taken away. In His resurrection, Christ has been exalted to the highest place, seated at the right hand of God, and given the name above every name. Soon, history itself will confirm what heaven knows for a fact. In the interim, a doomed, vanquished enemy continues to thrash and rage and inflict great pain on many multitudes, while simultaneously a holy kingdom continues to quietly spread like leaven in a lump of dough. This is a mystery. We live in this mystery. The sovereign plan of God dwarfs our ability to fully comprehend it.

During His earthly ministry, Jesus routinely demonstrated total supremacy over every challenging power. Not a single instance of concession, negotiation or compromise is recorded, whether with human leaders like Herod, by the pressure of his own friends, or Satan himself. He demonstrated total authority over every sphere of life...even *trees*, *waves* and *weather*. A legion of demons melted under His will like wax before a flame. Sickness and disease fled. Death retreated. Every clever scheme of man, every falsehood, was exposed. He was never tricked, never fooled, never lacking power for any occasion, and never afraid. If God-as-man continually drove demons from the real estate of man's dusty frame, He is committed to uprooting and displacing them wherever they may found amongst the dust of earth.

As this book makes plain, we have received His commission: rule.

---

## Only *His* rule is complete, *ours* is not.

---

However, only *His* rule is complete, *ours* is not. As we seek to boldly follow in His footsteps, it is important to humbly admit our limitations. Thus, as a final statement on ekklesia, we must temper our aspirations with a necessary caution against what may be called Triumphalism. Mind you, everything in this book stands. We cannot receive an ekklesial charge timidly, nor surrender to low expectations. But neither should we adopt an air of supreme authority. Quite the opposite, the truths of this book are not a license to stride into any situation like Dirty Harry, pointing our .44 Magnum of prayer at little punk demons, boasting, "Make my day." Any model of triumph defined by worldly standards will only hinder our ultimate purpose—conformity of all things to Christ—for the wisdom of the world is never in accord with the mind of Christ.

As we seek to grow in rulership, it is incumbent that we grow even more in humility. Our ways are not His ways, our thoughts are not His thoughts. The fullness of our authority is but a dim reflection of His. If the message of the ekklesia is managed improperly in carnal hearts, it can easily lend itself to an attitude of elitism, machismo and bravado. Friends, we are not the swaggering commandos of God, we are servants of the Most High. To counter any magnetic attraction of our hearts toward petty ambition or domineering and know-it-all egotism, an inverse relationship must be established, so that the inward character of our call must go as low as the heights of influence we might aspire to. We need to inoculate our hearts with truth. We don't need to temper Triumphalism, or minimize it, we need to completely deflate it. The three vaccinations that will keep us bowed low before the majesty of God are 1) The sacrificial nature of our service; 2) An understanding of necessary offense; 3) The call to be a faithful witness.

*1. Sacrificial Service.* Immediately after Jesus forms His triumphant government in Matthew 16, He immediately acts to counter any carnal, Triumphalist spirit that might already be stirring in his young band of disciples.[188] First, he forbids His new cabinet from issuing any press release. Generating headlines and personal acclaim is the last thing the ekklesia of Christ is to be concerned with. Second, He declares that his master plan for taking over the planet involves Him (gasp!)…dying? In other words, triumph will cost him His life. And not just any kind of death, mind you. Lord Sabaoth was about to be tortured and humiliated in the most cruel, degrading ways possible: mocked, spit upon, cursed, flayed, bruised, beaten, stripped, nailed to a tree, and run through with a spear, in full view of the public.

Peter, who emerged only three minutes prior from the euphoric whirlwind of divine revelation, in which he received a personal commendation from the planet's God-King, shows just how easily the new power can go to our head. Jesus proclaims the backwards kingdom of death as the path to life. Rulership emerges as acts of consecration and sacrifice. Victory goes to the weak and the humble, not the proud and the strong. The Way of the Cross is how we go with, rather than against, the grain of the universe. Unless a grain of wheat falls into the ground and dies, it remains alone, but if it is willing to follow the self-contradicting path in which it surrenders its own agenda and forfeits its own rights, it brings forth much fruit.

If you're like me, you can sympathize with the disciples for not getting this. Jesus declares their victory against Hades itself—travels all the way to Caeserea Phillipi to make the point—forms His first council, then tells them He must travel to Jerusalem, not in triumph as King, but as the prophesied Suffering Servant. Only in total contradiction to the enemy's pride and power-mongering will He can secure the authority by which His own council can rule effectively. And so we see our own path, in self-abnegation, the death of ego, the crucifixion of personal glory. These form their own moral authority, their own challenge to corrupt uses of power.

---

**We have no authority in prayer if
the Spirit of Christ does not prevail in our midst.**

---

It's a confounding message, utterly contrary to all our instincts. And that's the point. Rulership in the Kingdom of God must be predicated on extreme fidelity to Kingdom values. The Sermon on the Mount—"turn the other cheek, go the second mile, consider yourself blessed when men revile and persecute you"— offers Kingdom values that are utterly contrary to human nature. As such, the covenantal community must not interact casually with one another when we pray, prophesy, decree, teach and worship, as if the opposites of these virtues—jealousy, pettiness, vainglory, gossip, hatred, revenge—were trivial temptations. In an atmosphere rich with grace and love, fully aware of human weakness, we must lovingly and firmly challenge one another whenever Self begins to rear its ugly head and seek to take control of our legislative sessions. We have no authority in prayer if the Spirit of Christ does not prevail in our midst. The divine agenda is no place for pork-barrel politics.

We follow the Cross, *because it is the way* to the authority Christ promised.

A divine government shared among fallible mortals cannot, must not, operate any other way. In other words, the messianic identity of Christ must not be confused with the messianic modality of Cross. Dietrich Bonhoeffer said, "The figure of the Crucified invalidates all thought which takes success for its standard."[189]

Peter, who has been (and will be again), so instrumental in launching this new movement, just doesn't get it. Poor Peter! Poor me! Poor you! Having read this book, having written it, we, like Peter, may be so flush with ekklesial authority and visions of swift and painless triumph dancing in our head, that we may likely go out and totally blow it.

Peter actually tells Jesus that He's wrong! The Christ, revealed, is now the Christ corrected. Peter's got this all figured out.

> "Peter took Him aside and began to rebuke Him, saying, 'God forbid it, Lord! This shall never happen to You.' (To go to Jerusalem and die).
>
> But He turned and said to Peter, 'Get behind Me, Satan! You are a stumbling block to Me; for you are not setting your mind on God's interests, but man's.'" (v. 22-23).

We actually further the influence of Satan's counterfeit government if we seek to live, pray or govern apart from sacrificial servanthood.

> "Then Jesus said to His disciples, 'If anyone wishes to come after Me, let him deny himself, and take up his cross, and follow Me. For whoever wishes to save his life shall lose it; but whoever loses his life for My sake shall find it'" (v. 24-25).

The allure of worldly power, "might makes right", political schemes, status, money, along with building and protecting an impressive reputation, "my way or the highway" arrogance and autocratic dictates—even if these tactics and/or values are employed successfully for good and right causes—actually subvert, nay, spoil, the very kingdom triumphs we seek to achieve. N.T. Wright explains:

> "Paul's treatment of the cross (is) the means of the defeat of the powers. As everyone in the Roman world knew well, the cross already had a clear symbolic meaning; it meant that Caesar ruled the world, with cruel death as his ultimate, and regular, weapon. For Paul, throughout his writings, the cross is far more than simply the means whereby individual sins are forgiven, though of course it is that as well. It is the means whereby the powers are defeated and overthrown (1 Cor. 2:6-8; Col. 2:13-15). The resurrection demonstrates that the true God has a power utterly superior to that of Caesar. The cross is thus to be seen, with deep and rich paradox, as the secret power of this true God, the power of self-giving love which (as Jesus said it would) subverts the power of the tyrant (Mk. 10:35-45).[190]

When we follow the way of the Cross, we lay down the tyrant of Self. Your choices will cost you money, time, maybe even friendships. Setbacks await, perseverance will be needed. That's not meant to be predictive, merely honest. We live in a fallen world. We take our stand, and sometimes that stand is not popular, so we suffer for it. Sometimes we do it poorly, in pride or arrogance, and we are disciplined by God. Sometimes we do it well, and suffer anyway.

Is this so strange, when we follow One who "did not regard equality with God a thing to be grasped, but emptied Himself, taking the form of a bond-servant, and being made in the likeness of men... humbled Himself by becoming obedient to the point of death, even death on a cross" (Phil. 2:6-8)?

Veering from the way of the Cross will pervert our perception of justice, causing us to pray, bind and loose things with which Heaven does *not* agree, and will not ratify. Furthermore, we risk becoming arrogant in our relationships with one another, along with other ekklesia who are also commissioned to serve and rule. In this mode, houses of prayer become competitive with one another, full of posturing people with no real power or spiritual authority, because they departed the path of Christ the moment triumph became their goal.

This type of triumphalist mentality will eventually manifest as lording our convictions over others. We will prize our success and prowess in prayer, we will come to be defined by it, so much that we take it personally if God doesn't jump when we say jump. We will no longer internalize the burdens of injustice for which we intercede, but rather our own need for vindication. We will boast about our results, supposedly for God's glory, though really it is for our own visibility. Before long, our motivations will subtly shift. We will not be poured out for others, nor will we abide by kingdom values. Our goals will be personal gain.

Paul said, "Do nothing from selfishness or empty conceit, but with humility of mind let each of you regard one another as more important than himself; do not merely look out for your own personal interests, but also for the interests of others." He said we should "have this attitude in yourselves which was also in Christ Jesus..." (Phil. 2:3-4, 6).

The attitude of Jesus—Man, God, Lord, King and Christ—was more interested in others than Himself. He was Lamb and Servant. He carried a towel.

He did nothing unless it was on His Father's agenda. Satan tempted Him. Men tried to promote Him. Jesus declined every coronation of fame.

Be careful, friend. If you think of a ruling council as an authorization to pursue your own success, you stand *within* the gates of Hades. You have no power to topple them.

*2. Necessary Offense.* It may be argued by some that any message which urges believers to a militant, authoritative posture, sanctioned to bind and loose, told their efforts can shape history and break demonic strongholds, is only setting people up for offense should their "mission" in prayer fail. Lurking in this rather sensible warning, much like a parent trying to tamper their children's unrealistic dreams, is the expectation of failure. A parent has much more experience in the school of hard knocks, so it seems wise and loving to spare your kids the pain of disappointment. Don't aim too high, then the crash won't hurt so much. And partially, it is wise and loving, precisely because it's true. Failure is possible. With failure comes the risk of disillusionment.

Perhaps it is more fair to say: expect *both*, because to a certain degree, both are guaranteed. We are on a journey of rulership, convened not because Jesus trusts weak and foolish people to always get it right, but because He loves the process of growing us into maturity, and because He trusts the Holy Spirit to lead, guide, correct and heal our disappointments along the way. Not one person, nor any ekklesial band of brothers, is ever assured perpetual triumph. The reasons are numerous. We're imperfect. We're selfish and small-minded. We struggle to hear and understand. We lack faith. We drift into sin. We yell at our children or our spouse, then lose inner confidence that God hears our prayers. In sum, we do not always understand the larger purpose of God, nor do we fully comprehend the keys and strategies He wishes us to employ.

In spite of this, He still summoned us. He convened the council, put the keys in our hands, and told us to rule in our generation.

So…nothing ventured, nothing gained! Though our faith will not be weakened if we never fail, it will also never be strengthened if we never succeed. David's faith was ready for Goliath because he had already practiced his rulership against lions and bears. How will we stand before the Goliaths of our day, how will we not shrink back in fear when Goliath comes, if we have no history on which to draw?

A favorite quote attributed to General Stonewall Jackson is appropriate here: "Duty is ours; consequences are God's." Saint Augustine said it this way, "Pray like it all depends on God and work like it all depends on you."

But really, even this misses the point. Jesus said, "Woe to the world because of its stumbling blocks! For it is inevitable that stumbling blocks come; but woe to that man through whom the stumbling block comes!" (Mat. 18:7). In the context of the previous verses, many believe sins are the stumbling blocks ("offenses" KJV). Jesus had just called a child to His side. Tenderly, with the child in full view, he urges His listeners to become like children if they wish to "enter the kingdom of heaven." He urges them to humble themselves, and to receive such children in His name, and then He gives the woeful pronouncement about the world's stumbling blocks. While this should sober us, it may be inappropriate to make His caution a warning against sinful behaviors that prevent others from getting saved, as it is commonly understood. Woe to the one who causes one of these little ones *from entering the kingdom!* In the entire panoply of sins, we must not forget unbelief. In the book of Hebrews, unbelief is the predominant sin. Jesus constantly warned His disciples against unbelief. Paul said, "Whatever is not from faith is sin" (Rom. 14:23).

Though offenses will come, Jesus never preached a lesson to dampen our expectations. The Son of God never offered a theology for unanswered prayer. He simply told us to ask, seek, knock. Pray! Believe! When we invest ourselves enough in Heaven's values to forbid their antithesis on earth, we cannot help but expose our heart to disappointment, but if we do not believe enough to matter, then why pray? For the wise and cautious critics of radical prayer, I must ask, why would Jesus tell us to bind, loose, pray, forgive, permit, forbid, heal, exorcise, resurrect and influence if He did not mean for us to actually succeed in doing those things? So when we succeed, the kingdom is released externally. But when we fail, in the suffering of that moment, the kingdom is released *internally*. And this, too, is good.

The Lord is not so worried or concerned about the former that He will neglect the opportunities of the latter. Offense may not be pleasant or preferred, but sometimes it is necessary to remind us that "without Him we can do nothing." If we reach for nothing, if we strive to rattle no gates and storm no strongholds, then we forego the humbling work of "discipleship by disappointment," because part of the Lord's goodness and promises is to make all things, even failure, work together for our good.[191] It may seem wise and reasonable, but it is actually foolish to lower our expectations simply to avoid the possibility of offense. In God's wisdom, this offense serves to vaccinate us against pride.

In fact, sometimes the consequence of our failure is more glorious than the mode of our success. Other times, small failures become part of a larger tactical plan by which Lord Sabaoth seeks an even greater victory. Other times, failure in a minor test is the only way to prepare the ekklesia for greater tests to come. In all of these, God is supreme, and we are not.

*3. Faithful Witness.* The typical Western notion of "success" is far too short-term. In the 1980's, when American industry was floundering against the Japanese, I remember my business professor giving our college class a vivid illustration of short-term versus long-term thinking. At the time, the typical long-range strategic plan for American corporations was forecasted five to ten, maybe twenty years ahead. Meanwhile, the largest, multi-national Japanese corporations were developing 100 and 500 year plans. On the one hand, this is a ludicrous idea. But the point remains, we tend to view success as something that happens now, if not sooner. Since we are linear thinkers, we only succeed when we cross the finish line, not before. Furthermore, *when* we cross it, we expect to know that we have succeeded. But what if the finish line represents an unknowable? Do we have the will, tenacity and foresight to cross it anyway. Do we have the "assurance of things hoped for and the evidence of things not seen" at work in our souls, compelling us forward whether we ever realize "results"? This is a critical question for all those who aspire to become ekklesia, because while we are commanded to exercise dominion, we are not promised a total realization of it.

> "An outstanding example is provided by the career of the prophet Jeremiah. In the opening ten verses of the first chapter of Jeremiah, God declared that He had set Jeremiah apart as 'a prophet to the nations...to root out, and to pull down, and to destroy, and to throw down, to build, and to plant' (1:5, 10).

> What an exalted position for a young man, to be 'set...over the nations and over the kingdoms.' This is authority on a higher plane than the normal forces that shape secular politics. To judge by outward appearances, the subsequent career of Jeremiah gave little indication of such authority. On the contrary, his message was almost universally rejected, and he himself was continually subjected to indignity and persecution. For several months, he languished in prison, and at various times, he was at the point of death, either by execution or starvation.

> Yet, the course of history has vindicated the authority of Jeremiah and his message . . . Twenty-five hundred years have passed. In the light of history, it is now possible to make an objective evaluation. Throughout all the intervening centuries, the destiny of every one of those nations has followed precisely the course foretold by Jeremiah . . . by the prophecies that he uttered, he became the actual arbiter of their destinies."[192]

Time finally vindicated him, but only after Jeremiah was dead and gone. Under short-term scrutiny, the casual observer would assume he was a prophet of little stature.

So it goes. As with Jeremiah, the power is the word of God is not only in what we speak, but *also in the faithfulness of our witness.* We must be content to do our duty and leave the consequence to God. Time will tell the rightness of our positions. Many times we will be blessed to see immediate, favorable results. Sometimes we get it right, sometimes we get it wrong. In God's grace, both are "teachable moments" in the Holy Spirit. Listen to the tale of Clarence Jordan. Ever heard of him?

> "He had two Ph.D.s, one in agriculture and one in Greek and Hebrew. So gifted was he, he could have chosen to do anything he wanted. He chose to serve the poor. In the 1940s, he founded a farm in Americus, Georgia, and called it Koinonia Farm. It was a community for poor whites and poor blacks. As you might guess, such an idea did not go over well in the Deep South of the '40s.

> Ironically, much of the resistance came from good church people who followed the laws of segregation as much as the other folk in town. The town people tried everything to stop Clarence. They tried boycotting him, and slashing workers' tires when they came to town. Over and over, for fourteen years, they tried to stop him.

> Finally, in 1954, the Ku Klux Klan had enough of Clarence Jordan, so they decided to get rid of him once and for all. They came one night with guns and torches and set fire to every building on Koinonia Farm but Clarence's home, which they riddled with bullets. And they chased off all the families except one black family which refused to leave. Clarence recognized the voices of many of the Klansmen, and, as you might guess, some of them were church people. Another was the local newspaper's reporter. The next day, the reporter came out to see what remained of the farm. The rubble still smoldered

and the land was scorched, but he found Clarence in the field, hoeing and planting.

'I heard the awful news,' he called to Clarence, 'and I came out to do a story on the tragedy of your farm closing.' Clarence just kept on hoeing and planting. The reporter kept prodding, kept poking, trying to get a rise from this quietly determined man who seemed to be planting instead of packing his bags. So, finally, the reporter said in a haughty voice, 'Well, Dr. Jordan, you got two of them Ph.D.s and you've put fourteen years into this farm, now there's nothing left of it at all. Just how successful do you think you've been?'

Clarence stopped hoeing, turned toward the reporter with his penetrating blue eyes, and said quietly but firmly, 'About as successful as the cross. Sir, I don't think you understand us. What we are about is not success but faithfulness. We're staying. Good day.'"[193]

Finally let us note again the fact that we are given authority to prevail upon Hades, not Hell. This is a small, but consequential detail that helps realistically deflate Triumphalist notions. Hell, theologically identified as the final judgment upon evil (see Chapter 12), is a post-Millennial reality. As both a destination and a punishment, Hell speaks of the final authority of Christ alone. Our authority is limited in scope to shattering the gates of Hades (the powers and corruptions of death) in this life, but we have no mandate to execute final judgment. It is Christ who will cast Satan, the antichrist, death and Hades into the lake of fire at the conclusion of natural history. This is the inauguration point of the new age of eternal life, and the wedding feast of the Lamb. In other words, *we are eschatologically confined in the totality of our work.* We can and should liberally plunder Hades. Triumph should be the normal diet of the ekklesia, with the upper limit of what is possible having yet to be defined. We should pray in faith and live as faithful witnesses. Even so, we are given no warrant to rob Hell.

To what degree is dominion promised in this life? Biblically, I'm convinced we should assume 99 percent. Anything less and we will believe for too little. Someone has said that the problem with small goals is that you achieve them. Let's agree to push the upper limits of what the ruling council can achieve. Let's put the offense on the field and give the defense a rest. Let's dare to take the battle to the enemy, rather than continuing our present tactic of watching in horror as darkness spills over the gates, as cups of judgement fill to the brim.

Ultimately, rulership is about establishing a beachhead in every generation, culture and nation by being faithful the rule of Christ. Though we never relent in contending for His kingdom to come, nor do we artificially enforce it. We partner and proclaim. Real simple. We live with the expectation that our prayers are heard and acted upon. They matter. As this book closes, I trust you see that part of God's heart written in Scripture in a fresh, clear way. The ekklesia *was* and *is* His idea. He's not sorry for it, but He is waiting on it. Friends, there is no backup plan. We're it. Yet in spite of all this, in the end, *we do not rule because we succeed in total dominion, but because we are faithful to nothing less.*

To the critics, we simply say, "We're staying. Good day."

We live in days of prophesy and promise, when "the people who know their God shall be strong, and carry out great exploits" (Dan. 11:32).

Now go. Gather together. Love one another. Serve. And rule in His name.

# MY NOTES

# APPENDIX

## A Non-Comprehensive Review of the King James Version and Development of Church Culture

### A. A BRIEF HISTORY

1. The Greek word *"kyriakon"* is the generally accepted etymology of the later English word "church." This includes an extended variant, *"Kuriake Oikia"* (the "Lord's House"), which came into use sometime in the 4th century A.D.

2. For well over a thousand years, the Bible was accessible only to those who understood Hebrew, Greek or Latin, limiting its use to a small number of the wealthy, educated, or clergy, far beyond the reach of the common man.

3. The Authorized King James Version of the Bible was the third English translation to be approved by Church authorities in England. King Henry VIII commissioned the first, called the *Great Bible,* in 1535. The second was the *Bishops' Bible* in 1568. "A new English version was conceived in response to the perceived problems of the earlier translations as detected by the Puritans…James gave the translators instructions intended to guarantee that the new version would conform to the ecclesiology and reflect the episcopal structure of the Church of England and its belief in an ordained clergy. The translation was done by 47 scholars, all of whom were members of the Church of England."[194]

4. Prior, the first English *New Testament* was the Tyndale Bible, completed about 1524. Tyndale was a great reformer and

translator in England during the reign of King Henry. He was greatly influenced by Erasmus and Martin Luther and was the first to translate and print considerable parts of the Bible into English for public readership. The newly translated Bible was taken as a direct challenge to nearly every strata of the prevailing religious system, including the Catholic church, the English church and the state.

5.  Tyndale's Bible is credited with being the first English translation to work directly from Hebrew and Greek texts. Interestingly, he refused to use the English word "church" in his translation, save for two instances, and these two instances describe buildings devoted to idol worship—a sacred space or temple devoted to worship. In Acts 19:37, the word *heiron,* which Tyndale translated as church, was used elsewhere to describe both the Temple of Artemis of Ephesus, and the Temple in Jerusalem.

    a.  Acts 14:13 "Then Iupiters Preste which dwelt before their cite brought oxe and garlondes vnto the churche porche and wolde have done sacrifise with the people." (TYN)

    b.  Acts 19:37 "For ye have brought hyther these me[n] whiche are nether robbers of churches nor yet despisers of youre goddes." (TYN)

6.  As permutations of the Greek occurred over time, the word church began to enter the English language sometime prior to the 12th century. Early Anglo-Saxon forms were used in Bible translations as early as 1000 A.D.[195] The 1395 Wycliffe translation used the word "chirche" to translate ekklesia, but, as stated, the 1525 Tyndale version did not. Tyndale properly translated the Greek ekklesia as "assembly" or "congregation"—the literal meaning of the word (though lacking the critical context discussed in this book). Even so, one must ask, why would Tyndale's decision infuriate the state? Why would this make the

institutional church so mad that they would strangle him and burn his body? The reason is simple: power.

a. Kings and Caesars control land, buildings, armies and institutions. Historically, the church has either owned or controlled these things as well. Furthermore, religious notions of law, punishment, blessing and divine endorsement form an enormous power base to help consolidate and legitimize royal interests.

b. As an example of this mentality, consider the view of Constantine, who formalized Christianity as the state religion of Rome. "As *pontifex maximus,* Constantine I favoured the 'Catholic Church of the Christians'...because: 'it is contrary to the divine law...whereby the Highest Divinity may perhaps be roused not only against the human race but also against myself, *to whose care he has by his celestial will committed the government of all earthly things.'*" (emphasis mine)[196]

7. If we want to better understand why King James would authorize the shift towards mistranslation as a matter of official policy, we must sympathetically bear in mind the highly contentious political, religious and social milieu of medieval Europe from which it was born. During the time of his translation, James had a vested, material interest in a strong, state-sanctioned church possessing a well-defined hierarchy owing clear allegiance to the king, a view shared by nearly every European king throughout the Middle Ages. James was motivated partially by the noble goal of fortifying England as a Protestant bastion against Catholic hegemony, but also because the English line of kings (like most royal lines) operated on the notion of Divine Right. In contrast, as an assembly convened and governed directly by Christ, the ekklesia exists outside of state control. History records that James was a devout Anglican and learned Bible scholar who felt

responsible to God alone as "Defender of the Faith." Furthermore, as head of the State church, James faced opposition with the Puritans on the one hand and Catholic papal claims on the other. These may read like historical footnotes, but they were profoundly complicated, consequential royal concerns emerging from a highly charged political environment.

8.  For these reasons, it is said King James well understood: "No building, no bishop, no king." Partially to address this, he created fifteen rules which his translators were bound to follow. Article 1 laid out broad parameters, *"The ordinary Bible read in the Church, commonly called the Bishops Bible, to be followed, and as little altered as the truth of the original will permit."* Problem: the Bishops' Bible used the term congregation, so James narrowed the parameters with Article 3:

    a.  Article 3: *"The old Ecclesiastical Words to be kept, viz.* **the Word Church not to be translated Congregation** *etc."*[197] This rule became the *de facto* translation practice for Mat. 16:18, perpetuating the erroneous use of church in subsequent translations for the next 500 years.

## B. ADRIFT IN CHURCH CULTURE

1.  As the British Empire colonized the world, the influence of the KJV became the presumptive, definitive English translation of holy scriptures. Along with the works of William Shakespeare, the KJV is cited by scholars and historians as one of the greatest influences on the development of modern English. The beauty, forcefulness and structure of its syntax and style became a new, literary gold standard, dynamically influencing the greatest orators and authors of the 18th, 19th and early 20th centuries. As such, the KJV has long been considered the standard by which other translations are judged.

a.  The KJV directly contributed to the spread of Protestantism, which further shaped Evangelical, Pentecostal and mainline denominational paradigms.

2.  Because of the aura and reverence with which it has been treated inside the wider Judeo-Christian culture, the KJV has gone largely unchallenged. Few doubt its extraordinary contributions to the promulgation of the gospel and Western culture at large, nor that it was born out of sincere faith. For the same reasons, the consequences of such a revered translation replacing Jesus's word with the politically motivated dictates of an English king have led to the unchallenged, even unrecognized, growth of "church culture." No one even thinks to ask: is this the culture of Jesus? The mission, institution and trappings of church are the default understanding of popular Christianity. In other words, given our natural tendencies toward ideological entrenchment and habituation of the status quo, Jesus (via the accepted mistranslation of Matthew 16:18), is understood to be building Sunday Schools, "Seeker Sensitive" services, parking lots and TV empires.

3.  By far the most common understanding of the word "church" in the public imagination, both saved and unsaved, is that of the building—not the people, not the function. We stridently say and preach otherwise, precisely because we must continually redirect the flock away from the inherent gravity of our chosen identity. Unfortunately, this does little to modify our religious paradigm. Worse, such an association is not even technically in error, much less accidental. As denoting that which belongs to a lord (*kyriakon*, i.e. "church"), the correlation people make is fundamental to the phrasing we've adopted for the last four centuries. While the idea of "the Lord's house" may have once seemed useful in reference to the lordship of Christ over His people, the implications of property and ownership quickly displaced other

meanings. In popular thought, church is a system of property, location and dogma. We do not belong to Christ, we belong to the church. While it may offend to state it so bluntly, our interactions prove the point:

> Q. "Where do you go to church?"
>
> > A. "At First Assembly down on 5th and Main."
>
> Q. "How was church today?"
>
> > A. "The worship was good, but the sermon was dry."
>
> Q. "Mommy, what's that pretty building?"
>
> > A. "That's the church dear."
>
> Q. "I go to X Church, where do you go?"
>
> > A. "I go to Y Church. I don't agree with X."
>
> Announcement:
>
> > "Church members, we're starting a capital campaign for our new church building, so that we can more effectively be the church!"

4. Most of the dead religious notions of institutional Christianity can be traced to three toxic roots:

    a. With the Edict of Milan in 313 AD, Constantine elevated Christianity from a persecuted minority to an imperial religion. In 325, the First Council of Nicaea signaled a consolidation of Christian orthodoxy endorsed by Constantine. Christianity became a state-endorsed religion and, increasingly, a justification for the emperor's policies. The church became an arm of the empire. Critics of this "Constantinian shift" also see it as the point at which membership in the Christian church became associated with citizenship rather than a personal decision.

    b. Beginning in the 2nd and 3rd centuries AD—then expanding further as the Roman Catholic Church gained ascendency—a rigid, hierarchal system developed, riddled with human error, false doctrine and malpractice, evidenced in the sale of indulgences, and the buying and selling of clerical offices. The institutional church became legitimized as the intermediary between man and God.

c.  Both of the above factors combined to elevate cultural Christianity above authentic faith in the public mind. As English became the world's language, the expression of the error was further codified and sanctioned by the KJV, as previously discussed. Church culture multiplied globally, co-opting a Christian ethos and Christian values, yet often producing "members" more effectively than disciples with real devotion to Christ. Church became most associated with clergy, buildings, ritual and the civic obligations of well-mannered citizenry. Church culture became synonymous with Western Civilization.

## C. SUMMARY AND CONCLUSIONS

1.  While postmodern criticisms of church may be unfairly motivated by secular ideology, public (mis)perception is often well-deserved. Church culture can easily drift toward an insular, closed system, conservative in action and small in vision, as opposed to the bold, apostolic and prophetic witness which characterized first century believers. Negatively stated, churches *(kyriakos oikia)* meet 2-3 times a week mainly to reinforce a religious subculture by means of a rigid, well-rehearsed agenda. In its most positive expression, truth is preached, a local group of people are edified, pastoral concerns are address, the family unit is nurtured, community thrives, and worship and evangelism result. While these are vital and thoroughly Biblical aspects of body life, they are largely internal metrics which hardly convey the scope of mission, prayer and kingdom dominion resident within the local understanding of ekklesia in Jesus's day.

2.  The drift makes sense. Viewed from a certain vantage point, the church has actually done a fantastic job of building what it *thinks* Jesus committed to, i.e. if we understand Jesus to be building a *church,* our energies should naturally focus on attending to those who gather regularly to the Lord's house. A church can evangelize, feed the poor, build the family unit and run a great Sunday School program, but it takes an ekklesia to act with senatorial spiritual authority across their region. That's why the ekklesia is founded on apostles and prophets (Eph. 1:22, 23, 2:20), because the mindset is different. The chief values of the typical church are numerical growth and bigger buildings, rather than advancing a kingdom agenda. A local ekklesia definitely needs strong pastoral leadership, so the 5-Fold Ministry model remains vital. But it is considerably more difficult to harvest a culture of ruling prayer from a traditional church than it is to integrate pastoral care into an ekklesia. Quite often, a well-intentioned reformist within his local fellowship or even a well-known pastor will offer a critique of the Body of Christ, something like, "We need to quit playing games and *be the church.*" While their zeal is sincere, their diagnosis is entirely inaccurate. The problem is, we've been the church for hundreds of years! We need to be the ekklesia.

# END NOTES

1. Mixed ethnicities who repopulated after Assyria destroyed Israel's northern kingdom.

2. Towering above Caesarea Philippi is Mount Hermon, a region with a long history of idolatry. Israel's highest mountain was prime real estate for Baal worship, a fact attested to by modern archaeology, which has identified more than a dozen temples on and around the mountain. Various Old Testament references help paint the picture: "Baal-gad in the valley of Lebanon at the foot of Mt. Hermon" (Josh. 11:17); also "Baal-hermon" (Judges 3:3); "Now the sons of the half-tribe of Manasseh lived in the land; from Bashan to Baal-hermon" (1 Chron. 5:23). Some commentators believe these locations are one and the same, with the high place of Baal-hermon eventually becoming the village of Paneas, and later, the city of Caesarea Philippi. A mountainous area with multiple summits, Mt. Hermon was also given the names Senir and Sirion by various Canaanite tribes. Interestingly, Hermes, the wing-footed Greek messenger god who was also responsible for escorting departed souls to Hades, might be a derivation of the word Hermon. As Hermes was also the father of Pan, this etymology makes sense given what we know of Caesarea Philippi.

   But it gets worse. In 20 BC, Herod the Great furthered the idolatrous reputation of the city by building a white marble temple dedicated to the worship of Augustus Caesar, who proclaimed himself lord of lords and king of kings. By the time of Jesus, the village was expanded again under the rule of Herod's son, Philip, who renamed it in honor of both Caesar and himself. The ruins of the city are still visible in the contested Golan Heights region of Israel. Today, it's called by its Arab name, Banias.

3. In the context of what unfolds at Caesarea Philippi, the visit to Bethsaida is particularly interesting, since this was Peter's birth place and hometown (John 1:44). Did Jesus intend to subtly remind Peter of who he once was, and where he had come from, in hopes of adding significance to the personal commissioning that would soon follow?

4. See Mark 7:24. We are given hints of four reasons why Jesus might have wanted to "get away" to the far northern cities of Tyre and Sidon: 1) The recent death of John the Baptist (Mat. 14:9-13); 2) disciples weary of traveling (Mark 6:30-31); 3) Herod was hunting Him (Luke 9:9) and 4) the crowds were attempting to make Him king by force (John 6:15). In very human terms, Jesus needed some time away. This sabbatical forms a natural transition for the next phase of His ministry.
5. Eph. 5:25-29; Rev. 21:2
6. Heb. 2:10-12, 17, 3:6
7. Tony Campolo, *Let Me Tell You a Story* (Nashville: Thomas Nelson, 2000) p. 186
8. "Christianity agrees with Dualism that this universe is at war. But it does not think this is a war between independent powers. It thinks it is a civil war, a rebellion, and that we are living in a part of the universe occupied by the rebel. Enemy-occupied territory, that is what this world is. Christianity is the story of how the rightful king has landed...and is calling us all to take part in a great campaign of sabotage." — C.S. Lewis, *Mere Christianity* (1952; Harper Collins: 2001) p. 45
9. R. Arthur Mathews, *Born for Battle: 31 Studies on Spiritual Warfare* (Wheaton: Harold Shaw Publishers, 1976, 1999), p. 20
10. Eze. 10:12, Rev. 4:6, 8
11. 1 Cor. 13:12
12. Derek Prince, *Shaping History Through Prayer and Fasting* (New Kensington: Whitaker House, 2002) p. 38
13. 2 Cor. 12:2,4, 7; 2 Cor. 13:3
14. "Flesh and blood" idiomatically refers not to sinful, carnal knowledge, but human agency; in this case, human reasoning. Other examples of the phrase include Gal. 1:16, Eph. 6:12 and Heb. 2:14.
15. Rom. 11:33
16. 1 Cor. 2:10
17. Mahesh Chavda, *The Hidden Power of Prayer and Fasting*, 1998 (Shippensburg: Destiny Image) p. 148
18. Rev. 19:10
19. Gal. 1:12
20. 2 Cor. 5:7
21. Heb. 11:6

22. Given the witness of John 21:15, where Peter's father's name is stated to be John, we are intended to perceive another layer of insight. Might the naming of Simon as the "Son of Jonah" be intentional wordplay, as with the two forms of rock, *petros* and *petra?* This possibility will be discussed in Chapter 9.

23. Over a century ago, Richard Littledale summarized a number of common views. In his dispute with the Roman Catholic Church, he pointed out that the Creed of Pius IV bound Catholics "to interpret Scripture only according to the unanimous consent of the Fathers." Quoting Archbishop Kenrick of St. Louis in 1870, Littledale notes five different patristic interpretations regarding Matthew 16:18: "(1) That St. Peter is the Rock, taught by seventeen Fathers; (2) that the whole Apostolic College is the Rock, represented by Peter as its chief, taught by eight; (3) that St. Peter's faith is the Rock, taught by forty-four; (4) that Christ is the Rock, taught by sixteen; (5) that the Rock is the whole body of the faithful. Several who teach (1) and (2) also teach (3) and (4), and so the Archbishop sums up thus: 'If we are bound to follow the greater number of Fathers in this matter, then we must hold for certain that the word Petra means not Peter professing the faith, but the faith professed by Peter.'" — Richard F. Littledale, *Plain Reasons Against Joining the Church of Rome* (London: Society for Promoting Christian Knowledge, 1886), p. 24, note 1

24. Luke 5:8; John 1:41-42. Peter's name seems to be the most fluid of the entire New Testament. He is called at various times Simon, Simon Peter, Simon Barjona and Cephas. It is almost as if the different forms were more or less useful at different times, or perhaps Jesus enjoyed and used them as nicknames, friend to friend. In any event, well after the events of Matthew 16, after the crucifixion and resurrection, Jesus is again calling him Simon (John 21:14-17). I point this out because Petrine authority claims infer permanence both to and from the giving of his name, as a singular event, which Scripture simply does not support.

25. 2 Sam. 22:32. Other passages include: Deut. 32:15; 2 Sam. 22:3; Psa. 18:2, 46, 61:2-3, 62:6, 95:1; Isa. 17:10, 26:4, 44:8; Hab. 1:12

26. Mat. 7:24-25; cf. Luke 6:48

27. Rom 9:33, cf. 1 Pet. 2:8

28. 1 Cor. 10:4

29. Leonard Sweet and Frank Viola, *The Jesus Manifesto*, 2010 (Nashville: Thomas Nelson) p. 51)

30. *Jesus Manifesto*, p. 2-3

31. Another variation of this interpretation is less satisfying: rather than the dynamic, perpetual, confessional revelation of Christ being the foundation, it is the static summation of all sound doctrine upon which Jesus will build. I do not favor this view.

32. Nimrod, the "mighty one" (Gen. 10:8) was later deified, and may be the central, mythic figure behind the well-known *Epic of Gilgamesh,* as well as the foundation for many branches of Mesopotamian cultic religion. The Pharaohs of Egypt were first considered to be incarnations of the god, Horus, and later, sons of Amon-Ra. Babylonian, Persian and Assyrian rulers made god-like claims. In Daniel 3, Nebuchadnezzar's command to worship his statue is likely an attempt at self-deification; also see Artaxerxes' claim in Ezra 7:12. The great, dynastic rulers of China were all regarded as the "Son of Heaven," while Japanese Emperor Hirohito claimed divinity as late as the end of World War II.

33. Online article, "Lord of Lords" (http://www.followtherabbi.com/guide/detail/lord-of-lords)

34. Deification of the emperor was called *apotheosis.* "The deification of the Roman emperor eventually became a standard religious practice that was confirmed by senatorial vote...Herodian of Syria, a biographer writing during the third century C.E., composed an account...of the ritual ceremony of the apotheosis of Septimius Severus. The story mentions a funeral pyre and, at the climax of the ceremony, the releasing of an eagle to symbolize the emperor's ascent into heaven....A well-known scene carved on the Arch of Titus shows the Roman legion returning with the spoils of Jerusalem, but less well known is another scene that depicts the apotheosis of Titus. The apotheosis of Augustus is the subject of a very beautifully carved cameo, the Gemma Augustea, in the Kunsthistorisches Museum in Vienna." — Larry Kreitzer, "Apotheosis of the Roman Emperor," *Biblical Archaeologist,* Dec. 1990; p. 211. Upon ratification, the dead emperor's newly crowned progeny could also rightly proclaim himself a 'Son of God.' It is worth noting that the specific details of Jesus's ascension *preceded the apotheosis ritual by several decades.*

35. "The point bears repeating that, to have been crucified, Jesus must have gone up to Jerusalem and posed a significant threat to the Roman imperial order." — Richard A. Horsley, *Jesus and the Powers: Conflict, Covenant and the Hope of the Poor* (Minneapolis: Fortress Press, 2011), p. 168. Horsley's numerous works cast Jesus as a radical Jewish prophet of social change, bringing equity and redemption to the poor and oppressed per the time-honored model of Old

Testament Jewish prophets. While valuable, this view must be approached with caution. Jesus's mission was not a political-economic-religious attempt to liberate national Judea from Rome, but to emancipate mankind from Satan and sin.

Yet Horsley rightly attempts to ascertain the historic context in which Jesus operated, rather than imposing *ad hoc* Western assumptions and a religious worldview culled from 2,000 years of institutional thought onto the Gospels. Commenting on the commonly used term, *evangelion,* used in Greek cities such as Corinth to describe the salvation, peace and security afforded by the imperial savior Augustus and other, future Caesars, Horsley writes: "Equally outrageous was Paul's assertion that Christ, vindicated by God and now 'reigning' in heaven—where presumably only the greatest Greek heroes and deified Roman emperors joined the great gods in celestial glory—was about to 'destroy every rule and every authority and power' (1 Cor. 15:24-28)." — Richard A. Horsley, "Rhetoric and Empire—and 1 Corinthians," *Paul and Politics: Ekklesia, Israel, imperium, Interpretation,* ed. Richard A. Horsley, 2000; (Trinity Press International) p. 92.

36. N.T. Wright, "Upstaging the Emperor," *Bible Review,* February 1988.
37. Jesus self-confessed that He was both king (John 18:37) and son of God (Luke 22:70).
38. Deut. 18:15; 2 Sam. 7:14; Psa. 2, 16, 22, 34, 69 110; Isa. 7:14, 8:23-9:2, 9:5-6, 11:12, 53:5; Jer. 31:15; Eze. 37:26-27; Dan. 9:24-27; Hos. 11:1; Zech. 12:10; 9:9; Mic. 5:2; Hag. 2:6-9
39. Hebrews 5:6, 7:17, 7:21, 5:10, 6:20, 7:11, 7:15
40. For more, see the Appendix: A Brief History of the King James Mistranslation and the Establishment of Church Culture.
41. Opposition to God is increasingly in vogue among society's elite thinkers. As an example of blatant rejection of divine law, postmodern philosopher Richard Rorty rejoices in an America that refuses to "believe in the existence of Truth...(as) something which has authority over human beings." He celebrates the ideal of America as "the first nationstate with nobody but itself to please—not even God...We are the greatest poem because we put ourselves in the place of God...We redefine God as our future selves." As a result, Americans should express no interest in "anything which claims authority over America (since)...there is no standard, not even a divine one, against which the decisions of a free people can be measured." —Richard Rorty, *Achieving Our Country* (Cambridge, MA: Harvard University Press, 1999)

42. In one of the most famous examples of obedience to this command, Shadrach, Meshach and Abednego risked their lives by refusing to bow before Nebuchadnezzar's idol. (Dan. 3:10-18)

43. Larry J. Kreitzer, "When He at Last is First," *Where Christology Began: Essays on Philippians 2*, ed. Ralph P. Martin, Brian J. Dodd (Louisville: Westminster John Knox Press, 1998) p. 119

44. Deut. 6:4-5, a prayer called the *Shema,* is the great monotheistic rallying cry of the Jews: "Hear, O Israel! The Lord is our God, the Lord is one! And you shall love the Lord your God with all your heart and with all your soul and with all your might." In 1 Cor. 8:6, Paul boldly co-opts and recasts the Shema as a statement of Christ: "Yet for us there is but one God, the Father, from whom are all things, and we exist for Him; and one Lord, Jesus Christ, by whom are all things, and we exist through Him." To enhance this, Paul even goes so far as to gloss the term 'God' with 'the Father' and 'Lord' with 'Jesus Christ.' N.T Wright says, "Within his monotheistic argument, to make a monotheistic point, Paul quotes this, the best-known of all Jewish monotheistic formulae, and once again, he puts Jesus into the middle of it." — N.T. Wright, *Paul: In Fresh Perspective* (Minneapolis: First Fortress Press, 2009) p. 94.

45. "Philippians 2:5-11 and 3:19-21 can be seen to have explicit reference to the imperial cult and theme, with, once more, the main thrust that Jesus Christ is the true *kyrios* of the world, so that of course Caesar is not." — N.T. Wright, "Paul and Caesar: A New Reading of Romans," originally published in *A Royal Priesthood: The Use of the Bible Ethically and Politically,* ed. C. Bartholemew, (Carlisle: Paternoster, 2002) p. 173–193 found at http://www.ntwrightpage.com/Wright_Paul_Caesar_Romans.htm

46. Stanley Hauerwas, *With the Grain of the Universe* (Grand Rapids: Brazos Press, 2001).

47. 1 Cor 4:9

48. Col. 1:16, 20; 2:15; Eph. 1:10; 3:10. The throne of Christ is not second-tier. He fully possess the same kingdom as His heavenly Father, and sits on the same heavenly throne. In Revelations 3:21, He clarifies this, saying, "I also conquered and *sat down with my Father on his throne.*" (cf. Eph. 1:20-21; 1 Pet. 3:22).

    Gerald Hawthorne, quoting C.A. Wanamaker, says "Philippians 2:9-11 envisages Christ gaining equality with God in preeminence and function by virtue of the fact that God has appointed him vice-regent (cf. 1 Cor. 15:24-28). What Christ refused to grasp God has granted as a reward for his self-abasement and suffering." Gerald F. Hawthorne, "In the Form of God and Equal with God," *Where Christology Began: Essays on Philippians 2,* ed. Ralph P. Martin, Brian J. Dodd; (Louisville: Westminster John Knox Press, 1998) p. 103

49. "'Hosts' comes from a Hebrew word which means 'to wage war.' The Lord is the Commander of the hosts and heaven: the stars (Is. 40:26; Gen. 2:1), the angels (Ps. 103:20, 21), the armies of Israel (Ex. 12:41), and all who trust in Him (Ps. 46:7, 11)." — Warren Wiersbe, *The Wiersbe Bible Commentary: The Complete Old Testament* (Colorado Springs: David C. Cook, 2007) p. 1525

50. Francis Frangipane, *This Day We Fight,* (Grand Rapids: Chosen Books, 2010) p. 175

51. Daniel 10:5-8, Luke 1:12, 2:9, Mat. 28:3-4

52. Many scholars see the Ten Plagues as specifically tailored to humiliate Egypt's pantheon, as the following list demonstrates: Nile turned to blood (fish-goddess, Hatmeyt; also, the Nile water was considered to be the transformed life-blood of Osiris); Frogs (frog-headed goddess, Hekt); Flies or beetles (scarab-headed Khephera, regarded as a manifestation of Atum or Ra); Pestilence on livestock (Hathor, the cow-headed love goddess; also, the symbol of the bull was the symbol of Pharaoh himself); Boils (god of healing, Im-Hotep); Hail (sky goddess, Nut); Locust (locust-headed god, Senehem); Darkness (supreme sun-god, Amon-Ra); First-born (the next incarnation of Horus) — Manfred Lurker, *The Gods and Symbols of Ancient Egypt,* (London: Thames and Hudson, 1980)

53. Tremper Longman III and Daniel G. Reid, God is a Warrior (Grand Rapids: Zondervan Publishing House, 1995) p. 25

54. 1 Sam. 1:6-11

55. In the encounter with Joshua in ch. 5, the title, "captain of the host of the Lord," is clearly cut from the same cloth. Even so, the name, *Yahweh Tzevaot,* is not disclosed to history until Hannah's prayer.

56. 1 Sam. 3:19

57. In Gethsemane, when Peter took up arms to defend Jesus, the Lord refused to follow suit. By this we see the imperative of the Cross in the economy of God, and also the wisdom of weakness. "Put your sword back into its place; for all those who take up the sword shall perish by the sword." (v. 52)

58. Longman and Reid quoting Mennonite scholar M.C. Lind, *God is a Warrior;* p. 25

59. 2 Kings 19:31; Isa. 1:9-26; 2:12; 3:1-3, 21:10; 28:5; 31:4-5; 37:32; Jer 6:6; 7:3-7

60. Jeremiah 7:11, in which the Lord of hosts condemns the Temple being made into a den of robbers, is quoted in Mat. 21:13.

61. Jesus is revealed as Lord Sabaoth in both His first and second coming. Facing Pilate, Jesus said, "Do you think that I cannot appeal to My Father, and He will at once put at My disposal more than twelve legions of angels?'" (Mat. 26:53). Also, when He returns, we are told that "in righteousness He judges and wages war...And the armies which are in heaven, clothed in fine linen, white and clean, were following Him on white horses. And from His mouth comes a sharp sword, so that with it He may smite the nations; and He will rule them with a rod of iron" (Rev. 19:11, 14-15).

62. Not only does He denounce, He contends with them over breaking covenant. In this dreadful sense, rather than serving as her champion and defender, Lord Sabaoth becomes her enemy, warring against those who break covenant. He does this in faithfulness to Himself (Isa. 5:24–25; 10:23–33; Jer. 2:19; 9-10; 21-24; 9:7-9).

63. Isa. 9:7

64. 2 Kings 18-19; 2 Chron. 32; Isa. 36-37

65. The likely setting for this psalm is "on the fields surrounding Jerusalem where the Assyrian soldiers lay dead, their weapons and equipment scattered and broken. There had been no battle, but the angel of the Lord left this evidence behind to encourage the faith of the people...The Lord defeated and disarmed His enemies and destroyed their weapons, and they could attack no more" — Warren Wiersbe, *The Bible Exposition Commentary: Old Testament Wisdom and Poetry,* (Colorado Springs: Cook Communications, 2003) p. 184

66. We quote Psalm 46:10 all the time: "Be still and know that I am God." But do we notice the context? Peace in a violent, corrupt world ruled by dark forces and proud kings is not achieved apart from the masculine will and military strength of Lord Sabaoth. The stillness with which we are invited to contemplate God is a direct byproduct of His willingness to wage triumphant war on our behalf. Thus, Lord Sabaoth is the ultimate revelation of peace through strength.

67. 2 Cor. 12:29, also see 1 Cor. 1:25-27

68. Rev. 12:10–11

69. James S. Hewett, ed., *Illustrations Unlimited* (Wheaton: Tyndale House Publishers) p. 466

70. Rom. 8:37, 16:20; 1 Cor. 15:57; 2 Cor. 2:14; 1 John 4:4, 5:4

71. Josh. 1:3-6; 10:7-14, 24-25; 11:12; 18-20; 12:1-24

72. The main ruler to be dethroned is Self. This book primarily addresses the cooperative rulership of God's people *externally*, as those who manifest the triumph of Christ against injustice, false ideologies and false religions. Obviously, a more complete picture of rulership must also include inward dominion—letting Christ rule the inner man by cultivating the fruit of the Spirit and growing in surrender to God. "For this is the will of God, your sanctification... that each of you know how to possess his own vessel in sanctification and honor, not in lustful passion" (1 Thes. 4:3-5). Inner must precede outer. See John 14:30.

73. Psa. 110:1-2, 132:11; Isa. 9:7, 11:10; Jer. 23:5; Dan. 2:44

74. Victory: Rev. 11:15, ref. 20:4. Overcomers: 1 John 5:4-5; Rev. 2:7, 2:11, 2:17, 2:26, 3:5, 3:12, 3:21, 21:7. Reigning: Rev. 5:10; 20:6

75. C. S. Lewis, *Studies in Medieval and Renaissance Literature*, ed. W. Hooper (Cambridge: Cambridge Univ. Press, 1966), p. 137

76. Heb. 9:8. For example, the tabernacle's tripartite construction is a startling revelation of the Trinity. The Outer Court, which was most visible and accessible to the surrounding encampment of the twelve tribes, and also contained the altar of sacrifice, represented the incarnate nature and atoning actions of the Son, who was sent to Earth as the Lamb of God. The altar was the gateway of access to the Holy Place, where light and bread and the incense represent various aspects of the Holy Spirit's ministry within the human heart. Here, the inner realities of fellowship are cultivated, by which we enter the Most Holy Place, which is the throne of the Father's presence.

77. Moses's words are quoted in Heb. 8:5 from Exo. 25:40, then repeated in Exo. 26:30, 27:8 and Num 8:4. David's statement is made in 1 Chron. 28:19.

78. P. D. Miller, *Cosmology and World Order in the Old Testament: The Divine Council as Cosmic-Political Symbol*, HBT 9 (1987), p. 54.

79. I am much indebted not only to Sumner, but even more to the excellent research of Dr. Michael S. Heiser, available at www.thedivinecouncil.com. A more manageable introduction to the topic of the divine council can be found in both the full and abbreviated versions of Sumner's well-documented thesis, available at www.hebrew-streams.org/works/monotheism/council.html. Combined, Heiser and Sumner's insights collated a vast amount of research for the formulation of ideas contained in this chapter, though it must be noted that many of their conclusions, or at least applications, may differ from my own.

80. Closely related variants occur in Psa. 29:1 and Psa. 89:6, where the phrase *bene elim* is translated "sons of the mighty."

81. Compare 1 Peter 3:19-20 to Enoch 21:6. Also, in Revelation, while John draws many metaphors from Old Testament books such as Daniel, Ezekiel, Zechariah and Exodus, many scholars also see thematic language and paraphrased references to Enoch.

82. Prior to Augustine in the 5th century A.D., the common interpretation for "sons of God" was angels. Justin Martyr, Irenaeus, Athenagoras, Tertullian, Lactantius, Eusebius, Ambrose, and Philo of Alexandria all supported this view. "Later Judaism and almost all the earliest ecclesiastical writers identify the 'sons of God' with the fallen angels; but from the fourth century onwards, as the idea of angelic natures becomes less material, the Fathers commonly take the 'sons of God' to be Seth's descendants and the 'daughters of men' those of Cain." — footnotes to the *Jerusalem Bible,* Genesis 6 (New York: Doubleday, 1966). Which begs the question: if these were mortals, why not simply call them sons of Seth?

83. "The idea of a pantheon under the leadership of a supreme god is also clear in the *bene'elim,* "sons of gods," of Psa. 29:1...and 89:7 (where it is in parallelism to *qehal qedhosim,* "assembly of the holy ones," in v. 6, and *sodh qedhoshim,* "council of the holy ones," in v. 8)." — G. Johannes Botterweck, Helmer Ringgren, *Theological Dictionary of the Old Testament, vol. 2* (Grand Rapids: William B. Eerdman's Publishing Co., 1977) p. 158

84. Sumner summarizes facts common to the Throne Visions: 1) Each vision mentions or alludes to a *throne;* 2) They share a common theme: the *kingship of Yahweh;* 3) Each vision (except Exo. 24) refers to additional heavenly beings; 4) Throne visions historically *occur at crisis times* when affirmation of God's kingship is urgent to the nation; 5) The visions also affirm *God's choice of human leaders;* 6) The visions *confirm the authority* of those to whom God granted access to His council. The true prophet is one who hears the Word or Plan of Yahweh, then delivers it to Israel.

85. While "council access" is nowhere listed as a requirement for prophetic office, it does serve to validate true messengers. When Jeremiah challenges the false prophets around him, he rhetorically contrasts false with true prophets by asking, "Who has stood in the council of the Lord, that he should see and hear His word?" (Jer. 23:18). Jeremiah could have simply asked, "Who has truly heard the word of the Lord?" or even "who has received the counsel of the Lord?" But this is not counsel, it is council. Within the Bible's continuity

of revelation, the divine council is included from beginning to end. The fact that we reside in the middle of this span suggests that such revelation is meant to continue. Throne downloads of the divine council are never said to cease.

86. In this same vein, when Moses established a council of leaders on Earth, he appointed seventy elders. Why seventy? He was directed to this number by God Himself (Num. 11:16, 25). Ugaritic myths from the 2nd millenium B.C. may provide insight. "As the Father of the Gods, El is reckoned to have sired 70 sons...the entire pantheon is called *bn.ilm,* possibly to be rendered 'Sons of El'" — Alberto R.W. Green, *The Storm-God in the Ancient Near East: Biblical and Judaic Studies vol. 8* (Winona Lake: Eisenbrauns, 2003) p. 229. Interestingly, this legend describes the supreme god with his council of seventy. Could this be another example of pagan myths grasping at, and though perverting, also illuminating divine realities? Note how closely the cognate *bn'ilm* relates to *bene elyon,* "sons of the Most High."

87. "It is only by the Divine specific act of creation that any created being can be called 'a son of God.' For that which is 'born of the flesh is flesh.' God is spirit, and that which is 'born of the Spirit is spirit' (John 3:6). Hence Adam is called a 'son of God' in Luke 3:38. Those 'in Christ' having the 'new nature' which is by the direct creation of God (2 Cor. 5:17; Eph. 2:10) can be, and are called 'sons of God' (John 1:13; Rom. 8:14-15; 1 John 3:1)" — E.W. Bullinger, *Companion Bible: KJV, Large Print Edition* (Grand Rapids: Kregel Publications, 1999) p. 26.

     Adam was specifically created by God "in the likeness of God" (Gen. 5:1). Adam's descendants, however, were different; they were no longer directly in God's likeness, but Adam's. Adam "became the father of a son in his own likeness...and named him Seth" (Gen. 5:3). While Adam was a "son of God," his descendants were 'sons of men.' It is not until Christ that a wholly original Son of God is begotten again, and this time, not only in the image of God, but with truly divine parentage. He is conceived, not created. Begotten, not brought forth. Amazingly, in the mysterious act of regeneration, we are literally born-again by the very same Spirit that conceived Jesus in Mary's womb. Thus, "from now on we recognize no man according to the flesh...he is a new creature; the old things passed away" (2 Cor. 5:16-17).

88. Lewis Sperry Chafer, *Systematic Theology, Vol. 2* (Dallas: Dallas Seminary Press, 1947), p. 23.

89. John Loren Sandford, *Healing the Nations,* p. 133

90. From *Webster's New World Dictionary,* Third College Edition, 1988: "Church: Derived from the Middle English word *chirch/kirke,* which is derived from

the Old English word *cirice* (and the Old Norse *kirkja*), which is derived from the Germanic *kirika*, which is derived from the Classical Greek *kyriake* (*oikia*) which means 'lord's house,' and *kyriakos* which means 'belonging to the lord,' and *kyrios* which means 'ruler,' and *kyros* which means 'supreme power.'"

Dr. William Smith doubts even the connection to kyriakon. "The derivation has been too hastily assumed. It is probably *(more)* connected with Kirk." —*Smith's Bible Dictionary*, "Church"; available online www.smithsbibledictionary.org

Likewise, Liddell and Scott state, "How this Greek name came to be adopted by the Northern nations, rather than the Roman name ecclesia, has not been satisfactorily explained." — R. Scott, and H.G. Liddell, *An Intermediate Greek-English Lexicon* (Clarendon: Oxford University Press, 1999) p. 458.

91. *Smith's Bible Dictionary*, www.smithsbibledictionary.org
92. 1 Cor. 11:20, "Lord's supper"; Rev. 1:10, "Lord's day"
93. References in secular literature dating back to 1297, 1360, even Geoffrey Chaucer in 1390, employ "chirche" as denoting the building. Associations were likely made by virtue of pastoral admonitions such as, "But if a man does not know how to manage his own household *(oikos)*, how will he take care of the *ekklesia* of God...I write so that you may know how one ought to conduct himself in the household *(oikos)* of God, which is the *ekklesia* of the living God, the pillar and support of the truth." (1 Tim 3:5,15)
94. Nearly all modern translations of Scripture harbor this error, including: KJV, NKJV, NIV, NASB, NLT, ESV, CEV, NCV.
95. For the highly regarded Wuest translation, Kenneth S. Wuest explains church thus: "The word ekklesia appears in the Greek text where this word is found in the translations...The word 'assembly' is a good one-word translation of ekklesia" — Kenneth S. Wuest, *Word Studies in the Greek New Testament, Volume III, Vocabulary* (Grand Rapids, Eerdmans Publishing Co., 1973) p. 27
96. "In fact the word 'church' is not found in the Greek New Testament, nor was it used for some two hundred years after the New Testament was written." — J.A. Shackleford, *Compendium of Baptist History* (Louisville: Baptist Book Concern, 1892) p. 23-24. The antecedents of 'church' are considered Late or Medieval Greek. In other words, you can't reverse engineer them into Scripture.
97. Psa. 127:1
98. Solomon: Prov. 30:5-6. Paul: Rom. 3:4. Jesus: John 6:63, also 7:16
99. Winston Churchill, *The Second World War, Vol. 2: Their Finest Hour* (New York: Houghton Mifflin Co., 1949), p. 339

100. For example, it is hard to imagine that a doctrine as central as "grace through faith" could be lost for centuries, but it was. So God used Martin Luther to recover this truth, launching the Reformation. A more flagrant example of human error is a Bible published in 1631, nicknamed *Wicked Bible*. This reprint of the KJV contained about 1,500 misprints, including the omission of the word "not" from the command: "Thou shalt *not* commit adultery." The remedy was quickly addressed. The printer lost his license and was fined.

101. "...both in its original Greek and Hebrew usages, that sense (of a body of people being 'picked out' from the world) was not exclusive, but inclusive." — William Barclay, *New Testament Words* (Louisville: Westminster John Knox Press, 1974), p. 70

102. Acts 19:32, 39, 41

103. "Sunago: "to assemble" (sun, "together," ago, "to bring", is used of the "gathering together" of people or things; Sunagoge is, lit. "a place where people assemble...the building standing by metonymy for the people therein" — W.E. Vine, *Vine's Complete Expository Dictionary* (Nashville: Thomas Nelson, 1996) p. 42. Together, these words occur 119 times in the New Testament, which means they were certainly common and accessible enough to be useful if this is what Jesus intended.

104. Oskar Seyffert, *A Dictionary of Classical Antiquities: Mythology, Religion, Literature and Art* (New York: Macmillan Company) p. 202. Text available online through Google Books. Other definitions of ekklesia that are helpful to understanding its governmental function: "An assembly of citizens summoned by the crier, the legislative assembly." (Liddell and Scott, *A Greek-English Lexicon*); also "An assembly of the people convened at the public place of council for the purpose of deliberating" (J. H. Thayer, *A Greek-English Lexicon of the New Testament*).

105. The Septuagint, also called LXX, is the Koine Greek version of the Hebrew Bible. Translated between the 3rd and 2nd century BC, the LXX was held in great respect in ancient times. Philo and Josephus even ascribed divine inspiration to its authors. Since Koine Greek (along with Aramaic), was the common language of Jesus's day, the pre-Christian Septuagint provides invaluable insight by comparing key words and concepts between the Old and New Testament.

106. Though this claim is disputed by some, a number of strong arguments are in its favor, "because, to some circles of Greek-speaking Jewry, it replaced the

Biblia Hebraica, and thus became their Bible...In a historical perspective, it became, to an even greater extent than the Biblia Hebraica, the Old Testament of the New Testament...Until the process began which insisted on monopolizing Hebraica Veritas as the only authentic Bible text in respect of the Old Testament, the Jewish Bible was in fact both the Hebrew and the Greek text." — Mogens Müller, *The First Bible of the Church: A Plea for the Septuagint* (Sheffield: Sheffield Academic Press, 1996), 115-16, 120-21.

"It is clear that for all NT authors the Greek texts constitute authentic and authoritative Scripture, and that for most of them they are their only source...As well as providing direct quotations and recognizable allusions, the LXX exercises a profound influence on vocabulary and style, though this varies from writer to writer and is not all-pervasive." — Jennifer M. Dines, *The Septuagint: Understanding the Bible and Its World*" (London: T&T Clark/Continuum, 2004), p. 142-43

"Most of the Old Testament quotations in the New follow the text of the LXX in one of its known forms." — Natalio Fernández Marcos, "The Septuagint and the New Testament," *The Septuagint in Context: Introduction to the Greek Version of the Bible,* trans. W.G.E. Watson (Leiden: Brill, 2000), p.265

107. The word *qahal* is found in the Hebrew Old Testament 115 times. Of the 74 occurrences of the word *ekklesia* in the Septuagint, 66 are translations of qahal. Thirty-six times, qahal is translated as *sunagoge* instead.

108. William Barclay, *New Testament Words* (Louisville: Westminster John Knox Press, 1974) p. 69-70

109. Oskar Seyffert, referencing Aristotle's *Constitution of Athens* — *A Dictionary of Classical Antiquities: Mythology, Religion, Literature and Art* (New York: Macmillan Company) p. 202.

110. William Barclay, *New Testament Words,* p. 70

111. William Barclay, *New Testament Words,* p. 68

112. 1 Cor. 15:55. Of this event, Melito, Bishop of Sardis, penned the following approximately 170-190 A.D.: "Who will contend against me? Let him stand before me. It is I who delivered the condemned. It is I who gave life to the dead. Who will argue with me? It is I, says Christ, who destroyed death. It is I who triumphed over the enemy, and having trod upon Hades, and bound the Strong Man, have snatched mankind up to the heights of heaven. I, he says, am the Christ."

113. Erwin Raphael McManus, *The Barbarian Way* (Nashville: Thomas Nelson, 2005) p. 3-4

114. Deut. 28:48

115. Winston Churchill, *The Second World War, Vol. 5: Closing the Ring* (New York: Houghton Mifflin Co., 1951), p. 64

116. P.T. O'Brien, "The Church as a Heavenly and Eschatological Entity" in D.A. Carson ed. T*he Church in the Bible and the World* (Exeter: Paternoster Press, 1987) pp 88-119.

117. H. Thielicke, *The Evangelical Faith 3: Theology of the Spirit,* trans. and ed. Geoffrey W. Bromiley (Grand Rapids: Eerdmans, 1982), p. 206-207

118. Again, reference Psa. 2, 110. In the New Testament, passages such as Hebrews 12:22 and Galatians 4:24-26, 6:16 interpret OT references to Zion bringing nations to God in light of the ekklesia. Also compare Amos 9:11-12 and Acts 15:15-19.

119. *By the Still Waters* (Old Tappan: Flemming H. Revell, 1934). Quoted in Guideposts, October 1981, p. 5

120. R. Lightner, *Truth for the Good Life,* (Denver: Accent Books, 1978), p. 115-6

121. Stephen Ambrose, *Citizen Soldiers* (New York: Touchstone, 1997), p. 40

122. Psa. 89:14, 97:2

123. Rev. 20:10-15

124. Molech was worshiped by the Ammonites, and came to be worshiped by Israel (Lev.18:21; 1 Kings 11:3,5,7; 2 Kings 23:10; Amos 5:26; Acts 7:43). In Jeremiah's day, the Hinnom ravine was connected to Molech's worship (Jer.32:35). Josiah, king of Judah, destroyed the high places of Molech (2 Kings 23:10,13), which incorporated human sacrifice, including the sacrifice of children by fire (2 Chron. 28:3, 33:6) on altars erected within the valley of Hinnom.

125. Gen. 37:35, Num. 16:30-33; Psa. 86:13; Ecc. 9:10, Isa. 38:17-20

126. Ezek. 31:14-17

127. Job 10:21-22

128. Acts 2:27, 31

129. Rev. 1:18, 6:8, 20:13-14

130. The technical distinction is helpful as a counter-argument against ultimate dominion, or triumphalism. See later section: "Reality Check: A Caution Against Triumphalism."

131. Gen. 19:1; Psa. 69:13; Ruth 4:1-2

132. "Prevail" is a rather loose English rendering of the more specific Greek 'katischyo,' which means to overpower in the sense of holding back, holding down, detaining, suppressing, etc. The thing which is held back is clearly not the ekklesia.

133. Israel Ministry of Foreign Affairs online, "Index of Archaeological Sites," entry 'Dan' at www.mfa.gov.il

134. R. Arthur Mathews, *Born for Battle: 31 Studies on Spiritual Warfare* (Wheaton: Harold Shaw Publishers, 1976, 1999), p. 20

135. Rom. 8:17

136. "Gates of death" are also mentioned in Psalm 9:13.

137. "He that is in possession of (keys) has the power of access, and has a general care of a house. Hence, in the Bible, a key is used as a symbol of superintendence, an emblem of power and authority." — Albert Barnes, *Barnes' Notes on the Bible*, 1832 (online at: www.ccel.org/ccel/barnes/ntnotes.iv.xvi.xix.html).

    Also "By the kingdom of heaven, we may consider the true Church, that house of God, to be meant; and by the keys, the power of admitting into that house, or of preventing any improper person from coming in." — Adam Clarke, *Clarke's Commentary on the Bible*, 1832 (online at: www.godrules.net/library/clarke/clarkemat16.htm

138. While admitting the existence of an invisible "gate" is perhaps the biggest leap for post-modern, rationalist Christians, it shouldn't be. Hades is invisible, the battle is invisible, the keys are invisible, yet Jesus described them all as exerting real and visible influence in the earth. The prevailing worldview of scientific materialism has erroneously divorced visible and invisible realities in the public mind, including the minds of many believers. This represents a victory of monumental proportions for the enemy. Such a false, humanistic paradigm is itself a gate which must not prevail.

139. "In Jeremiah 33:3, 'Ask of Me and I will show you great and *mighty* things...' the word 'might' (Hebrew: *batsar*) is better rendered 'isolated' or 'inaccessible.' The suggestion is that God would give Jeremiah 'revelational insight' that otherwise might be inaccessible or isolated. Such 'revelational insight' always has been essential for a clear understanding of victorious spiritual warfare." — Dick Eastman, *Spirit Filled Life Bible*, gen. ed. Jack Hayford (Nashville: Thomas Nelson, 1991) p. 1108, note on Jer. 33:3.

    The rendering of cities or walls being 'batsar'—*fortified* or *fenced* in Isa. 2:15, 22:10, 25:2, 27:10, 36:1, 37:26—conveys a similar concept.

140. The Lord wants His name known—every name, but certainly Lord of Armies, Lord Sabaoth. "This time I will make them know My power and My might; and they shall know that My name is the Lord...'Not by might nor by power, but by My Spirit,' says the Lord of hosts" (Jer. 16:21; Zech. 4:6).

141. Mat. 11:12

142. "Outside this gate, five undressed stones (up to 60 cm. in height) were found standing erect. They served as *matzevot* (erect stones) marking a cultic place." Israel Ministry of Foreign Affairs online, "Index of Archaeological Sites," entry 'Dan'

143. A number of demon gods are named in Scripture, including: Baal, Ashtoreth, Astarte, Chemosh, Dagon, Artemis and Molech. Other references to false worship include the golden calf, household idols, heavenly bodies and people, along with the Beast, False Prophet and Antichrist of Revelation.

144. 1 Kings 11:7, 14:22-24; 2 Kings 23:13

145. also see Lev. 26:30; Deut. 24:4; Jer 2:7; Eze 36:17-18

146. A.W. Tozer, *A.W. Tozer on Worship and Entertainment,* James L. Snyder, ed. (Camp Hill: Christian Publications, 1997), p. 152-153

147. A. T. Robertson, *Word Pictures in the New Testament* (Grand Rapids: Baker Book House, 1930), p. 134; note on Mat. 16:19.

148. Adam Clarke, *Clarke's Commentary,* note on Mat. 18:18.

149. John Lightfoot, *A Commentary on the New Testament from the Talmud and Hebraica: Vol. 2* (Peabody: Hendrickson Publishers, 1979), p. 236-241; note on Mat. 16:19.

150. Charles B. Williams, *The New Testament: A Private Translation in the Language of the People,* (Chicago: Moody Press, 1960)

151. Mathews goes on to say, "My purpose is to intensify the inner realities and to encourage God's people to derive their value systems from the direct teaching of the Word itself and then to surrender themselves to the truth as the Holy Spirit applies it and to use it in prayer. If we do this, then there can be no fear that the cutting edge will be blunt." *Born for Battle,* p. 60

152. W.E. Vine, *Vine's Complete Expository Dictionary* (Nashville: Thomas Nelson, 1996)

153. F. Brown, S. Driver, C. Briggs, *The Brown-Driver-Briggs Hebrew and English Lexicon* (Peabody: Hendrikson Publishers, 1996), p. 3

154. C. S. Lewis, *The Abolition of Man* (New York: Simon and Schuster, 1996), p. 37

155. Gen. 2:21-23

156. 1 Cor. 11:11

157. John Eldredge, *Wild at Heart* (Nashville: Thomas Nelson, 2001)

158. God remains committed to this goal, as He promises through the prophet Isaiah that "the Lord will comfort Zion; He will comfort all her waste places. And her wilderness He will make like Eden" (Isa. 51:3).

159. Eph. 5: 25, 27, 29, 32

160. C.S. Lewis, *That Hideous Strength,* (New York: Macmillan, 1965) p. 316

161. Mat. 26:31; Luke 12:32; John 10:16; 1 Pet. 5:2. An exception to this is Acts 20:28.

162. 1 Cor. 3:9, 16, Eph. 2:21, 1 Pet. 2:5

163. Mat. 5:13-14

164. Rom. 8:14, Eph. 1:5, Gal. 4:6

165. References to bondservants (Rev. 7:3, 22:3-5) and faithful martyrs (Rev. 20:4) are gender neutral. Again, it is the masculine nature that is inferred in the previous examples, not the male gender.

166. Mat. 25:31

167. Perhaps this subject matter sheds light on other difficult passages? For example, was it an historically appropriate reinforcement of ekklesial dominion for Paul to assert a primarily masculine leadership of the ekklesiai? Both genders were fundamental to ekklesial community life, with clear spheres of value and service. We are even given examples of indirect, but high female influence, including the three Marys, the four prophetess daughters of Philip, Dorcas and Priscilla, Anna the prophetess, and Junia the apostle, not to mention Old Testament examples such as Sarah, Miriam, Deborah, Ruth and Esther. Jesus and Paul were countercultural in their fair and equal treatment of women. Yet with regard to Mediterranean expectations of propriety, combined with the familiarity of the ekklesial format, Paul thus proclaimed, "It is improper for a woman to speak in ekklesia" (1 Cor. 14:35).

168. R. Arthur Mathews, *Born for Battle: 31 Studies on Spiritual Warfare* (Wheaton: Harold Shaw Publishers, 1976, 1999), p. 25

169. And all the while we must remember, in Christ "there is neither male nor female, for you are all one" (Gal. 3:28).

170. Mat. 22:21; Rom. 13:1-7; 1 Tim. 2:1-3; Tit. 3:1; 1 Pet. 2:13-15

171. R. Arthur Mathews, *Born for Battle: 31 Studies on Spiritual Warfare* (Wheaton: Harold Shaw Publishers, 1976, 1999), p. 20

172. R. Arthur Mathews, *Born for Battle: 31 Studies on Spiritual Warfare* (Wheaton: Harold Shaw Publishers, 1976, 1999), p. 30, 33

173. Ray Vander Laan, "Lord of Lords," www.followtherabbi.com

174. The importance of sacrifice and ritual cleanness are evident in Joshua 5 and 1 Sam. 13. The need for spiritual preparation is also evident in the story of David and Bathsheba (2 Sam. 11-12). After committing adultery, David twice "tries to lure Uriah into the bed of his wife, but twice Uriah refuses. His refusal is based on his need to be spiritually prepared to reengage in holy war." Furthermore, the authors point out how "seemingly banal law(s) in the book of Deuteronomy (are) actually charged with theological significance in light of holy war and the divine warrior." The laws in question, conveyed in Deut. 23:9-14, involve purification that must occur if a warrior ejaculates the night before battle, and also the inappropriateness "to have a latrine in the midst of the camp for reasons of purity...'For the Lord your God moves about your camp to protect you and to deliver your enemies to you.' (Dt. 23:14)" — *God is a Warrior*, p. 35-37

175. 1 John 3:10

176. Dan. 7:13-27

177. Luke 10:1

178. While this is expressed in the negative sense in Deuteronomy 32:30, the balance of other verses seems to suggest that the principle is actually neutral, and can be utilized either for good or evil.

179. Gen. 32:24-28

180. *Spirit Filled Life Bible;* p. 865, note on Psa. 126:5-6.

181. *Mere Christianity* (New York: Macmillan Publishing Co., 1952), p. 51

182. Jen Miller, "Busboy Arrested For $80 Million Theft Attempt," The Brooklyn Ink, Nov. 28, 2007 (online at archives.jrn.columbia.edu/2009/thebrooklynink/brooklyn/busboy-arrested-for-80-million-identity-theft-attempt.html)

183. "Since god fights for Israel...in the ethos of the Old Testament, a large army and superior weapons technology are a liability. Israel cannot boast in its own strength, but only in the power and might of the Lord, who gives victory in spite of overwhelming odds." — Longman and Reid, *God is a Warrior;* p. 37

184. Judges 8:10

185. Judges 5:2

186. Luke 11:26

187.  Derek Prince, *Shaping History Through Prayer and Fasting,* p. 39, 44-45

188.  Mat. 16:20-26

189.  Bonhoeffer, *Ethics* (New York: Simon and Schuster, 1995), p. 78

190.  N.T. Wright, *A Royal Priesthood: The Use of the Bible Ethically and Politically,* ed. C. Bartholemew (Carlisle: Paternoster, 2003) p. 173–193. Online at www.ntwrightpage.com/Wright_Paul_Caesar_Romans.htm

191.  Rom. 8:28

192.  Derek Prince, *Shaping History Through Prayer and Fasting,* 2002 (New Kensington: Whitaker House) p. 33-35

193.  Tim Hansel, *Holy Sweat,* (Dallas: Word Books Publisher, 1987) p. 188-189.

194.  http://en.wikipedia.org/wiki/King_James_Version

195.  Corpus Christi manuscript 140 dated circa 1000 A.D. and the Anglo-Saxon Gospels Hatton Manuscript 38 circa 1200 A.D

196.  Beard, M., Price, S., North, J., *Religions of Rome: Volume 1, a History* (Cambridge University Press, 1998); p. 370 (*"Official Letter from Constantine, dated 314 CE"*)

197.  "This is one of the words which was not translated by King James' translators, but 'kept' under his third rule which required all the old ecclesiastical words to be kept and not translated." J.A. Shackleford, *Compendium of Baptist History* (Louisville: Baptist Book Concern, 1892) p. 23-24

## ABOUT THE AUTHOR

Dean Briggs is a husband, father, teacher and intercessor. He leads the Ekklesia Prayer Communities network of contending prayer. Dean is also a trainer at TheCall's Spiritual Air Force Academy (SAFA) on the campus of Frontier Ventures (formerly The US Center for World Missions) in Pasadena, CA. He is married to Jeanie. Together, they have eight children. **DeanBriggs.com**

# OTHER BOOKS BY DEAN

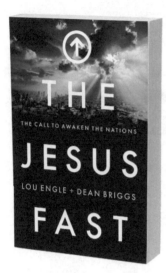

### The Jesus Fast
### by Lou Engle & Dean Briggs

The original Jesus movement that exploded with signs, wonders, miracles and salvation was preceded by extended fasting. Both a war manual and global summons to revival, *The Jesus Fast* is your guide to the most explosive weapon in the Christian arsenal: humility, expressed in fasting, combined with prayer. Join the next great Jesus Movement!

### *Consumed* by Dean Briggs

Have you contemplated fasting, but not known where to start? *Consumed* is about the journey. Less a how-to manual and more a daily companion, *Consumed* was written during the author's own 40-day fast. Short devotionals will speak to you in "real time" right where you are, in the middle of the struggles and weakness, yet filling you with courage and practical guidance.

## The Legends of Karac Tor
*Fiction for Champions*

Made in United States
Troutdale, OR
02/10/2024

17540129R00149